Chinese Earth-Sheltered Dwellings

Chinese Earth-Sheltered Dwellings

Indigenous Lessons for Modern Urban Design

Gideon S. Golany

University of Hawaii Press / Honolulu

92   93   94   95   96   97   5   4   3   2   1

Library of Congress Cataloging-in-Publication Data

Golany, Gideon.
   Chinese earth-sheltered dwellings : indigenous lessons for modern
urban design / Gideon S. Golany.
     p.   cm.
   Includes bibliographical references and index.
   ISBN 0–8248–1369–3
   1.   Earth sheltered houses—China.   I.   Title.
NA7448.G6   1992
728'.0473'0951—dc20   91–21496
                             CIP

*Dedicated to the memory of my sister
Hanna, who died at an early age and
never enjoyed life fully.*

CONTENTS

FIGURES

TABLES

PREFACE

Since the growth of awareness about the world-wide energy crisis, the nations of the world, particularly the technologically advanced countries, have been seeking ways and means to reduce energy consumption. To achieve this goal architects, urban designers, and developers have been searching for efficient designs with appropriate energy-saving locations. Earth-sheltered habitats in the United States, belowground shopping centers in Japan and Canada, and subterranean industrial plants in Sweden are good examples of design that promotes energy saving, efficient land use, and conservation. Since their introduction, much experience has been gained throughout the world that can be applied in the execution of similar building designs such as subterranean libraries, hospitals, public gathering halls, offices, entertainment centers, schools, and the like. The old/new idea of belowground space usage needs no proof today of its efficiency, affordability, and far-reaching positive impact on the modern city sprawl. The challenge we face now is to improve belowground space design, efficiency, and thermal performance, so as to meet the demands of modern standards and design norms. Some obvious ways of doing this are through experimentation (which consumes resources) and/or through monitoring, researching, analyzing, and drawing conclusions about the ancient-through-contemporary experience of belowground space usage. An excellent observatory in this regard is the Chinese belowground habitat. The Chinese themselves have only recently become aware of the wealth of information to be gleaned from their own cave dwellings. Yet, there is still a noticeable lack of knowledge in the West about the Chinese earth-sheltered vernacular habitats, the so-called *yaodong* or cave dwellings of China. This volume is the first of its kind to introduce them in a comprehensive manner.

The goals of this work are to acquaint the Western scientist and lay reader with one of the world's unique types of vernacular housing through comprehensive documentation of the data on its features; to introduce ancient lessons in regard to design and thermal principles; to point out the deficiencies of Chinese cave dwelling design and offer applicable solutions; and, last, to introduce some relevant lessons from the belowground experience of the past to modern urban design. Thus, this book is a general comprehensive treatment of Chinese belowground dwellings. Unique to this manuscript are the documentation of various factors affecting the design of these dwellings —especially the correlations between soil and climate conditions—and the descriptions of variation in design and construction techniques. The book also contains many illustrations that have been redrawn based on personal photographs. The modern city's dispersed land use patterns require the introduction of innovative solutions to their design, construction, and maintenance problems. The cost savings to be realized through the innovative use of belowground space can ease the financial burden of building and maintaining today's cities so that more of the available resources can be diverted to upgrading the social quality of life. The introduction of belowground space concepts within modern cities for nonresidential usage is a promising prospect. The Chinese experience has been an excellent source of information for study in this regard. Chinese designers have recently realized this fact and have tremendously accelerated the use of modernized belowground space in Beijing and several other cities.

Belowground dwellings are commonly known to be the most ancient form of shelter used by man. Such shelters were used extensively in southern Italy, Iran, Mesopotamia, Spain, France, and North America (by Indians and Eskimos). Some large-scale belowground communities have existed almost without interruption since their development and down through the millennia until our time. Among the many regions of the world where large-scale belowground communities still exist, the most outstanding are located in Tunisia, Cappadocia (Turkey), and China.

In Tunisia, about twenty such communities are located in the southern part of the country on the Matmata plateau, which borders the northern Sahara desert. Research in Tunisia points out that the Berber people of north Africa introduced their concept of belowground habitats within this region as a defensive tool against Arab-Islamic invasions of the seventh century. Their subterranean shelters proved an excellent form of housing, responding positively to the climatic harshness of the Sahara. In any case, these communities emerged as integrated Berber-Arab societies that were confined to the defensible Matmata plateau. The typical north African habitats use both the pit-type and the cliff-type belowground dwelling designs. The Romans learned the use of belowground shelters from the Berbers and constructed an impressive belowground city complex in their own style at the city of Bulla Regia. This city was located in northern Tunisia, where the Mediterranean climate prevailed.

In Cappadocia, central Turkey, there is a remarkable historical development of cliff-type belowground dwellings. Approximately forty cliff-dwelling communities exist in the semiarid climate of the Göreme valley, some 400 kilometers southeast of Ankara, the capital of modern Turkey. Such space has been used by succeeding civilizations almost without interruption during the

four millennia since the time of the Hittites. These dwellings are excavated in a unique landform that is shaped by environmental constraints. This landform is made of *tufa* soil (lava) that is abraded by dry winds, a process that results in landforms having the appearance of a forest of conic stones, each measuring more than 50 meters high. The cliff dwellings are carved into the acute slopes of the cones. This design made accessibility difficult and protected the communities against the invaders of ancient times. The cliff dwellings are interconnected with each other and with various other communities in a sophisticated manner, forming an intensive and extensive belowground traffic network that is well known to the native inhabitants. This feature adds to the remarkable defense capability of the dwellings. In addition, the dwellings promote a comfortable indoor ambient climate that helps inhabitants cope with the especially harsh outdoor climate of summer. Today much of the belowground space is used for residential purposes, while some is also used as a national center for citrus refrigeration. The cliff dwellings are also a tourist attraction because of the ancient Byzantine churches found within.

In China, belowground habitats are commonly called "cave dwellings" (*yaodong*), even though they are actually entirely man-made, earth-sheltered environments. The Chinese cave dwellings are of interest especially because of the scale of their distribution. These cave dwellings developed in the same region that is known as the cradle of Chinese civilization. Most Chinese researchers date the first cave dwellings to earlier than 2000 B.C. and believe they may have preceded the appearance of aboveground housing. The estimated thirty to forty million contemporary Chinese cave dwellers are confined to the loess soil ("yellow soil") region that stretches along the mammoth Yellow River (Huang *he*) in northern China, from the northwest to the eastern part of the country. The loess soil is structurally uniform, free of stone, and presents an ideal condition for relatively easy digging and stable structural form. The Chinese case is especially intriguing because it introduces a variety of elaborate design conditions.

During my research on Chinese cave dwellings, I was able to review most, if not all, of the literature published on this subject in Chinese through special translations to English that I commissioned. In some cases, complete texts of books were translated so that I could become acquainted with specific geographical and cultural conditions. I also reviewed the limited amount of literature published in English. My primary sources of information were personal observations, surveys and maps, thermal measurements, interviews, and photographs. I became well informed through my field research and by reading the available literature on the subject. With the help of the Ministry of Metallurgical Industry, I was able to move around the country without any of the limitations usually imposed upon a tourist. I was accompanied by a local government representative and a Chinese assistant and was able to personally select the sites for research as well as the dwellings to be visited in different geographical regions. Usually, I obtained full cooperation from residents in the villages where the research was conducted. Some of the cave dwellings were then surveyed and mapped. I also measured diurnal and seasonal temperatures. Thus, this book is the culmination of more than one and one-half years of field work in China, preceded by several years of preparatory activities. To assist the reader, both Chinese and English designations have been used in this volume for many geographical names, for example, Banpo *cun* Village, Wei *he* River, Gong *xian* County, and Liupan *shan* Mountains.

A major problem was the lack of detailed statistical information about cave dwellings at the county, township, or commune level. Much of this information was obtained through collaboration with my Chinese colleagues by means of special surveys conducted in the five provinces where the cave dwellings are dispersed. Detailed information on the historical evolution of the cave dwellings in China was also in short supply. Only recently have Chinese authorities, and especially members of the Architectural Society of China, become aware of the wealth of information that can be obtained on the use of belowground space. The problems posed by the cave dwellings in contemporary China demand special and innovative solutions in order to bring them up to our modern standards of design.

One of the basic advantages of belowground space is its thermal performance. In general, dwellings that utilize such spaces provide residents with cool summers and warm winters. The daily temperature remains stable during all seasons and this provides a comfortable ambient environment. Typically, belowground dwellings do not need cooling systems in summer and may require only a minimum amount of heating in winter. These conditions are a result of the time lag that operates as heat or cold travels down from the soil's surface to the space belowground. The optimal response of belowground space occurs primarily in warm, dry climates (as in the Sahara or other desert areas), and in cold, dry climates (as in north-central Canada and Siberia). The Chinese cave dwellings are located primarily in the warm and dry climate of a semiarid region.

ACKNOWLEDGMENTS

THE field research that provided material for this book was financed by the United States National Academy of Sciences through the Committee on Scholarly Communication with the People's Republic of China. Preparation of the manuscript for publication was supported by funds provided by The Pennsylvania State University's Vice President for Research, Dr. Charles Hosler, who was decisive and efficient in securing the necessary financial resources and encouraging to me throughout the creation of the book. I am thankful for his financial contribution and his moral commitment. Dr. James Moeser, Dean of the College of Arts and Architecture, showed constant support for this project as well as my other scholarly activities, and I am very grateful to him. I am thankful also to the late Professor Raniero Corbelletti, my former department head, who stood behind me throughout the project. Sincere thanks also must go to my colleague, Professor Peter Magyar, for his advice on the design of a dust jacket for this book.

I would like to express deep thanks to my graduate assistants, Wu Hua, Yang Xiaohui, and Deng Dong, who followed my instructions in drawing the final illustrations from my drafts here at Penn State. My thanks also to my graduate assistant, Wang Jianzhong, who helped me with data gathering before and during my visit to China and who drafted some of the final drawings after returning to the University; and to Huang Changshan, graduate assistant in the Department of Landscape Architecture, who also helped with the drawings. Professor Shirley Wood of Henan University in China, Luke Leung, graduate stu-

dent in Architectural Engineering at Penn State, and Dr. Y. S. Li from Tongji University, Shanghai, have all helped immensely by translating many background texts from Chinese to English. My thanks and appreciation to my friend, Nan Yingjing, an engineer associated with the Investigation Group on Chinese Cave Dwellings, Architectural Society of China, for his careful reading of the full manuscript and his valuable comments.

I would also like to take this opportunity to express my sincerest thanks to those who helped me realize my research plan, both before and during my stay in China, including:

Mr. Robert Geyer, former Director of the National Program for Advanced Study and Research in China sponsored by the Committee on Scholarly Communication with the People's Republic of China at the National Academy of Sciences, Washington, D.C., and his former Program Assistant, Mr. Jeff Filcik. Their help was instrumental to the success of this project.
The staff of the Chinese Ministry of Metallurgical Industry in Beijing, who sponsored my itinerary and stay in China. A large number of their key personnel facilitated every detail of my project plans, and without their dedicated help this research could not have been done. Among them were: Mr. Wang Zucheng, Director of the Education Department; Mr. Li Wenjian, Vice Director of the Education Department; my friend Mr. Yang Songtao, Engineer, Foreign Affairs Department; and Mr. Li Fuqin, Translator, Division of Higher Education.
Many staff members of the American Embassy in

Beijing gave important help, including: Dr. Jack L. Gosnell, former Counselor for Science and Technology, and his former assistants Mr. Christopher J. Marut and Mr. Douglas B. McNeal; Dr. Karl F. Olsson, First Secretary and Cultural Affairs Officer; and Mr. Lynn H. Noah, Counselor for Press and Cultural Affairs.

The Architectural Society of China, which, along with the Ministry of Metallurgical Industry, was most effective in managing my itinerary. Some of the many people involved were: Mr. Huang Xinfan, Director of the Academic Affairs Division; Mr. Gong Deshun, former Secretary of the ASC; Ms. Xi Jingda, Director of the Department of Foreign Affairs; Mr. Jin Oubo and Mr. Zeng Jian of the ASC; and Professor Chen Zhanxiang of the China Academy of Urban Planning and Design.

Also the many people from Xi'an Institute of Metallurgy and Construction Engineering: President and Professor Zhao Hongzuo; my friend, Professor Hou Jiyao, who was most helpful with advice on arranging my project plan; Mr. Zhang Guang and Mr. Zhang Pei-xue of the Department of Foreign Affairs; members of the Department of Architecture, Professor Guang Shikui, former Head, and Professors Zhang Sizan and Xia Yun and my assistant, Mr. Qiao Zhen, architecture student. Mr. Qiao acted as my faithful assistant during the field survey. He gathered the data with me, measured the temperatures, and mapped and surveyed the buildings.

The large number of people at Tongji University in Shanghai, among them: Professor Hou Xue-yuan, Head of the Department of Geotechnical Engineering, and my assistants, Mr. Su Yu and Mr. Peng Fristo.

Others at Beijing University of Iron and Steel Technology were: President and Professor Wang Run; Professor Yu Zongsen, Dean of the Faculty of Physical Chemistry; Professor Huang Wudi, Head of the newly developed Graduate Program on Environmental Design; Professor Qiao Duan; and Mr. Yang Dali and Mr. Zhao Yonglu, interpreters.

In Shanxi Province: Architect Zuo Guobao of the Institute of Building Science; Mr. Lin Yishan, Director of the Institute of Building Science; Mr. Li Minhong and Mr. Qiao Shuangwang, both of the Taiyuan City Construction Committee; Mr. Jia Kunnan of the Architectural Society of Linfen Region; and Mr. Lian Peng, interpreter with the Foreign Affairs Office of Linfen Region.

In Shaanxi Province: Mr. Wang Zhengji, Head of Fenhui Team, Liquan County; Mr. Wang Yangchang, Leader at the Foreign Affairs Division; Mr. Li Jianqian, Architect from Yan'an; Mr. Wei Tanqing, Construction Engineer of Yan'an Region; and Mr. Zhang Zongqiang of the Foreign Affairs Office.

In Gansu Province: My friends, Mr. Ren Zhen-ying, Chief Architect of Lanzhou City and Head of the Investigation Group on Chinese Cave Dwellings; Mr. Nan Yingjing, Translator and Engineer, Lanzhou City; Mr. Jing, of the Qingyang Regional Government; and Mr. Wang Jiuru of the Architectural Society of Qingyang Region and Head of the Office of Urban and Rural Construction and Environmental Protection.

In Henan Province: Professor Shirley Wood, Dean of the Foreign Language Department and Honorary Director of Graduate Studies, Henan University, Kaifeng; in Zhengzhou, Architect Li Liansheng of the Architectural Society of Henan, and Mr. Zhou Peinan of the Architectural Academy of Zhengzhou City; in Gong County, Ms. Zhang Chongrong and Mr. Li Jinlu, engineers with the Department of Construction; and in Luoyang; Mr. Li Chuan-zhe and Mr. Wang Anmin of the Architectural Society of Luoyang Region.

Last, at Qinghua University, Beijing: Professor Li Daozeng, Dean of the Department of Architecture, and Professors Cai Junfu and Wu Huan-jia, both of the Department of Architecture.

To all, my deep thanks and appreciation for their perceptive help, advice, and warm hospitality.

Last but not least, I am grateful to my editorial assistants, Grace Pérez, who worked closely with me in the early stages of the manuscript preparation, and Barbara Labinsky, who worked with me on the final stages of this manuscript; also to my assistant Amy Zhang, who was dedicated to the romanization of the Chinese names and the preparation of the index with much accuracy. I would like to thank them for their perseverance and attention to detail while working on this book. My thanks also to Linda Gummo for her careful typing of the text. I am grateful for and appreciative of the assistance I received from all of these people. This volume would not have been realized without their help.

ONE

Introduction: Evolution of the Chinese Cave Dwellings

THE area of China covers approximately 9.6 million square kilometers and takes up nearly one-fifteenth of the world's total land surface. This makes China the third largest country in the world after the Soviet Union and Canada. Its territory extends 5,500 kilometers from north to south, and 5,000 kilometers from west to east. Topographically, the land rises from the eastern seacoast to the western Tibetan mountains. Within this vast, confined country, a great number of belowground habitats evolved during the last four millennia. This unique housing type is distributed along the northern zone of China within the fertile, yet mostly dry, loess soil. In the course of time, much experience has been accumulated by the dwellers and passed down from one generation to another. Based on this experience, the cave dwellers have developed two major types of housing. These are the pit and the cliff types.

Pit-type and cliff-type cave dwellings constitute a unique form of shelter among Chinese vernacular habitats. Although they are commonly called cave dwellings, they are actually entirely man-made earth-sheltered environments, an outgrowth of environmental, technological, and socioeconomic conditions that have operated together through history. Chinese vernacular aboveground architecture has always been distinctive and offers remarkable design examples, especially in its use of local materials for construction. The study of cave dwelling architecture should be viewed within the overall context of Chinese vernacular architecture and the forces that shape it. There is a unity and continuity in the basic principles of Chinese house design, a tradition that has been adhered to in most geographical regions of China. For example, the roots of the principal cave dwelling design motifs are also to be found in the so-called Beijing house and in the Nanjing round dwelling (*yuanzhai*) typical of Fujian province. All these forms are derived from earlier prototypes of the courtyard house.

The pattern of cave dwelling development in China has been reinforced by certain aspects of the national culture. Cave dwellings make an ideal setting for the familiar extended family structure. The traditional patriarchal family, with its intimate ties and interrelationships, was strengthened by the closeness of the cave dwelling environment. The designs of the dwellings themselves also reflect a tradition of communal living, limited interaction with outsiders, and enclosure and protection of family members, a tradition that fosters a sense of unity.

The following three types of cave dwellings were developed in China: (1) cliffside-type cave dwelling (a horizontal space dug on the edge of the cliff); (2) sunken courtyard-type cave dwelling (a large square or rectangular excavated pit with cave dwelling units dug around the perimeter); (3) vaulted cave dwelling (a stone or brick building covered with earth having one or two stories above ground) (Li Xiaoqiang 1985, 215).

The term "cave dwelling" (*yao dong* or *di xia jian zhu*) is commonly used in China for space dug deep below the ground, whether in cliff or pit form. The same term as used in this book means an entirely subterranean space used for habitation, in either cliff or pit form. "Semisubterranean cave dwelling" (*ban di xia jian zhu*) describes

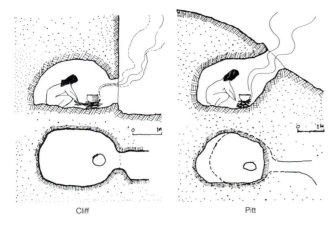

Cliff

Pitt

a   PROTECTIVE PRIMITIVE NEST SHELTER

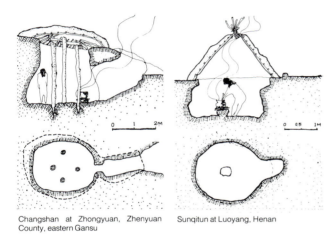

Changshan at Zhongyuan, Zhenyuan County, eastern Gansu

Sunqitun at Luoyang, Henan

b   TROGLODYTE DWELLING

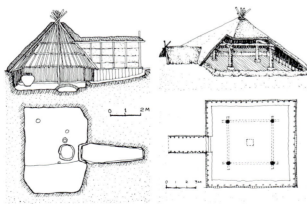

Yangshao site at Banpo Neolithic village

c   SEMISUBTERRANEAN ELABORATIVE HABITAT

Fig. 1.1   Assumed evolutionary stages of belowground space usage. Scale is approximate.

a structure built partly below and partly above the ground. "Earth-sheltered habitat" (*yan tu jian zhu*), as used here, denotes an aboveground structure built with a stone or brick vault and covered by a layer of earth that is one-half meter in thickness or more.

In terms of historical development, Chinese cave dwellings evolved over a period of more than four millennia in a distinct region of China. In general, residential dwellings have evolved from belowground to aboveground structures. The assumed stages of this evolution are as follows: (1) nomadism (no fixed dwelling); (2) nest shelter (man-made niche or pit dug in the earth for protection); (3) troglodytism (habitation in natural or artificial caves); and (4) cave dwelling as an organized lifestyle (fig. 1.1). Evolution from one stage to the next represented great progress in the civilization of mankind. In the case of China, the loess soil fostered what became Chinese civilization. It is in the loess soil environment that Chinese Neolithic village culture and permanent agricultural settlements appeared.

As in other Stone Age civilizations, Chinese Paleolithic man may have used natural caves as seasonal dwellings during the period when he was a hunter and wanderer. He may have used wood, then available in large quantities, for building semi-shelters as well. The remains of man-made dwellings of this period have not yet been discovered in China. But it can be assumed that man-made pit dwellings began to appear in the late Paleolithic period (ibid., 210). In any case, existing archaeological evidence shows that the Chinese Paleolithic and Mesolithic sites are located primarily within the Yellow River (Huang *he*) watershed (fig. 1.2).

During the Neolithic age, mankind began to assume tribal or clan social forms. Animal domestication and agricultural development both required pasturage and necessitated the creation of settlements. Seasonal shelters developed first into year-round dwellings and then into permanent ones. Early Neolithic remains have been found at Zishan in Hebei province and at Egou in Mi *xian* County, Henan province. The findings at these sites reveal the construction of circular, oval, or square half-pits covered with cone-shaped roofs made of wood. The interiors of the pits are flat

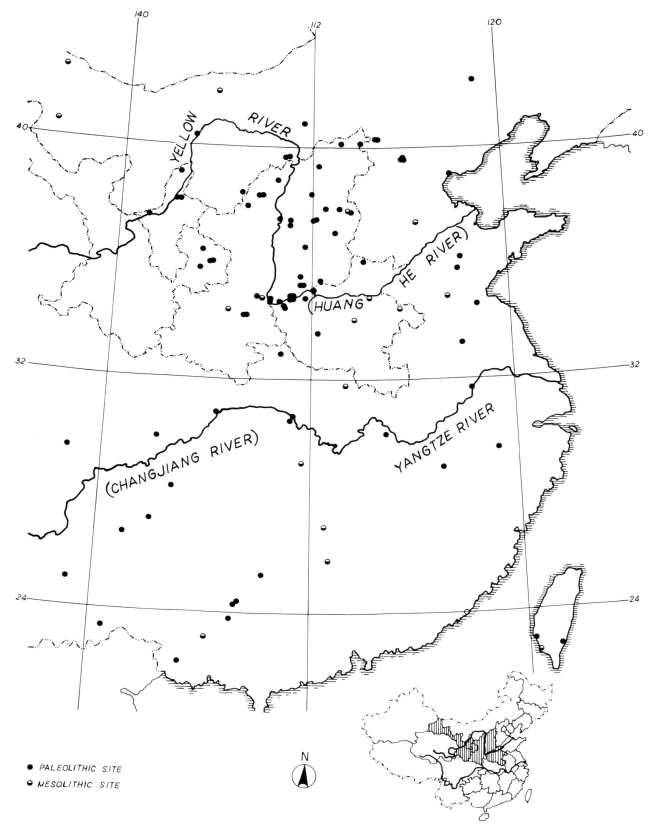

● PALEOLITHIC SITE

◐ MESOLITHIC SITE

N

Fig. 1.2 Paleolithic and Mesolithic sites in China. Note the high concentration within the loess soil zone around the Yellow River where cave dwellings evolved. The inset shows the five provinces where existing cave dwellings are chiefly distributed.

with evidence indicating the presence of ovens (ibid., 211).

A good example of these semi-belowground pit shelters can be found in the Neolithic village of Banpo at Xi'an, the capital of Shaanxi. The village is now a covered museum (fig. 1.3). Banpo *cun* (sometimes Pan-p'o-ts'un) is a semisubterranean village constructed on a flat site. The lower parts of the dwellings are dug belowground while the upper portions are built aboveground. The village is separated from its surroundings by a deep ditch for defense and protection. The site is located 800 meters east of the Chan *he* River, about nine meters above the level of the riverbed, in the suburbs of Xi'an. The settlement covers a 50,000-square-meter area. It has an irregular oval shape oriented on a north-to-south axis. The houses and pits are clustered in the center. The ditch or moat that surrounds the site measures five to six meters in depth and width. The village cemetery is located outside the site to the north (Kwang-chih Chang 1977, 100). Banpo *cun* Village is located in the loess soil zone, where the earth is suitable for digging and cuts easily. Cliff cave dwellings dating back 4,000 years have been found in Xia *xian* County, Shanxi province.

It can be assumed that Chinese cave dwellings evolved from primitive troglodytism. Historically, the two earliest examples discovered—at the above-mentioned Neolithic village of Banpo, and at Xiafeng *cun* Village in Xia *xian* County—can be traced back five or six thousand years (Ren Zhenying 1985a, 318). At Hougang, near present-day Anyang in the northern part of Henan, another form of pit shelter had been developed during Paleolithic times. This shelter, known as the bottle-shaped pit, became popular with the rise of Yangshao culture.

The plain around the Wei *he* River in Shaanxi province was the center of the Yangshao culture (fig. 1.4). The Yellow River valley region in general is considered to be the center of the earliest Neolithic culture of China as a whole. It was during the Neolithic period that agricultural community settlements developed here in the form of villages. Evidence of the Yangshao culture was first discovered in 1920 by farmers of Yangshao *cun* Village, Mianchi *xian* County, in northwestern Henan. This culture was prevalent all along the Yellow River from southern Hebei and northern Henan in the east to eastern Gansu in the west; and from northern Shaanxi and Shanxi in the north to southern Shaanxi and Henan in the south. Authorities agree that the best-preserved sites of this culture include Banpo *cun* near the city of Xi'an, Jiangzhai near Lintong, Yuanjunmiao in Hua *xian*, and Beishouling near Baoji, all in Shaanxi, and the Xia *xian* sites located in Shanxi

Fig. 1.3   Sketched model of Banpo, a Neolithic semisubterranean village near Xi'an. Note the deep defense ditch around the settlement.

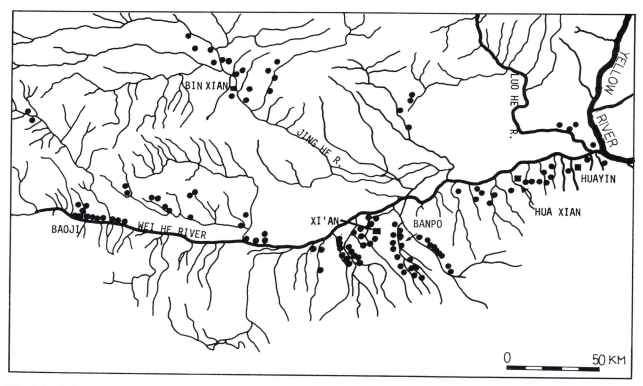

Fig. 1.4   Distribution of Neolithic Yangshao sites in the Wei *he* River region. There is a major concentration near Xi'an. Present-day cities are indicated by squares.

(Chang 1977, 91–93). This area, known as the cradle of Chinese civilization, is the same region where the existing Neolithic cave dwellings have been found (fig. 1.5).

It is not surprising that this region, encompassing the middle reaches of the Yellow River, is also the area richest in relics of the Neolithic culture in China; here, artifacts such as painted pottery and bones have been found in large quantities (Wang Yongyan and Zhang Zonghu 1980, [unpaginated]). The early villagers who inhabited the valleys of the Yellow River drainage system often built adobe shelters in the lowest loess terraces along the riverbanks. This semi-belowground housing also included food storage pits. At Banpo, 46 dwellings and more than 203 excavated pits were found occupying only about one-fifth of the total area of the settlement, which suggests that more than one hundred dwellings had actually been built. Commonly, the houses measured 3 to 5 meters across and were square, oblong, or round in shape with plastered floors. The roofs were supported by small to large wooden posts (Chang 1977, 101–102).

Cave dwellings continued to be developed in the loess soil of China throughout the historical periods. Textual references to cave dwellings are to be found in the *Book of Changes* dating from the Western Zhou period (eleventh to eighth century B.C.) and in the *Book of Poetry* dating from the Spring and Autumn period (eighth to fifth century B.C.). According to the *Book of Poetry*, people predicted the coming of rains by observing the high humidity in their caves (Li 1985, 213–214). Cave dwellings were also used extensively during the Warring States period (fifth to third century B.C.). As recorded in the *Book of Rites*, ancient Chinese kings "had no palaces in which to live in the past. They used to dwell in underground caves in winter and nests in summer" (Zhang Yuhuan 1985, 469). Pit dwelling references are found occasionally for the Qin and Han dynasties (third century B.C. to third century A.D.), when cliff cave dwellings were apparently in common use (Li 1985, 214).

Thus, cave dwellings in China probably appeared during the Xia dynasty, which can be characterized as a Bronze Age culture that flour-

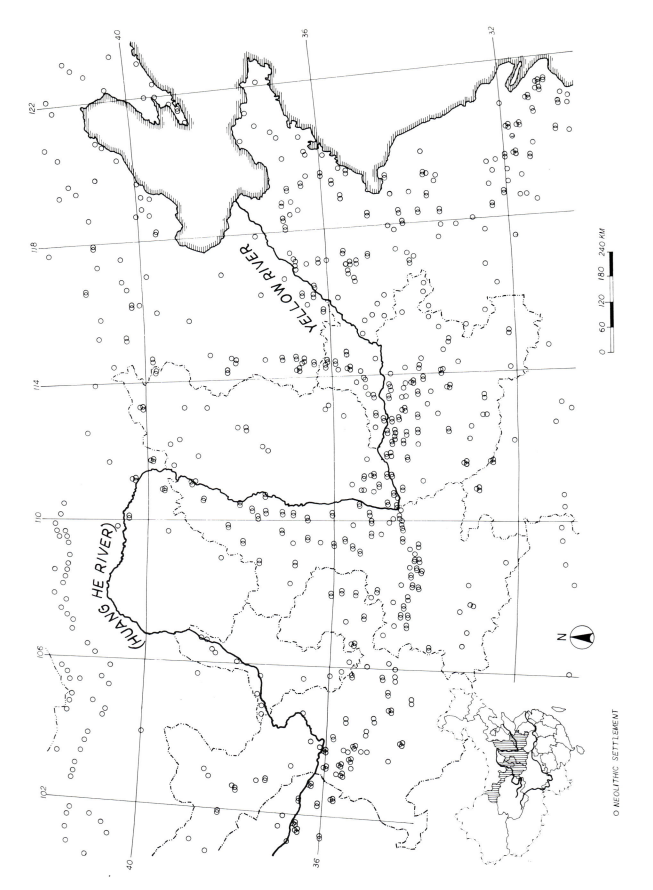

Fig. 1.5 Neolithic settlements in China. Similar to later cave dwelling distribution, there is a greater concentration along the middle reaches of the Yellow River.

○ NEOLITHIC SETTLEMENT

ished around the beginning of the second millennium B.C. However, it is assumed among Chinese researchers that widespread construction of cave dwellings began only during the Han dynasty (206 B.C.–A.D. 220) and that cave-building techniques reached a mature stage only by the time of the Sui (A.D. 581–618) and Tang (618–907) dynasties. The large-scale proliferation of cave dwellings in the loess soil zone did not occur, however, until the period of the Ming and Qing dynasties (1368–1911). By this time forests had been depleted, causing a critical shortage of timber. Harsh climate, population growth, and a large number of homeless refugees fleeing from war all accelerated the need for, and excavation of, subterranean dwellings (Zhao Sude 1985, 479). As a result, habitation in cave dwellings has become increasingly common in China during the last five centuries (Nan Yingjing 1982b, 109).

Textual references to cave dwellings for the Ming-Qing period are to be found in chapters 12 and 42 of the *Book of Qingyang,* a chronicle of local history which records, for the winter of 1556, that the province adjacent to Qingyang was jolted by an earthquake possibly of a magnitude close to 8.5 on the modern Richter scale. According to the text, "buildings collapsed [and] uncountable numbers of cave dwellers were killed. . . ." This report provides evidence that a large number of cave dwellings were in use during the period. And today, there are old cave dwellings still in use that claim a history of two or three hundred years (Ren Zhiyuan 1982b, 9–10).

All through the ancient historical periods the armies of different dynasties acted as a major force in the accelerated development and construction of cave dwellings. From the Warring States period (475–221 B.C.) to the Qin and Han dynasties (221 B.C.–A.D. 220) through the Sui and Tang dynasties (581–907) and onward to the close of the Ming dynasty in 1644, many wars were fought in the area around Luoyang, one of the five famous capitals of ancient times. At the end of the Sui dynasty, for example, an army of 300,000 troops was amassed on a mountain north of Luoyang to face a decisive battle. Since it was impossible to construct shelters for such a large number of men in a short time, the only solution was to use caves for shelter. At the same time, many of the city's residents took refuge in the countryside, where they also dug cave shelters in the loess soil for temporary accommodation. Thus, the number of cave dwellings increased abruptly, while aboveground homes were destroyed (Ren Zhenying 1985a, 320). In 1984, a report from the Liujianzhuang Brigade of the Huanghe Commune in Hejin *xian* County, Shanxi, claimed a history of 1,300 years for one of its local cave dwellings. According to the report, General Xue Rengui of the early Tang dynasty once lived in this cave (Xiao Tihuan 1982).

Subterranean cave dwellings in China, with underground tunnels connecting their sunken courtyards, also served a significant function in the Chinese campaign against Japanese occupation during World War II. They were often used for storing ammunition and food, and also as shelter for soldiers. During the 1930s, the Communist Party headquarters and numerous Red Army soldiers were accommodated in the well-known caves around the city of Yan'an.

Curiously, throughout the entire ten thousand kilometers that make up the loess plateau, there are no ruins of temples inside caves. The Chinese apparently believed that their temples would be defiled if they were housed inside a cave made of soil. Temples were built exclusively aboveground. It was also usual for the wealthy to build their homes aboveground. But occasionally, rich landowners were attracted to cave living, and they developed villas and granaries belowground. Still, for most of their history cave dwellings have been associated with poverty and the lot of poor farmers. The usual interpretation is that poor people inhabited cave dwellings because they had no other choice (Nan 1982b, 110). The correlation between high concentration of cave dwellings and poverty is documented for the backward region of Qingyang, eastern Gansu, while in western Henan, with a richer economy, many more houses are built aboveground in both urban and rural areas. A high percentage of cave dwellings can still be found in rural Chinese communities where poverty has been dominant until only recently. In any case, poverty has been clearly associated with cave dwelling throughout Chinese recorded history. Today, however, subterranean space no longer has the same connotation, and it is increasingly used not only for dwellings but also for universities, schools, hospitals, factories, libraries, shops, granaries, garages, and many other nonresidential functions (Jin Oubo 1983, 63).

For China, exploitation of belowground space is one of the few options left for future development that will not destroy valuable agricultural land. And, the very size of the population requires innovative solutions for the expansion of already built-up areas as well. Experience gleaned from the tradition of cave dwelling can form the basis for development of modern belowground settlements, both urban and rural. Modern technology can respond well to most of the problems connected with belowground space usage.

We have seen that the development of Chinese cave dwellings has been limited primarily to the loess soil zone. However, increased interest in the use of belowground space in China has resulted in the development of some major belowground projects in Shanghai, Beijing, and other cities located outside the loess soil region. In general, the area surrounding the middle reaches of the Yellow River is identified as the regional concentration of Chinese cave dwellings (fig. 1.6). This region has an area of approximately 275,600 square kilometers and it encompasses the provinces of Gansu, Shaanxi, Shanxi, and Henan, as well as the Ningxia Hui Autonomous Region. Geographically, the cave dwellings are distributed throughout the region that is bordered by the Wushao *ling* range of mountains on the west, the Taihang *shan* range on the east, the north slope of the Qin *ling* range on the south, and the Great Wall of China on the north (Wang Fu 1982, 117). The land of this region has eroded into a variety of landforms ranging from mountains and valleys to hills and mesas, and to gullies and cleavages.

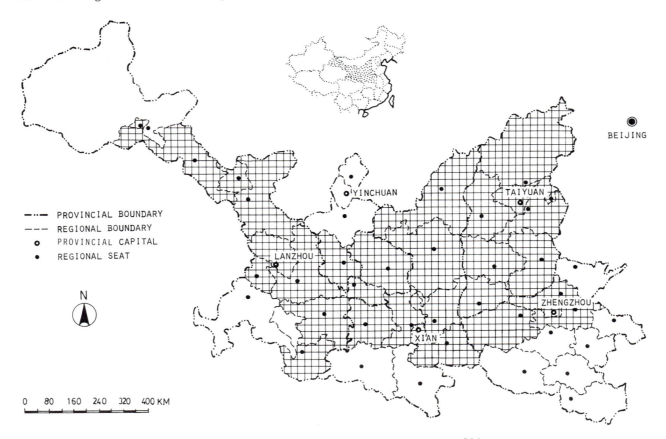

Fig. 1.6   Distribution of cave dwellings in the loess soil of five provinces in northern China

More than eight million Chinese people are employed in the building and construction trades, and they account for about 7 percent of the nation's workers. In housing, as with most other types of construction, building materials constitute the bulk of the expense. Since the cost of labor is low, many Chinese believe that mechanization or automation is not a particularly necessary or desirable trend in the building industry. However, heavy work such as may be involved in excavating sites, building foundations, or transporting materials can hardly be accomplished by manual labor alone. The use of fired brick (a staple of Chinese building materials) will continue because of its low cost, durability, and ease of production. In 1982, 160 billion fired bricks were produced in China. However, fired brick production could still benefit from technical improvements for the sake of quality and variety. The tendency today is to develop hollow bricks as a means of reducing soil and coal consumption, lessening the structural load, and improving the thermal properties of buildings. Future developments will probably witness an increase in use of reinforced concrete (Xu Ronglie and Wu Jialiu 1984, 1–6). In light of these facts, the use of belowground space for residential and nonresidential purposes (now accepted practiced in China) amounts to a practical response to the country's conservation, economic, and construction problems.

From 1978 to 1981, 1.5 billion square meters of housing were constructed throughout China. In 1980 alone, 45,800 new cave dwelling units were built in the area of Yan'an *shi,* Shaanxi—more than the total number that were built during the preceding ten years. There are 150,000 persons living in pit-type cave dwellings in Gong *xian* County, Henan. In 1984 almost all the members of the Zhongtou Team of Mangshan Commune near Luoyang *shi,* Henan, were inhabiting subterranean cave dwellings (Ren Zhiyuan 1983, 82). In Qingyang, east Gansu province, 60 to 80 percent of the area's courtyards are subterranean.

The existence and use of cave dwellings throughout the long history of China resulted from a combination of environmental, social, economic, and technological factors. Cave dwellings became popular because they were simple and easy to build under China's favorable loess soil conditions. Durability, low demand for maintenance, and reduced energy requirements (for heating and cooling) all contributed to their practicality.

Additionally, there are some significant environmental factors whose influence has had a major impact on the development of Chinese cave dwellings. The most important of these factors are the soil and climate conditions that prevail in the loess soil zone. The correlation between these factors and Chinese cave dwelling use and development are discussed in chapter 2.

TWO

Regional Environmental Determinants

LIKE other types of vernacular settlements and shelters, cave dwellings have been influenced by their natural environment. They represent man's effort to cope with nature and, with minimum modifications, to live in harmony with it. The desire to maintain harmony is also influenced by the farmer's practical concern with preserving the natural resources necessary for survival. For purposes of this book, natural resources will include China's existing geomorphological configurations, its loess soil, climatic pattern, and hydrological system. To a significant extent, these environmental factors have determined the development and distribution pattern of the Chinese cave dwellings.

Physical Features

Chinese cave dwellings are distributed over the northern and northwestern parts of the country. Administratively, this region includes the five provinces of Gansu, Shaanxi, Shanxi, Henan, and the Ningxia Hui Autonomous Region. Some cave dwellings can also be found in the neighboring provinces of Hebei in the east, Qinghai in the west, and the Xinjiang Uygur Autonomous Region in the northwest. The cave dwelling region follows the distribution of loess soil across an approximately 2,000 x 600-kilometer strip in northern China. The region is characterized by the special physical features of its geological formations. These features have a direct impact on the climate and soil and ultimately affect the cave dwelling pattern. Physical features, loess soil, and arid climate are the three components that inter-

influence one another and correlate to form the unique landscape where the environment favoring cave dwellings prevails.

The major mountain ranges of the area are the Qilian *shan* in the northwest (more than 4,000 meters high), the Qin *ling* in the south, the Helan *shan* in the west (more than 2,000 meters high), the Yan *shan* in the northeast (more than 2,000 meters high), the Taihang *shan* (averaging 1,500 meters high) in the east, and the Liupan *shan* in the southwest (more than 2,500 meters high) (fig. 2.1). To the far north lie the Yin *shan.*

The barrier of the Qin *ling* range has the greatest impact on the cave dwelling region. These mountains extend 1,500 kilometers across central China from the Gansu-Qinghai border in the west to central Henan in the east. They range in elevation from 2,000 to 3,000 meters above sea level. The main peak is Mount Taibai (3,767 meters high) in Shaanxi. The Qin *ling* range makes it difficult for the summer's moist ocean air to penetrate deep into the loess region to the north; it also keeps the cold, northern-continental winter air of central Asia from penetrating very far to the south. This range of mountains defines not only the limits of the eolian loess soil zone, but also the aridity of the region's southern borders, and consequently determines the agricultural economy of the regions on both sides of it. In short, the Qin *ling* range forms a natural divider between the northern semiarid zone of the loess region (with an economy based mainly on the dry farming of wheat) and the southern warm and humid zone (with an economy based mainly on irrigated rice farming).

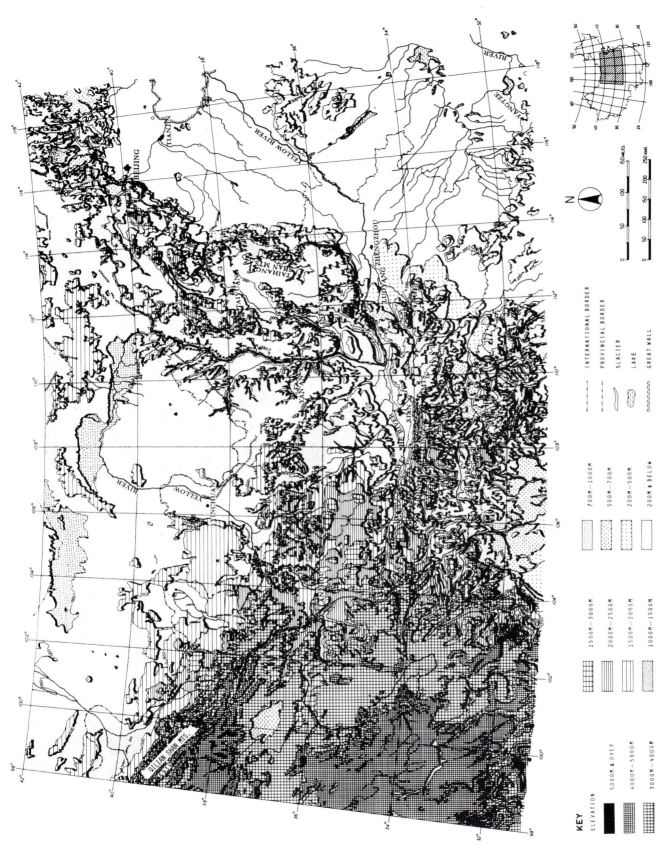

Fig. 2.1   Generalized map of important mountains and topographical form of the cave dwelling region

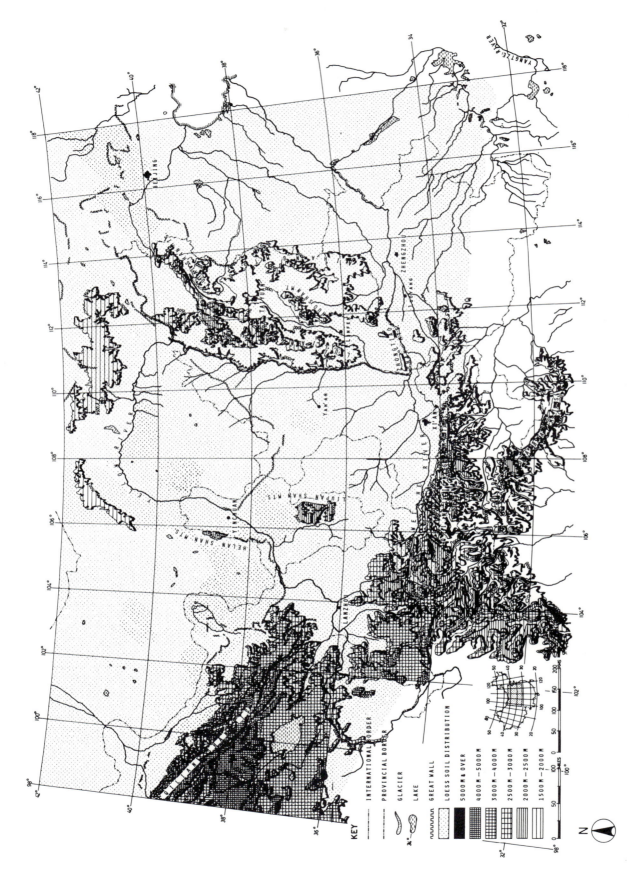

Fig. 2.2   Physiography of the cave dwelling region. The distribution of loess soil is generalized. East and north of this area there are only large patches.

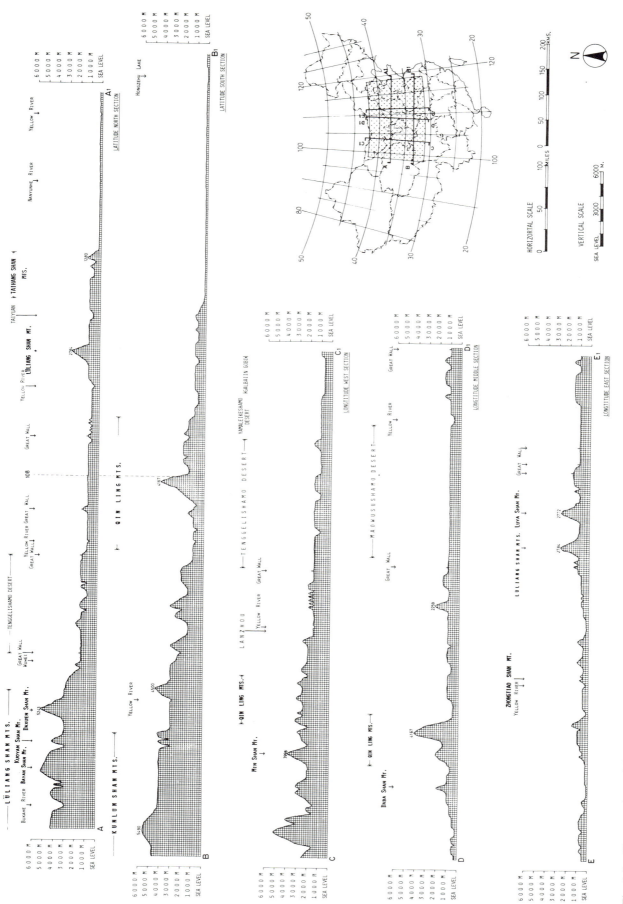

Fig. 2.3   Cross sections of the cave dwelling region

The physiography of the region is that of a central plateau surrounded by high mountains. The general tendency is for the height to decrease toward the east. The central part is composed of eastern Gansu, central and northern Shaanxi, and the Ningxia Hui Autonomous Region, which together form the loess plateau (fig. 2.2). The Yellow River winds through this entire region. The highest mountains, rising more than 5,000 meters above sea level, are located in the west and southwest. The second-highest mountains are located in the south and range in elevation between 1,500 and 2,000 meters. Lowest in altitude are the mountains to the east which rise only to a height of between 1,000 and 1,500 meters. The plateau itself is no higher than 1,000 meters at its center (fig. 2.3).

Impact of the Loess Soil

The loess or yellow soil of China is mainly distributed between thirty-three and forty-seven degrees north latitude and is confined by the direction of the east-west mountain systems, especially the Qin *ling,* Funiu *shan,* and Dabie *shan* ranges on the southern border of the region. This loess soil lies in an arid and semiarid climatic belt where annual precipitation varies between 250 and 500 millimeters, evaporation exceeds 1,000 millimeters per year, and where winter temperatures average below 0°C while summer temperatures exceed 35°C.

The loess strip covers an area of 631,000 square kilometers and accounts for approximately 6.6 percent of China's total land area. Loess soil is found mainly at altitudes of 200 to 2,400 meters above sea level. The main plateau is situated along the middle reaches of the Yellow River and extends over 2,000 kilometers to the west of the Liupan *shan* range. The altitude in the east varies between 1,000 and 2,000 meters above sea level. An altitude lower than 1,000 meters is found in some of the eastern basins and plains and scattered along some of the piedmonts in the west.

The Chinese plateau is the largest loess region in the world. Worldwide, loess soil is found in only a few places: the USSR (Siberia); the United States (Mississippi valley); Germany; southern

Israel; and China. The Chinese deposit seems to be the largest and most developed of all. Written Chinese records of the loess region date back some 2,000 years. Loess soil is common in more than four of China's provinces, but it is primarily concentrated in Henan, Shanxi, Shaanxi, and Gansu. It varies in quality and composition—in some places it is soft while in others it tends to be dense and heavy.

Two different processes are thought to have produced loess soil. The eolian model assumes that loess was primarily formed from dust that was generated by deflation in an adjacent desert area and then carried out by winds and deposited far from its origin. Such is thought to have been the case in China and also in the Negev of southern Israel. In North America, Germany, and the south-central USSR, loess soil is thought to have resulted from fluvial deposits that were left after the retreat of glaciers.

The existing loess soil zone in China, then, resulted from action of northwesterly winds originating in the desert regions of Asia (the Gobi, Mongolia, and Inner Mongolia). Such dry wind blows during most seasons of the year and carries with it fine particles of sand and dust (see climate section below). The Taihang *shan* range to the east and the Qin *ling* to the south prevented the dust from continuing further and caused it to be deposited in this zone (*see* figure 2.1). The eolian process is a continuous one. It was recently proven, for example, that the loess soil deposits of southern Israel still accumulate additional dust blown in from the Sahara and north Africa (Dr. Eli Ganor, personal communication, Tel Aviv University, summer 1983). As long as the combination of aridity and wind velocity prevails, such a process continues to build up loess soil areas. It can be assumed that the Chinese loess soil is also being built up continually. The major deposits occurred during the Quaternary period over a major part of northern China (fig. 2.4).

Except for a few high mountains, the plateau formation dominates the loess area with the yellow soil forming its core. The plateau itself covers 400,000 square kilometers and forms the bulk of the loess soil region, rising 800 to 2,000 meters above sea level. Topographically, the zone can be

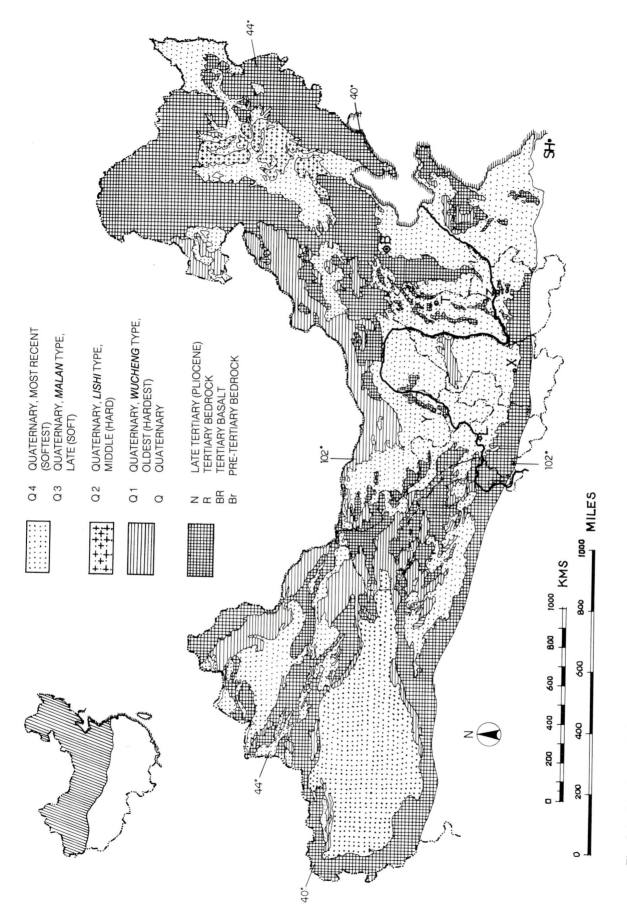

Fig. 2.4 Distribution of the Quaternary and Tertiary soil in northern China. Note the preponderance of Quaternary loess. Cities are indicated by their initials: Beijing, Lanzhou, Shanghai, Taiyuan, Xi'an, and Yan'an.

Q 4   QUATERNARY, MOST RECENT (SOFTEST)
Q 3   QUATERNARY, *MALAN* TYPE, LATE (SOFT)

Q 2   QUATERNARY, *LISHI* TYPE, MIDDLE (HARD)

Q 1   QUATERNARY, *WUCHENG* TYPE, OLDEST (HARDEST)
Q   QUATERNARY

N   LATE TERTIARY (PLIOCENE)
R   TERTIARY BEDROCK
BR   TERTIARY BASALT
Br   PRE-TERTIARY BEDROCK

MILES

KMS

N

divided into four parts: (1) the central Gansu plateau; (2) the eastern Gansu and northern Shaanxi plateaus; (3) the Shanxi plateau; and (4) the western Henan highlands. The loess plateau drops off sharply at its edges, where there are many gorges and gullies. Since timber for housing construction is scarce in this region, and because the soil is uniform and relatively soft, cave dwellings have become a distinctive form of shelter here.

ORIGIN

At the end of the nineteenth century, F. von Richthofen pointed out that the loess soil in northern China is composed of dust particles that originated in neighboring regions and were deposited by the action of wind. Thus, the loess is an eolian deposit. At the beginning of the twentieth century, V. A. Obruchev observed that the primary or main loess originated from deposits made by wind from central Asia and the neighboring deserts, and that the secondary loess was formed by other forces such as alluvial depositing or flooding; he called the latter type locally originated loess. Later, Anderson, Roque, Deljin, and others who have studied the Chinese loess of Shaanxi, Gansu, and Shanxi provinces developed the hypothesis of wind formation further. They clarified the distinction between eolian and fluvial loess. After the 1930s, Chinese scholars began their own investigations. Ma Rongzhi, who has researched the distribution of Chinese loess, is convinced that it was formed by wind. He bases his belief on: the common distribution pattern of loess in valleys as well as in high mountains and on plateaus and terraces; the relative balance of topographic development at the higher and the lower levels; the fact that the main components of the soil are powdery sand and not coarse sand or fine gravel; and that all deposits contain lime although the amounts and ratios differ in various places. Other geologists who followed Ma Rongzhi have confirmed the hypothesis that the Chinese loess is of eolian origin (Zhai Lisheng 1983, 3–4). This hypothesis does not exclude the involvement of other forces such as water in the reformation of some secondary loess (ibid., 2–3). But many Chinese geologists have continued to research and reinforce a hypothesis that water was

not the main factor in the origin of the Chinese loess soil, and they also believe that a dry climate has contributed to the deposition and formation of loess (fig. 2.5).

In 1959 Zhang Zhonggu introduced the "multiple causes" approach, which was complemented in 1963 by the work of other Chinese geologists. Following this approach, China's loess can be analyzed into the following ten types: (1) alluvial; (2) slope deposition; (3) flood deposition; (4) wind deposition; (5) ice deposition; (6) lake deposition; (7) flood-slope deposition; (8) alluvial-flood deposition; (9) remained-slope deposition; and (10) alluvial-slope deposition. This multicause formation hypothesis encompasses both the primary and secondary types of loess. The main area of dispute concerns loess formation in high mountains and plateau areas rather than formation in river valley basins (ibid., 5–7).

COMPOSITION

Loess soil is composed of salty minerals from loamy sands rich in the nitrogen, phosphorus, and potassium that support agriculture. The looseness of the soil, its lack of vegetation cover, and torrential summer rains intensify erosion. On the margins of the plateau, especially along the Yellow River, the soil forms ridges, gullies, and mounds. Destruction of the dense ancient forests has also contributed to the erosion process. Summer rain runoff washes away fertile topsoil at the rate of 0.5 centimeters per year. Ninety percent of the Yellow River mud and silt, totaling more than one billion tons per year, comes from the loess plateau. The river becomes clogged, causing disastrous floods (China Handbook Editorial Committee 1983, 47–48).

The constituent materials of loess include component particles, minerals, soluble salts, and trace chemical elements. The component particles are smaller than 0.25 millimeters in size and usually make up 10 to 25 percent of the total soil bulk, up to a maximum of 30 percent. The early Quaternary loess has a higher proportion of clay particles and a lower proportion of fine sand than that of the late Quaternary period.

Loess is rather complicated in its mineral composition. Light minerals make up 90 percent or

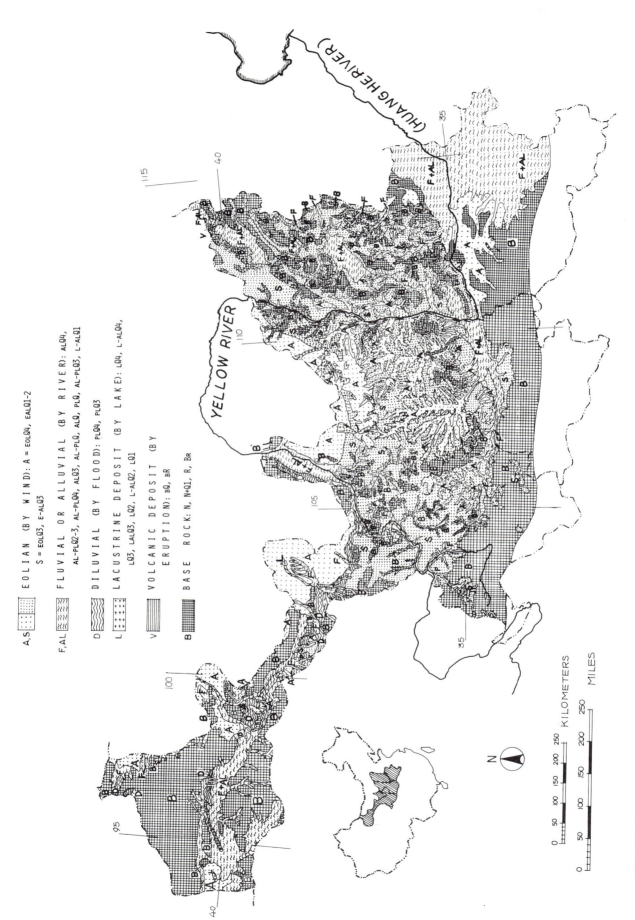

Fig. 2.5　Deposition of loess soil by origin

more of the total mineral content, while the quantity of heavy minerals is generally less than 10 percent. The heavy minerals mostly grade between 0.05 and 0.01 millimeters. The clay mineral most common in loess is illite. Calcium carbonate is one of the most common soluble salts found, ranging from between 10 to 16 percent of the total salts (Wang Yongyan and Zhang Zonghu 1980, [unpaginated]).

GEOLOGICAL STRUCTURE

Chinese loess soil was first formed during the Pleistocene epoch, the earliest stage of the Quaternary period (fig. 2.6). This period was characterized by the rise and recession of continental ice sheets and by the appearance of humans. The Pleistocene loess is composed of an early Pleistocene (Q1) layer (formed between 1,200,000 and 700,000 years ago) with a total thickness of 40 to 100 meters; a middle Pleistocene (Q2) layer (deposited between 700,000 and 100,000 years ago) with upper and lower sublayers and a total thickness of 50 to 70 meters; and a late Pleistocene (Q3) layer (formed between 100,000 and 5,000 years ago) with a thickness of about 10 to 30 meters. Holocene loess (Q4) is only 2 to 3 meters deep and lies on the upper part of the soil, distributed over the surface. It is loosely cemented and contains a remarkable proportion of unstable heavy minerals. The Holocene deposits date back 5,000 years (ibid.).

These four geological layers of the Quaternary loess soil are schematized as follows (fig. 2.7): (1) Q4 Quaternary, the Holocene layer, is the most recent and forms the upper layer. It is the softest form of loess and therefore the most unsuitable for cave dwelling construction; (2) Q3 Quaternary is the late Pleistocene layer. Known to archaeologists as the *ma lan* layer, it is a late deposit of loess where medium-width cave dwellings can be constructed; (3) Q2 Quaternary is the middle Pleistocene layer. Known as the *li shi* loess layer, it is of medium strength. *Li shi* loess is the main wind-deposited layer in China. Most of the Chinese cave dwellings are located here, including the very old historic ones; (4) Q1 Quaternary is the early Pleistocene layer. Known as *wu cheng* soil, it is the oldest loess. It is seldom exposed since it is buried quite deeply, and very few (if any)

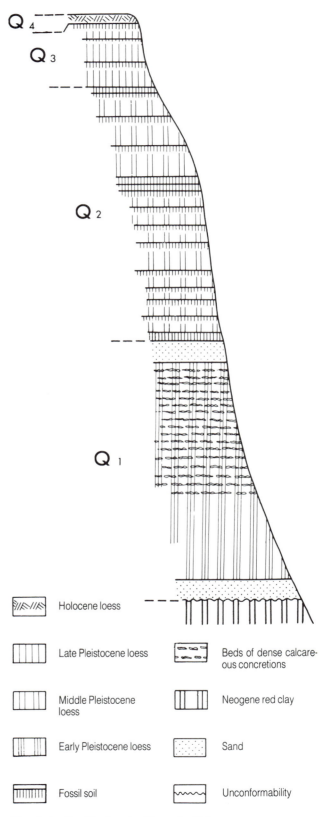

Fig. 2.6   Profile sketch of loess in China

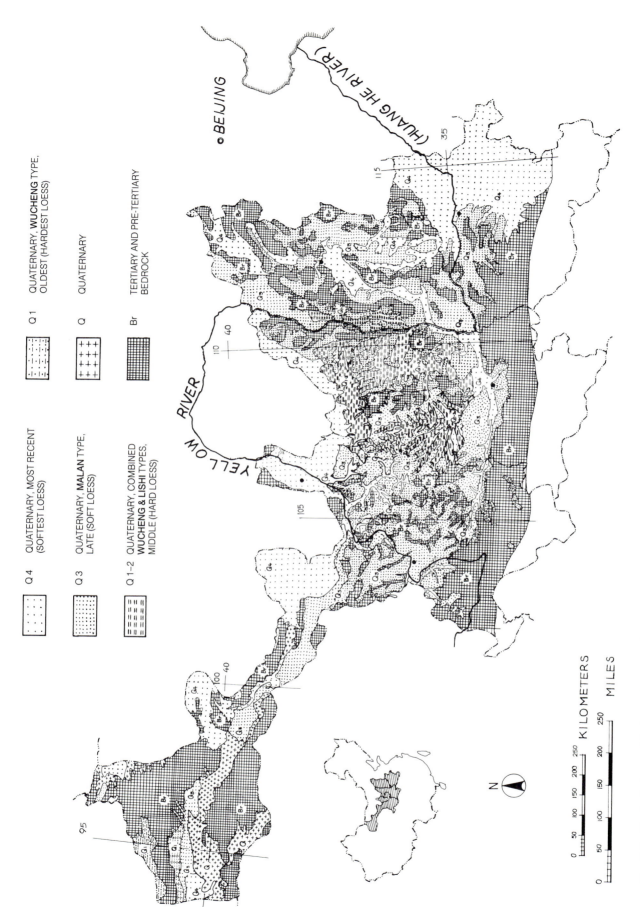

Fig. 2.7 Geological age of the loess plateau in the provinces researched

Q 4   QUATERNARY, MOST RECENT (SOFTEST LOESS)

Q 3   QUATERNARY, **MALAN** TYPE, LATE (SOFT LOESS)

Q 1–2   QUATERNARY, COMBINED **WUCHENG & LISHI** TYPES, MIDDLE (HARD LOESS)

Q 1   QUATERNARY, **WUCHENG** TYPE, OLDEST (HARDEST LOESS)

Q   QUATERNARY

Br   TERTIARY AND PRE-TERTIARY BEDROCK

KILOMETERS

MILES

N

BEIJING

(HUANG HE RIVER)

YELLOW RIVER

Table 2.1 Depositional Loess Strata: Petrological Features in Lanzhou, Xi'an, and Taiyuan

Place	Strata	Layers	Buried Weathered Layer	Stratification	Porosity	Granule Uniformity
Lanzhou	two strata 5–20 meters thick	many	has	clear	not apparent	not uniform
Xi'an	three strata 12–27 meters thick	rare	has, and has fine buried soil profile	not clear	most apparent	comparatively uniform
Taiyuan	one stratum 10–22 meters thick	a few	lacks	comparatively clear	apparent	not uniform

Source: Zhai Lisheng 1983, 15.

cave dwellings are found in this type of soil. Each of the above layers can be further analyzed into sublayers. There is also basement rock beneath the loess soil which was formed during the Tertiary and pre-Tertiary periods. The basement is likewise further divided into the late Tertiary or Pliocene (N); Tertiary bedrock (R); Tertiary basalt (BR); and pre-Tertiary bedrock (Br) layers.

In the *li shi* loess soil (Q2) there is frequently a red horizontal layer followed by a harder calcium core layer. This calcium layer protects the tops of the cave dwellings. The cave dwellers have learned this from experience and many have purposely constructed their caves beneath this calcium layer. Similar layers also are found in *ma lan* loess soil (Q3).

Throughout the course of the eolian process, the percentage of sand in the soil of the middle Yellow River basin decreases from west to east and from north to south. This trend leaves the loess soil stronger, lessens the number of cracks and the amount of soluble salts (carbonic acid, chloride, and sulphuric acid), increases soil density, and improves soil mechanics (Wang Fu 1982, 118). This overall quality improves soil stability and thus enhances the stability of cave dwellings themselves.

Most parts of the Chinese loess plateau are composed of *ma lan* (Q3) and loess accumulated in modern times (Q4). The intensity of the earthquakes in some regions, as in Ningxia, has also changed the original outer layer of the loess deposits and has resulted in softening and destabilizing of the soil. The quality of the loess soil varies from region to region and it has different

mechanical properties under different climatic conditions. Generally the older the loess, the more dense it is (table 2.1). Moving from the upper layer to the lower, the quality of the loess improves. It becomes more stable, stronger, denser, and has a lower degree of moisture. According to Luo Wenbao, the mechanical properties of loess in different regions are different; for example the shear strength and dry density of loess in Shanxi and Henan provinces are greater, while in the loess of Shaanxi province they are inferior, and in that of Gansu province and the Ningxia Hui Autonomous Region they are the lowest (Luo Wenbao 1985, 234).

The basic characteristics of China's loess soil are captured by describing its uniformity, composition, hardness, color, and propensity for vertical erosion. Loess soil is uniform in that it is generally free of stones. This is especially true of loess soil that originates from eolian dust deposits. The uniformity of the soil makes it especially well suited to excavation for cave dwellings.

The granular composition and plastic index of loess soil are unique in that this soil is made up only of fine particles. It normally contains more than 55 percent calcium carbonate and powdery matter with no granule larger than 0.25 millimeters in size. These small particles increase the soil's porosity and enable straight, even cutting for the construction of cave dwelling walls (Zhai 1983, 1).

Loess soil is very hard when dry, and during the dry season it has a characteristic crust measuring 20 to 30 centimeters thick. This hard, dry crust prevents the escape of moisture from lower soil strata, promoting a cool space within cave dwellings that makes an excellent living environment during the hot dry season.

Loess soil is typically yellow, brownish yellow, or grayish yellow in color, which makes it appear similar to desert soil. The presence of certain minerals in the soil contributes to this coloration. The color of the loess soil lends its name to the Yellow River, the main waterway that runs through this region.

Finally, loess soil is characterized by a propensity for vertical erosion. The erosion process in loess soil is unique and the landforms resulting from it are distinctive. The soil is largely porous and not covered by vegetation. Thus, water penetrates deeply into the ground creating sinkholes, funnels, tunnels, cliffs, columns, and cavities. This erosion process is unusual in its intensity, accelerating during the brief torrential rains that are typical of the region and increasing the ratio of runoff.

Of all the loess soil characteristics, its propensity for vertical erosion is of special concern because of its impact on the development of cave dwellings. Vertical erosion can cause sudden collapse of cavities or cave dwellings and creates special landforms such as ridges, bluffs, and gullies. Eroded soil, carried by rivers and their tributaries, establishes a high percentage of loess mud in the waters and results in deposits on the floodplain and riverbanks. Although this process provides land well suited to agriculture, it is essential to set up a controlled drainage system within and around a complex of loess cave dwellings to minimize it.

Loess soil requires a special pattern of agricultural cultivation and a special maintenance system to minimize erosion. Because of the intensity of vertical erosion, loess is among the least suitable soils for aboveground residential construction. The upper layer of loess soil, especially the Holocene (Q4) layer, is recent, only 2–3 meters thick, and relatively loose. It contains a high proportion of light minerals, soluble salts, and particles. Rain penetration into this layer is quick and intense and therefore destructive. This deficiency has traditionally been understood by Chinese farmers and it may have contributed to the evolution of cave dwellings as alternative residences. In

the southern part of the Ningxia Hui Autonomous Region, residential construction has been severely restricted in its development. Most residences in this area are either earth-and-wood constructions, pit cave dwellings, or cliff cave dwellings, all of which belong to the category of earth-sheltered buildings (Bai Mingxue 1985, 56–57). The difference between cave dwellings and aboveground housing is that cave dwellings create open space that does not require the use of building materials, while aboveground dwellings confine open space and require building materials for construction. Recent Chinese research on loess soil was primarily motivated by the practical needs of constructing railways, bridges, et cetera, in the loess soil zone (Zhai 1983, 11–14).

THICKNESS

China's loess soil ranges between fifty and three hundred meters in thickness. The thickest is that found along the middle reaches of the Yellow River (fig. 2.8). West of the Liupan *shan* range and northward, from the terrain between the Huajialing and Mahanshan elevations to the vicinity of Lanzhou and west of the Baiyu range, it is up to two or three hundred meters thick. To the east of the Liupan *shan* and west of the Lüliang *shan* ranges, the thickness is between one and two hundred meters. On the northern piedmonts of the Qilian *shan,* Tian *shan,* and Altun *shan* ranges, the loess is less than fifty meters thick. On the north China plain the loess deposit is interlaced with other alluvial sediments and not especially thick (Wang and Zhang 1980 [unpaginated]).

The general features of the loess deposits closely follow the paleotopography of the underlying bedrock. The formation process began in the early Pleistocene epoch, or about 1,200,000 years ago (ibid.). The loess soil varies in depth throughout the Chinese plateau. The maximum thickness is found in the Qingyang region of eastern Gansu and in the adjacent Yan'an region of northern Shaanxi. In some parts of eastern Gansu and northern Shaanxi provinces the loess layer is 150 meters thick. The shallowest deposits are in the areas of Jinnan (southern Shanxi) and Yuxi (western Henan) (fig. 2.9) (Ren Zhiyuan 1985a, 333).

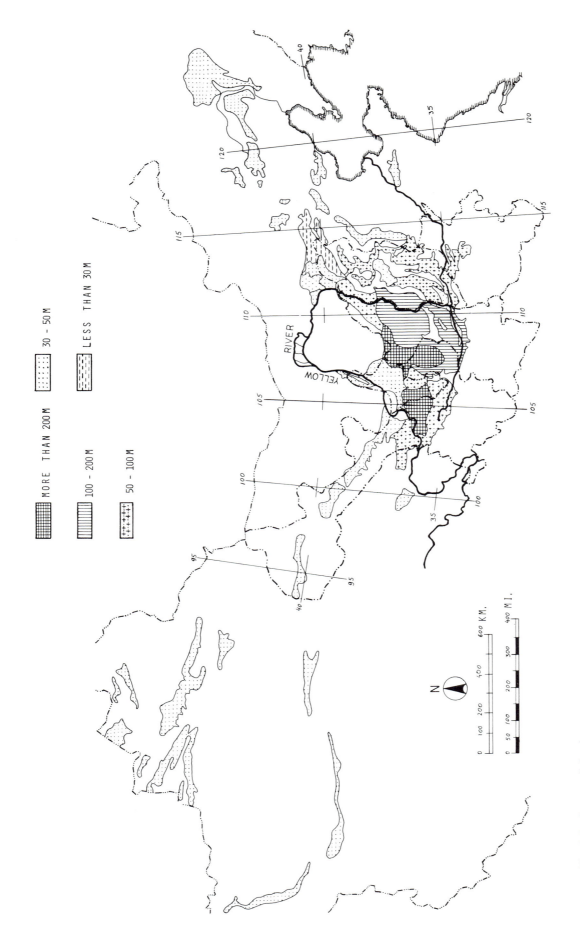

Fig. 2.8   Loess soil depth

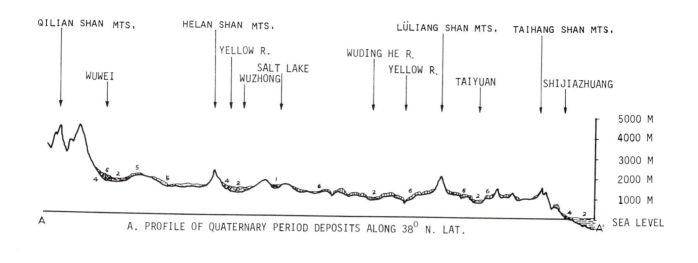

A. PROFILE OF QUATERNARY PERIOD DEPOSITS ALONG 38° N. LAT.

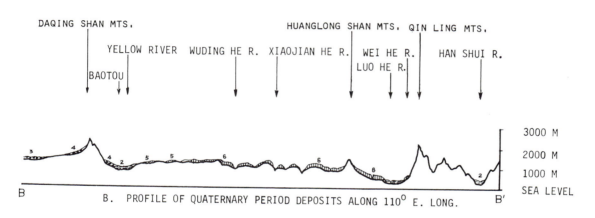

B. PROFILE OF QUATERNARY PERIOD DEPOSITS ALONG 110° E. LONG.

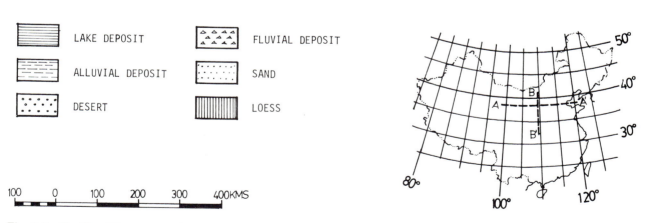

Fig. 2.9   Profile of Quaternary deposits in the main areas of loess distribution

A. *YUAN* : HIGH TABLELAND

B.*LIANG* : ELONGATED MOUND

C.*MAO* : ROUND MOUND

D. GULLY : VERY NARROW, STEEP VALLEY

E. CLIFF

F. LANDSLIDE

G. SINKHOLE

H. BRIDGE

I. FUNNEL

J. CRACKS

K. COLUMNS

L. EOLIAN : SAND

Fig. 2.10   Landforms in the loess soil region

REGIONAL ENVIRONMENTAL DETERMINANTS 25

ENVIRONMENTAL FORCES

In analyzing the Chinese loess soil all contributing natural forces must be considered comprehensively. These forces include climate, landforms, stratification, structural properties, hydrological conditions, and physical as well as geological features. Of all these factors, the structural properties of loess—especially its physical and mechanical behavior—are the most important because they determine construction measurements.

Climate. The dry or semidry climate that prevailed while the Chinese loess was formed has determined the physical and geological features of the region, the water table, the level of moisture within the soil, and the composition of the soil. The climate reveals the regional structure, both in horizontal and vertical terms. The climate itself is influenced by altitude and distance from the ocean. In any case, the climate of this region is basically the same today as it was during the Quaternary period when the loess soil accumulated. The same may be said for the topography and the mountain forms within and surrounding the region. But the special topography of the loess plateau in northern Shaanxi—the basins of Guanzhong (the Wei *he* River region), Taiyuan, and the Yellow River—took shape in several stages. Moreover, each type of loess soil developed at a different time and resulted from the action of different forces.

Landforms. Another factor defining loess formation is the landform. Loess is a continental accumulation. The formation of both the landform and the loess itself is one integrated process. Landforms such as basins or sand dunes reflect the accumulation process. Through analysis of their historical formation and their patterns of distribution, we can understand the landforms. Topographically, the loess region is surrounded on three sides by a number of mountain ranges: the Taihang *shan* in the east, the Qilian *shan* in the west, and the Qin *ling* to the south. The northern side is almost free of mountains. Within the region, a number of mountain ranges divide the land, including the Lüliang *shan,* the Liupan *shan,* the Bai *shan,* and the Zhongtiao *shan.* Various other landforms also characterize this area, in-cluding river valleys, terraces, watershed plateaus, hilly plains, slide slopes, sinkholes, funnels, loess karsts, gullies, and eolian sand forms (fig. 2.10).

The loess landforms are generally analyzed into four major types, and each landform type has an impact on cave dwelling development.

(1) *Yuan,* or high tableland. A broad, flat, and high plateau surrounded by deep gullies and cliffs (fig. 2.11). This form is primarily spread over northern and central Shaanxi and the neighboring area of eastern Gansu. Cave dwelling villages are commonly associated with the *yuan* landform.

(2) *Liang,* or elongated loess mound. A long, narrow landform usually more than ten kilometers in length (fig. 2.12). Its width at the top may be from ten to several hundred meters. In its upper elevations are residual narrow terraces. *Liang* usually emerges in places between *yuan* and *mao* landforms. It is found in western and eastern Gansu, and in northern Shaanxi. Cave dwelling villages are not usually constructed within such a landform. *Liang* is mostly distributed in the northern and western parts of the plateau.

Fig. 2.11 Aerial view of the world's largest loess plateau, located in eastern Gansu: the *yuan* landform is a broad, flat, high plateau surrounded by cliffs. Note the pit cave dwelling patios in the foreground.

Fig. 2.12   The *liang* form is an elongated loess mound

(3) *Mao,* or round loess mound. This term refers to the arched loess and hilly topography where there are circular and elliptical shapes. The angle of the slopes varies between fifteen and thirty-five degrees. *Mao* generally merges with neighboring *yuan* and *liang* landforms. Cave dwelling villages are not usually constructed within such a landform. *Mao* is found in western and eastern Gansu, and in northern Shaanxi.

(4) River valley landform. Primarily formed by depositional loess with wide or narrow terraced surfaces, this landform appears as a meandering or straight riverbed. It is found in central and northern Shaanxi, western Henan, and in Shanxi. Many cities and towns with cave dwellings are located within the low river valley landform terraces, for example the cities of Yan'an in Shaanxi province and Taiyuan in Shanxi. The valley or the plain form represents the final stage of the progressive loess erosion process. Loess river valley basins are found along the middle reaches of the Yellow River, in the northern Ningxia Hui Autonomous Region, in central and southern Shanxi, and within certain other river basins.

There are important differences between the landform formation process assumed for the plateau region of western Gansu and northern Shaanxi and that assumed for the basin area of central Shaanxi, Taiyuan, and the Yellow River (Zhai 1983, 8–10). Other distinctive landforms also resulting from erosion include: (1) Sharply vertical cliffs that drop abruptly from the plateau; (2) vertical cavities, funnels, sinkholes, and underground spaces that cause collapses and in turn change the face of the plateau or slope (fig. 2.13); (3) bridges and columns formed as a result of the combined actions of vertical erosion and cavities, or from cracks in cliffs; (4) gullies or narrow canyons that drop abruptly from the plateau; (5) eolian landforms such as sand dunes; and (6) terraced forms.

Cave dwellings have been built in the slopes of gullies, although neither the slopes nor their lowlands are suitable for agriculture. Residents of such cave dwellings suffer from lack of ventilation and high indoor temperatures during the summer. Landslides and cliff wall collapse due to gravity or erosion are common in such lowland areas, and cliff cave dwellings built here can also suffer the collapse of their facades.

Stratification. The circumstances of loess deposition inferred for each time period are distinct. The early, middle, and late epochs of the Quaternary period show different types of stratification.

Fig. 2.13   Vertical erosion and sinkholes in loess soil

The epoch also determines rock formation. The rocks of the oldest epoch, for example, are the strongest and show little or no deformation.

During the early Pleistocene epoch (Q1), loess accumulation emerged in the Guanzhong area of Shaanxi province, while in Shanxi only a gravel accumulation appeared. During the middle Pleistocene epoch (Q2), a great quantity of loess accumulated in Shaanxi. Loess in Shanxi was scattered in zones surrounding a few basins. The accumulation of loess in western Gansu was sparse and rare. During the later Pleistocene (Q3), loess accumulation in Shaanxi continued. A comparatively thin layer of loess appeared in a continuous pattern. The loess accumulating in western Henan during this epoch was so thin that it left the surface of the ground visible beneath.

Hydrological Conditions. It is essential to understand the hydrology of the loess since survival in cave dwellings depends on the degree of moisture in the soil. Usually the permeability of loess creates favorable conditions because of its high porosity. But underground water may lead to karsts, cavities, or funnels. In the loess plateau, that water may flow out of a spring and thereby induce the formation of karsts and landslides. In the valley basins the water table depth is usually shallow, and it is subject to change according to different landforms, intensity of irrigation, and the amount of precipitation (ibid., 15–24).

Structural and Physical Properties. The characteristics of loess soil provide several advantages for cave dwelling construction. Loess is relatively easy to cut or excavate quickly. As a result, cave dwelling construction in this type of soil requires only simple technology and/or tools.

Because loess soil is firm and hard when dry, it makes a durable material, and cave dwellings, when properly excavated in it, can last for anywhere between thirty and four hundred years. But cave dwelling excavation must be performed over an extended period of time rather than all at once. This permits the soil to dry and become hard enough to hold its shape. If the cave is excavated too quickly, the soil remains moist and soft and the structure is prone to collapse, especially in regions where the soil is high in moisture content as in Henan province.

Traditional methods of cave dwelling construction do not require any building materials other than the soil itself. Fired or adobe bricks and wood are not necessary and consequently the construction of a cave dwelling allows a considerable savings on building materials. The use of wood in construction of windows and doors for cave dwellings is only a recent phenomenon.

Since constructing a cave dwelling requires only a few relatively simple tools and no additional building materials, the overall construction cost is low. This fact, coupled with the ease of construction, makes cave dwellings affordable for farmers and others in similar economic circumstances.

Another construction advantage offered by loess soil is its excellent thermal performance. Loess functions well as both insulator and heat retainer. Its seasonal thermal performance provides a cool ambient environment in summer and warmth in winter.

During cave dwelling construction the loess soil must be kept as dry as possible. The nature of loess is that it softens when moist and hardens and solidifies when dry. The builder of cave dwellings must avoid sites where the soil is soft, especially on slopes created by landslides and earthquakes. The following are some guidelines for cave construction and site selection in relation to soil type:

*Q3/1 *Ma lan* loess soil of the epi-Pleistocene. Here caves with small spans can be excavated. In the lower part of *ma lan* loess there is often a thin brown layer of soil that has a calcium tuberculous layer beneath it. Because the calcium layer has good cementlike qualities, it lends strength and structural support to caves dug beneath it.

*Q2 The upper and lower layers of the *li shi* loess, of the middle Pleistocene epoch. Caves with large spans can be excavated here. In *li shi* loess are some embedded red layers with calcium layers beneath. Here too, the calcium layer adds strength when it is above the cave.

*Q1 The Eocene-Pleistocene loess. Rarely are caves excavated here because the earth layer is very deep and little exposed except in a few isolated areas.

*Q4 Loess representing the whole Pleistocene epoch. Cave dwellings cannot be excavated in this type of soil because it is not firm enough and collapses often occur.

*Q3/2 Upper part of the *ma lan* loess. Caves cannot be excavated here since collapse often occurs in this type of soil also (Wang Fu 1985, 405).

Li shi loess is the most common wind-distributed loess soil in China. Within this layer the majority of Chinese cave dwellings are found. In the middle section of the Yellow River basin—where *li shi* loess is also found—there is a tendency for certain changes to occur in the loess soil as the wind moves across it toward the east and south. Toward the east and south of this middle section the proportion of sand particles, ratio of cavities, and amounts of chloride, sulfate, and

heavy carbonite in the loess soil decrease, while the clay particle content, index of plasticity, soil density, and physical or structural capabilities increase. These amount to major differences in the quality of the loess. Cave dwellings constructed in this southeast region are less prone to collapse and safer because of these qualitative changes. Thus, careful consideration of site selection is essential to the building of safe cave dwellings (ibid., 405–406).

A good example of incorrect site selection is the one that was chosen for construction of a public school in 1974 at Fenghuo Brigade in Liquan *xian* County, southern Shaanxi, some 80 kilometers northwest of Xi'an. Although the school's design was integrated into the natural slope configuration of the site, the seven terraced levels of belowground rooms survived for only a few years, finally collapsing after a heavy rain. The school was constructed in soft *ma lan* soil (fig. 2.14). Because schools require large classrooms with natural light, the Chinese government permits schools in caves only when economic conditions in the particular county

Fig. 2.14   The seven-story belowground elementary school in Liquan *xian* County, southern Shaanxi. View from the north.

are poor. Part of this structure is used today only to house some of the teachers and for a few student activities. The ceiling of the teachers' residence is almost seven meters thick. The upper floors of the school are drier than the lower floors because the lower soil layers contain more moisture and are softer than the upper layers. In 1981 this school of six hundred students and teachers was moved to an aboveground structure. Across the hills to the west, there are many abandoned cave dwellings. Even though their roofs were considered to be sufficiently thick, the dwellings collapsed as a result of irrigation on the land above. Some cave dwellings in the same county are situated on flat land, but building here is discouraged by the government because it uses too much precious agricultural land.

Climate Pattern

The Chinese describe the climate of the researched region as encompassing four different types: moist in the south and southeast; semimoist in the north; and semidry and dry further north and northwest (fig. 2.15). The researched region is characterized by long, cold, and dry winters and short, hot, and rainy summers. In fact, the region as a whole is a geographical zone in itself that falls between two distinct climatic regions. To the north of the zone lies the continental desert region (Mongolia and the Gobi), and to its south is the humid region of China, bisected by the Qin *ling* range of mountains.

The climate pattern of this geographical zone is

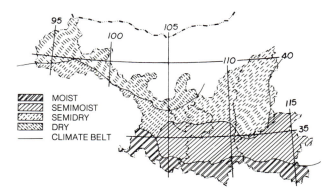

Fig. 2.15   Climate pattern in the researched region

defined as arid and semiarid. Arid zones are areas where the rate of moisture evaporation exceeds precipitation, resulting in a defict of humidity. These zones also show a marked difference between temperatures recorded in the afternoon and in the late night hours.

Usually, precipitation in arid zones is variable and does not support dry farming. The rainfall is characteristically brief, torrential, and sparse. The intensity of the rain results in very little of the water actually seeping into the ground, which causes a high proportion of runoff. This condition often causes flooding and erosion of the loess soil.

Also characteristic of such zones is an absence of vegetation. This detracts from the soil's capacity to absorb rain runoff and intensifies the erosion process. It also increases the likelihood of dust storms. In short, the characteristics of arid zones constitute an environment that is hostile to human, animal, and plant life. Thus, the arid zone environment necessitates special design considerations for shelter.

The Chinese cave dwellings are located in such an arid and semiarid geographical zone, where the temperature in winter months is usually below freezing. The average annual precipitation is between one hundred and eight hundred millimeters while the rate of evaporation is over 1,000 millimeters annually. The climate is defined as warm-temperate in most of the loess soil area. The autumn and spring seasons are short and moderate, and the duration of the frost-free period is from five to eight months. In this zone, the difference between minimum and maximum diurnal temperature is great and there is much windblown dust in the spring and fall.

The Qin *ling* range, bordering the southern part of the loess region, has a significant influence on the climate. Along with the Huai *he* and Bailong *jiang* (both rivers in the west), it forms a natural geographic and climatic barrier between southern and northern China. North of this range, temperatures fall below 0°C in the winter and rivers freeze, while south of the range, temperatures remain above freezing and rivers flow freely. Summer precipitation south of the range averages 1,200 millimeters (China Handbook Editorial Committee 1983, 77–78).

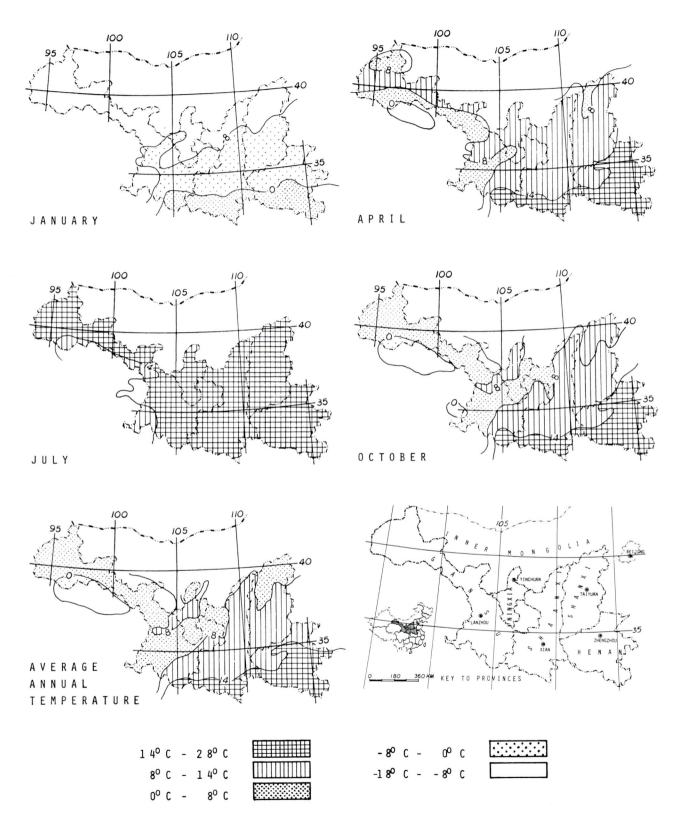

JANUARY

APRIL

JULY

OCTOBER

AVERAGE
ANNUAL
TEMPERATURE

KEY TO PROVINCES

14° C – 28° C		-8° C – 0° C	
8° C – 14° C		-18° C – -8° C	
0° C – 8° C			

Fig. 2.16   Average monthly and annual temperatures

TEMPERATURE

The highest annual average temperatures occur in southern Shaanxi and Henan, in the southernmost part of the region. Temperatures drop off toward the north, especially during winter (fig. 2.16). Monthly records show extreme differences between the coldest temperatures (-18°C——8°C) in January and the warmest temperatures (14°C—28°C) in July. The quarterly average temperature record shows that January is the coldest month of the year for the whole region and July the warmest (fig. 2.17). These seasonal temperature conditions encourage a preference for cave dwellings because such structures provide a comfortable ambient temperature year-round.

In arid regions, the number of frost days throughout the year is quite high (fig. 2.18) and frosts at night are common. Because the air is dry, when temperatures begin to fall they drop off sharply through the evening. The dryness or aridity of the air accelerates temperature diffusion during the night and frosts result. As the temperature drops and the air cools, it becomes stagnant and sinks. In this region a high frequency of frost (more than 100 days per year) is common in the relatively low land of Gansu and on the loess plateau that is surrounded by high mountains on

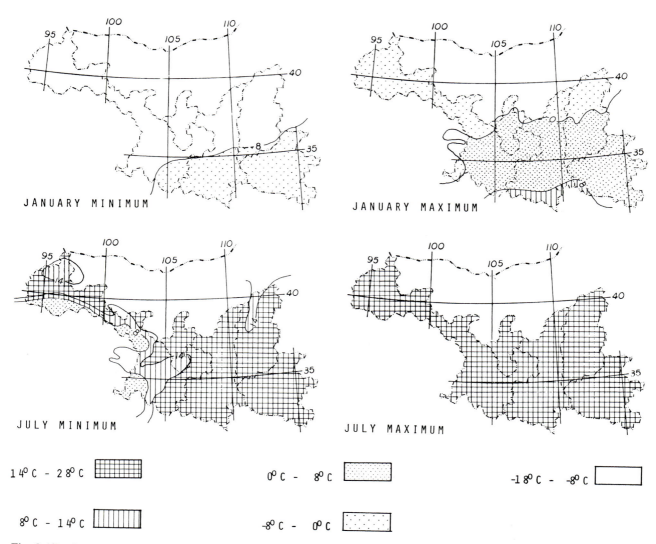

JANUARY MINIMUM

JANUARY MAXIMUM

JULY MINIMUM

JULY MAXIMUM

14°C - 28°C

8°C - 14°C

0°C - 8°C

-8°C - 0°C

-18°C - -8°C

Fig. 2.17   Average quarterly minimum and maximum temperatures

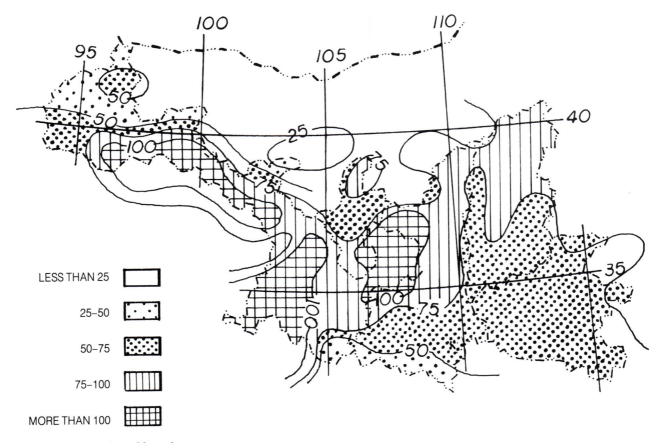

Fig. 2.18   Number of frost days per year

three sides. Here too the high number of frost days shows the importance of the cave dwellings as shelter, especially during the later hours of the night. Cave dwellings provide an ideal shelter from this hostile environment because they provide comfortable, stable indoor temperatures. An aboveground dwelling in this region would be very cold during the later half of the night, especially in winter, and overly warm during summer afternoons.

WIND

Wind velocity differs greatly from one part of the region to another (fig. 2.19). In general it can be said that spring and autumn are windy and dusty throughout the whole region and that high wind velocity (four meters per second) prevails in the northwestern part of the region throughout the year. The dominant wind comes from the north. It is very strong, cold, and dry in winter and

warm in summer. This is the wind that once brought deposits of loess soil to the region. It is generally assumed that this north wind still continues to bring particles from the dry regions of Mongolia and the Gobi. The direction and velocity of the wind in the north support the hypothesis that the origin of the loess soil was eolian and that it came from central Asia (fig. 2.20). From July through September, strong winds come to the middle and southern part of the loess region from the east, southeast, or southwest. This wind is warm and moist and it increases the high relative humidity in these areas.

The combined effects of heat and humidity during the summer create an uncomfortable ambient environment within the cave dwellings that poses a serious problem and real challenge to the designer. Adding to this, the lack of ventilation and otherwise cool temperature within the cave often results in condensation on its walls. The

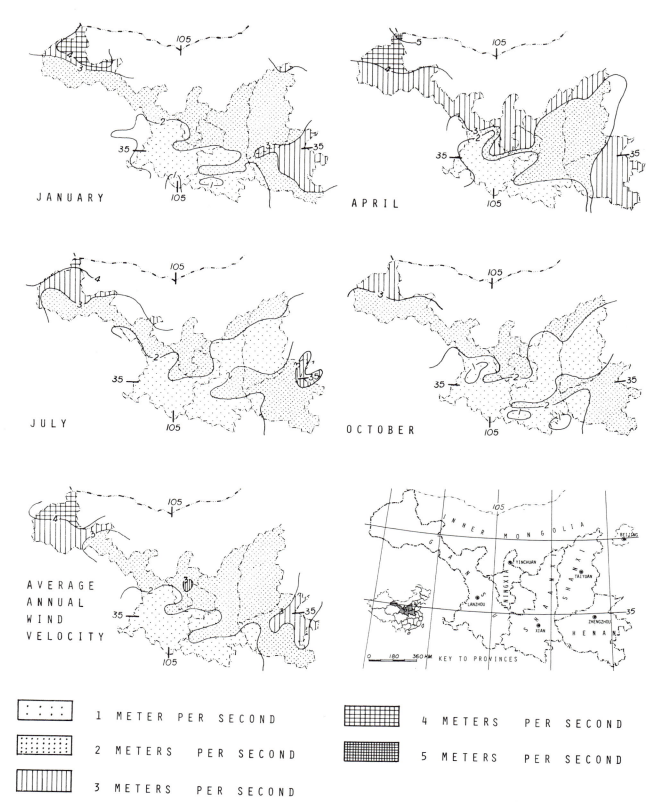

Fig. 2.19   Average monthly and annual wind velocity

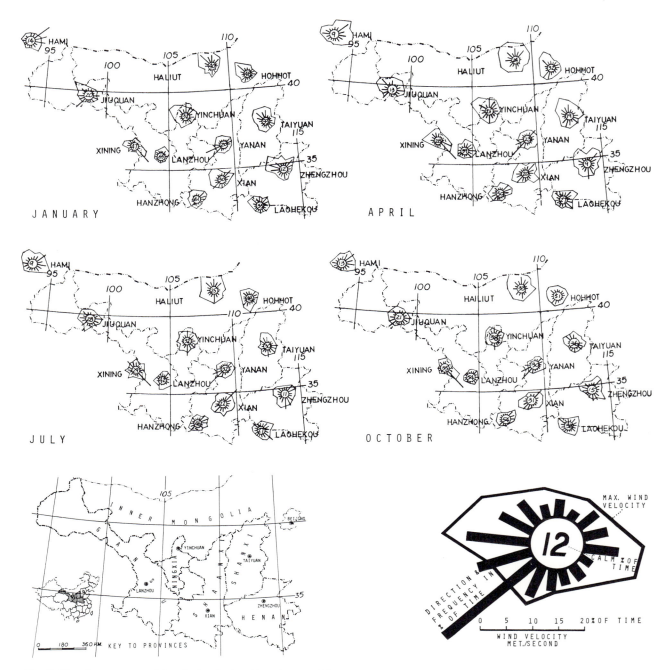

Fig. 2.20   Average monthly wind velocity, direction, and frequency

moisture content of the loess soil itself increases the relative humidity within the cave dwellings even more. In other parts of the world where cave dwellings have developed, the climate is warm and dry during the summer. Consequently, the non-Chinese belowground communities do not have the same humidity/moisture problem in their cave dwellings.

The number of dusty and stormy days can be as high as twenty or more per year in the northern part of the region (fig. 2.21). This is a much higher incidence rate than is typical in the south. The cause of this difference is to be found in the physiographical structure of the whole region, as shown in figure 2.1 where the lack of naturally occurring barriers leaves this area open to the arid

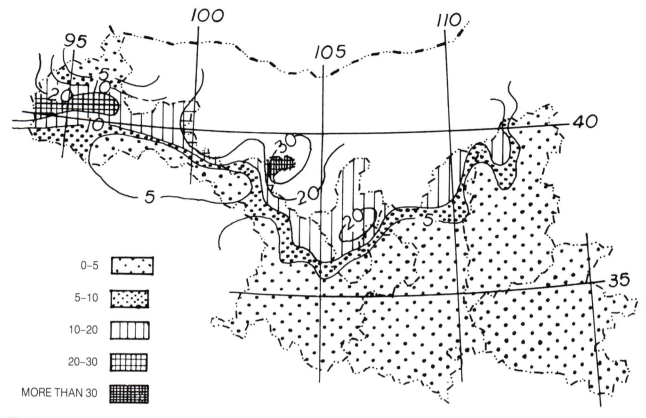

Fig. 2.21   Number of duststorms per year

and dusty air of the north. Beijing, for example, suffers from dust storms in both winter and spring. A few years ago, the Chinese government decided to implement a green belt along its Mongolian borders to minimize the negative effects of these northern dust storms. Arid regions are prone to suspension of fine dust particles in the air, increasing the likelihood of dust storms.

The dust also has an impact on aboveground buildings in the region. Dust particles abrade the buildings and weaken their foundations. Cave dwellings, on the other hand, are not harmed by the dust.

PRECIPITATION

Average annual precipitation is from four hundred to six hundred millimeters in the southern part of the region and one hundred to three hundred millimeters in the north and northwest. Because the southern rainfall takes place only during the summer, it alone is not sufficient to support the region's agriculture and must be sup-

plemented by irrigation. Most of the rainfall occurs during July and August. In general, there is less rainfall in the arid north and northwest and more in the semiarid south and southeast (fig. 2.22). The winter snow is generally sparse but the air is made very cold by the north wind.

Average monthly relative humidity in the region is very high during the summer and fall seasons, from July through November. It is low during the winter and spring seasons, from December through June. Because of the high altitude of the Qin *ling* range, the southern portion of the region has 60 percent or higher relative humidity throughout the year (fig. 2.23).

In the four capital cities of the region, as in Beijing, the number of solar hours is very high in summer and low in winter (fig. 2.24). The percentage of precipitation and the number of sunny hours and rainy days are all similar. The average annual relative humidity is highest at the end of summer and lowest in winter.

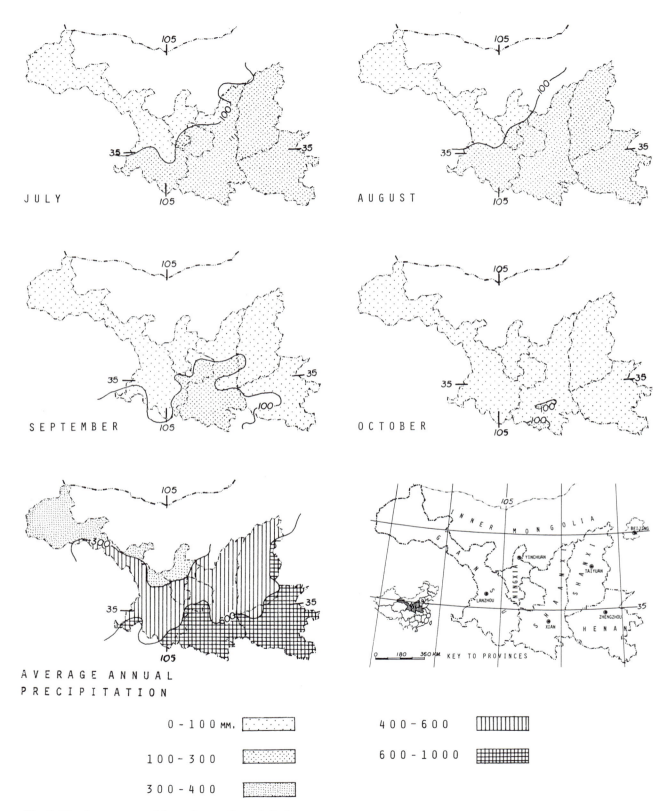

JULY

AUGUST

SEPTEMBER

OCTOBER

AVERAGE ANNUAL
PRECIPITATION

0 - 100 мм.

100 - 300

300 - 400

400 - 600

600 - 1000

KEY TO PROVINCES

Fig. 2.22   Average monthly and annual precipitation

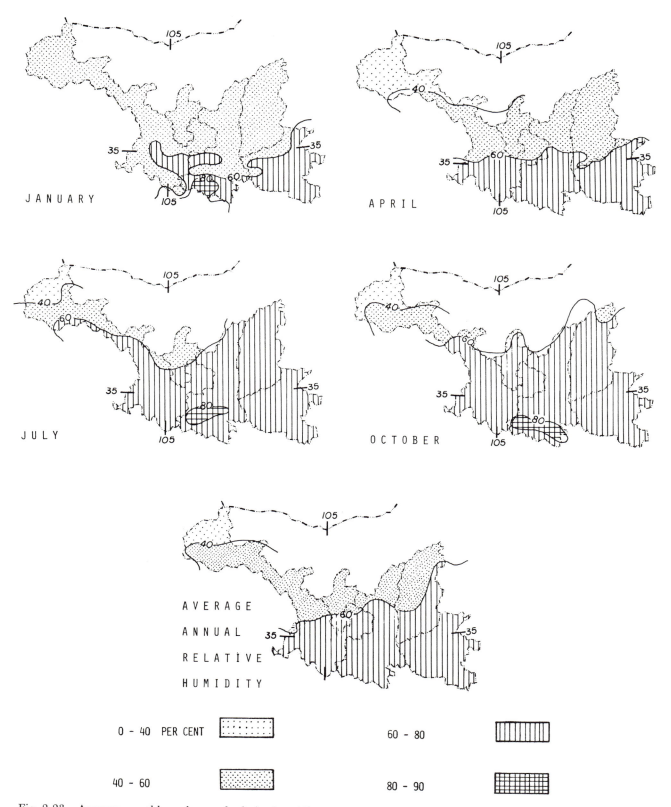

JANUARY

APRIL

JULY

OCTOBER

A V E R A G E

A N N U A L

R E L A T I V E

H U M I D I T Y

0 - 40 PER CENT

40 - 60

60 - 80

80 - 90

Fig. 2.23   Average monthly and annual relative humidity

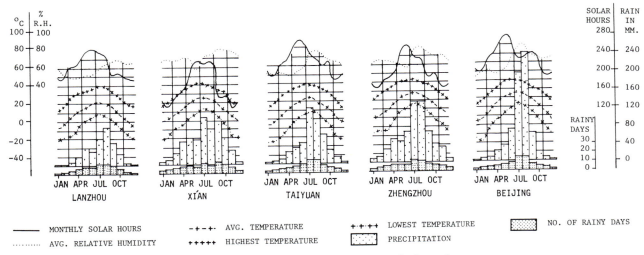

Fig. 2.24   Basic climate information for Beijing and capitals of the researched provinces

The Region's River System

The Yellow River is one of the region's two main rivers and it is centrally located. The other is the Wei *he*, a major tributary located in the southern part of Shaanxi. Another tributary is the Fen *he* River in Shanxi province. The agriculture of the region is based primarily on irrigation from the Yellow and Wei rivers.

The Yellow River is the second-largest river system in China and its valley has traditionally been referred to as the cradle of Chinese civilization. There are more than 19,995,953 hectares (49,410,000 acres) of cultivated land in this river basin, which amount to one-fifth of the total cultivated area of the entire country. The following nine provinces are included in the Yellow River watershed: Qinghai, Sichuan, Gansu, Ningxia, Inner Mongolia, Shanxi, Shaanxi, Henan, and Shandong. The region is well developed and densely populated, and it has many unmined mineral deposits. Major cities along the river are Lanzhou, an industrial city and the capital of Gansu; Baotou, an industrial city of Inner Mongolia; Zhengzhou, the capital of Henan; and Jinan, the capital of Shandong.

The Yellow River changes its course frequently. It is bounded by the Yin *shan* range in the north and the Kunlun–Qin *ling* ranges in the south. The river is 5,464 kilometers long and drains an area that measures 752,443 square kilometers. It is not

a main artery of commerce. From its headwaters in Qinghai province, the river descends 4,400 kilometers to Shandong, where it joins the Bo Hai Gulf (fig. 2.25). The average annual flow is 48,000 million cubic meters with a total power potential of more than 40 million kilowatts. In general, the southern rivers in China have had higher water levels than the northern ones. The Yellow River has been the source of devastating floods (especially on the north China plain) until recently, when flood control measures were taken.

In summary, the review of this region's environmental determinants—its physical features, the unique properties of its loess soil, its arid climatic pattern, and its hydrological system— shows that these have come together so as to lend strong support to the historical development of cave dwellings in an area that was the cradle of China's civilization. Each one of the four environmental elements has contributed, in different degrees, to the continuing development of such dwellings. All of these environmental determinants are correlated, and together they have fostered the evolution of cave dwellings and assured their dominance as a form of shelter in this region. Among the four environmental elements, the soil and the climate have the strongest impact. The soil's uniformity and plasticity permit the dwellings to maintain a firm structure and to be excavated easily, yet the dryness of the climate supports the specific conditions of the dwellings.

Fig. 2.25   Map of the Yellow River basin

The loess soil's determining characteristics are therefore also dependent on the arid and semiarid climatic conditions, and this is reflected in the particular development of cave dwellings in the researched region.

There is a noticeable correlation not only among the four regional environmental determinants but also between their combined effects and the high ratio of cave dwellings that we find in this type of environment. Each one of the determinants can be evaluated singly on a scale of best-to-worst influence and mapped. Where all of them coincide in their most ideal forms, such conditions encourage the development of cave dwellings and determine their distribution within the entire region. As will be shown in the following chapter, the major concentration of cave dwellings for this whole region is found in its central part, where the combined environmental conditions are most favorable.

THREE

Distribution of Cave Dwellings and Dwellers

Distribution of Cave Dwellings

CHINA'S cave dwellings are distributed throughout the loess soil region. This area stretches more than 2,000 kilometers from east to northwest, and 800 kilometers from north to south. This loess region encompasses the four provinces of Henan, Shanxi, Shaanxi, and Gansu, as well as parts of the Ningxia Hui and Xinjiang Uygur autonomous regions. Also included are portions of Qinghai and Inner Mongolia (Zhao Sude 1985, 478). The quality of the loess soil in this region provides excellent structural support for cave dwellings, but the more northerly locations such as Ningxia are subject to earthquakes. The loess plateau (*huang tu gao yuan*) is located at the center of the loess region.

The following are the locations of six major concentrations of cave dwellings in this region: (1) central Shanxi; (2) central Inner Mongolia; (3) the Yan'an region of northern Shaanxi; (4) the Yuxi area of western Henan; (5) the Jibei area of northern Hebei province; and (6) the Longdong area, comprising several counties of eastern Gansu. In different locations the cave dwellings are identified by the name of their region, for example: Jinzhong *yao dong* (in central Shanxi); Chahaer *yao dong* (in central Inner Mongolia); Yan'an *yao dong* (in northern Shaanxi); Yuxi *yao dong* (in western Henan); Jibei *yao dong* (in northern Hebei); and Longdong *yao dong* (in eastern Gansu) (Zhang Yuhuan 1981, 48).

Certain types of cave dwellings are referred to by different terms depending on the region. For example, pit-type cave dwellings are called "dim courtyards" (*an zhuangzi*) in the Qingyang and Pingliang regions of Gansu; in the Changwu and Qian counties of Shaanxi they are referred to as "dugout courtyards" (*xia wa yuan*); in the Yuncheng region of Pinglu County in Shanxi, they are called "underground courtyards" (*di jiao yuan*); and in the Luoyang region and Gong County area of Henan, they are called "sky-well yards" (*tian jing yuan*) (Ren Zhiyuan 1983, 75).

Chinese cave dwellings are either dug into a cliff with an open terrace in front or designed as a group of belowground rooms that surround a large rectangular or square-shaped open pit. In general, China's pit cave dwellings are dug deeply below the surface of the loess soil—usually to a depth of six or more meters. They have a minimum cover of earth above their vaulted ceilings that measures three or more meters thick. The interior of the cave extends deep into the ground with a horizontal length of five or more meters. There are also some local design details that are characteristic of dwellings in each region, design features of the windows, facades, and arches in these cave vaults.

The regional concentration of cave dwellings is dependent upon the following three major factors: (1) Quality of the loess soil. Stronger soil such as the *li shi* type (Q1 or Q2) will more safely support the construction of cave dwellings. Softer soil such as the *ma lan* type (Q3) is less safe in cases of heavy rain or earthquakes. (2) Stressful climate. In general, the more harsh the climate, the more often cave dwellings are developed as a typical form of shelter in a region. Accordingly, the northwestern part of this particular region would be most likely to have a high concentration of cave dwellings. (3) Level of technology and degree of isolation. Regions far from urban centers lack building materials and tools for construction. Since cave dwellings require only simple tools and no additional building materials, they have become the preferred form of housing. The dominant factor among these three, however, is the quality of the loess soil.

Distribution of Cave Dwellers

China's one billion people constitute more than 23 percent of the world's total population. Generally, the human density is calculated at 107 persons per square kilometer; however, the population is not distributed evenly. At the end of 1981, 72 percent of the Chinese population was employed in agriculture, 13.4 percent in industry, 4 percent in commerce, 3.8 percent in the combined fields of scientific research, education, public health, and social welfare, 2.9 percent in construction, and the remainder in transportation or management of other governmental agencies. Life expectancy has increased from 35 years, during the period prior to the Revolution of 1949, to 69 years in 1980. Less than 20 percent of the population is now illiterate.

Although there is no official government census of the total population living in cave dwellings throughout the loess soil region, most researchers estimate the number to be between thirty and forty million people. Many scholars have settled on thirty-five million as a realistic figure (Wang Zuoyuan and Tong Linxu 1985, 420). Ren Zhenying, head of the Cave Dwelling Research Investigation Group appointed by the Architectural Society of China, estimates that the population living in what he terms "cave dwellings and raw soil buildings" is about 100 million, with at least thirty million people concentrated in the 150 or so counties of the loess plateau (Ren Zhenying 1985a, 320). Alternatively, Konishi and Aoki state that around forty million people live in so-called cave dwellings in China while around 100 million people use earth for dwelling construction (Shiro Aoki and Toshimasa Konishi 1985, 17).

Within the five provinces of Henan, Shanxi, Shaanxi, Ningxia, and Gansu (where the bulk of the loess soil is concentrated), there was a total population of more than 152 million in 1984, distributed as follows:

Province	Population
Shanxi	25,291,389
Henan	74,422,739
Shaanxi	28,904,423
Gansu	19,569,261
Ningxia	3,895,578
Total	152,083,390

(Foreign Languages Press, ed. 1984, 2)

Each province has its own research group which forms one part of the national Cave Dwelling Research Investigation Group. The estimated figure of forty million cave dwellers in China comes from both the Henan research group and the Gansu group. According to the national research group, out of the total population for each of the five provinces listed above, this figure of thirty-five to forty million cave dwellers can be roughly divided as follows: in Gansu, 26 percent of the population is cave dwelling; in Shaanxi, 20 percent; in Shanxi, 30 percent; in Henan, 24 percent; and in Ningxia, 75 percent (fig. 3.1). However, there are different definitions of cave dwellings and this can result in different figures. Thus the larger number of forty million probably refers to a mixture of buildings, including those made of stone and covered with earth (Nan Yingjing, personal communication, Lanzhou, summer, 1984).

The majority of China's population is composed of persons claiming Han ethnicity. Except for members of the Hui ethnic minority, which makes up the majority of the population in the Ningxia Hui Autonomous Region, cave dwellers are predominantly Han people and their primary occupation is farming. The Hui ethnic group is considered to be essentially the same as the Han except that they are Muslims—Islam was introduced by Arab merchants and soldiers about 1,200 years ago.

Throughout most of its history, China's rural

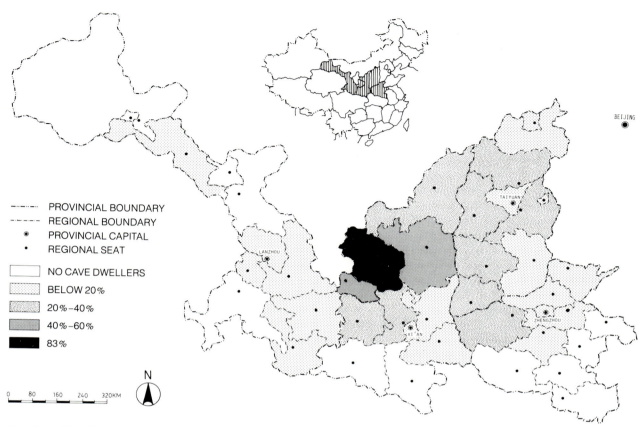

Fig. 3.1   Distribution of cave dwellers in the loess soil zone of Henan, Shanxi, Shaanxi, and Gansu

population has been poor and barely able to satisfy its own nutritional needs. Under such circumstances housing became a secondary issue to survival. Cave dwellings, since they were easier and more economical to build, suited the populace better than aboveground housing. Caves were also historically used for refuge during periods of war and local conflict, or by unfortunate people who needed to hide. These factors all contributed to the development of the cave dwelling life-style and gave rise to an architectural style that has become a typical feature of northwestern China. Of the nearly four million people living in the Ningxia Hui Autonomous Region, almost three million live in earth-sheltered buildings (Huo Fuguo and Cao Shaokang 1985, 115). The region suffers from very little rainfall and an extreme shortage of wood. These earth-sheltered structures are characterized as "cave dwellings, vaulted caves [made] with sundried bricks and

some single-story houses with flat roofs on earth-bearing walls" (ibid.). In each county of Ningxia, 16 to 35 percent of the total population lives in cliff-type cave dwellings. And, vaulted caves constructed with sun-dried bricks constitute 30 to 45 percent of the buildings in several counties of Ningxia (ibid., 116).

In general, recent agricultural and rural reforms have noticeably improved the income of Chinese farmers. As a result of their increased incomes, China's farmers have begun to demand more and better housing. Their improved standard of living has also allowed them to purchase such modern amenities as sofas, beds, televisions, and refrigerators. The farmers need larger living quarters to accommodate such furnishings, and some would now like to move into more fashionable aboveground homes.

General factors that have influenced the development of cave dwellings, especially among farmers, can be summarized as follows: they are simple and quick to build, and their construction requires very little technology and few if any building materials. Cave dwellings are also practical in other ways, since they permit dual land use and are easily expanded to meet the needs of a growing family. In addition, they demand only minimal amounts of fuel for heating purposes.

Although many of the existing Chinese cave dwellings were developed by farmers and villagers, growing numbers are being constructed for use in urban settings as well. In the famous city of Yan'an in Shaanxi province, more than 50 percent of the residents live in cave dwellings or other earth-sheltered structures.

The Provinces and Their Cave Dwellings

GANSU

This is a long, narrow province that lies in the upper Yellow River valley of northwestern China. The province has an area of more than 450,000 square kilometers and a total population of nearly twenty million, with 11 percent living in urban centers. The dominant ethnic group is of Han stock while various minorities make up the remaining 7.8 percent of the population.

The eastern part of the province is composed of an undulating loess plateau drained by the Yellow River and its tributaries (fig. 3.2). The mountainous area along the Gansu-Qinghai border generally rises more than 4,000 meters above sea level. Although the greater part of the provincial "corridor" is desert and semidesert with an arid climate, there are contiguous oases that benefit from snow melt draining from the Qilian *shan* range. Here farming and animal husbandry are practiced. A natural passage, well known as the historic Silk Road that led from the heartland of China (beginning at Xi'an) to Xinjiang and central Asia during ancient times, the Gansu corridor is today crossed by the Lanzhou-Xinjiang Railroad. Gansu's economy is greatly enhanced by the large number of mineral ores found there and by its textile, power, and other manufacturing

industries (China Handbook Editorial Committee 1983, 242–244).

Gansu has the marked transitional characteristics of a temperate continental climate. It has an annual mean temperature of 0–10°C, with great differences between the northwestern and southeastern parts of the province. The annual mean precipitation is 0–400 millimeters, with greater amounts in the southeast than the northwest. The cultivated area of 3,547,282 hectares (8,765,334 acres) is located mostly to the east of the loess plateau. Gansu also has a forested area of 3,425,973 hectares (8,465,580 acres), and a grassland area in excess of 13,330,635 hectares (32,940,000 acres), or nearly 30 percent of the province's total acreage.

The eastern part of Gansu province is commonly known as Longdong. This area includes the regions of Qingyang, Pingliang, and Tianshui. In these combined regions the major concentration of China's cave dwellers can be found. In the Qingyang region especially, the ratio of cave dwellers to non–cave dwellers is the highest found anywhere in China.

Because precipitation is low in this part of Gansu province, the loess soil stays hard and dry —making cave dwellings here more stable and safe than those built in other loess regions. Only the facades of the dwellings are covered with brick to prevent collapse of the entrances and windows. Otherwise, the strong, dry soil supports the structure by itself and holds the cave's interior walls firmly in place.

The Qingyang Cave Dwellings. The Qingyang region, where most of Gansu's cave dwellers are found, is located east of the Liupan *shan* range. Elevation of the region is from 1,200 to 1,600 meters above sea level and topographically it forms a basin. Land to the west, north, and east has a still higher elevation. Qingyang is divided into seven counties and has a total area of 27,000 square kilometers. Seventeen percent of the land here is agricultural (fig. 3.3). The loess zone of Qingyang is divided among three characteristic subzones (fig. 3.4 and table 3.1): (1) the southern loess cleavage: hard, dark soil, an agricultural area with semihumid climate; (2) the northern

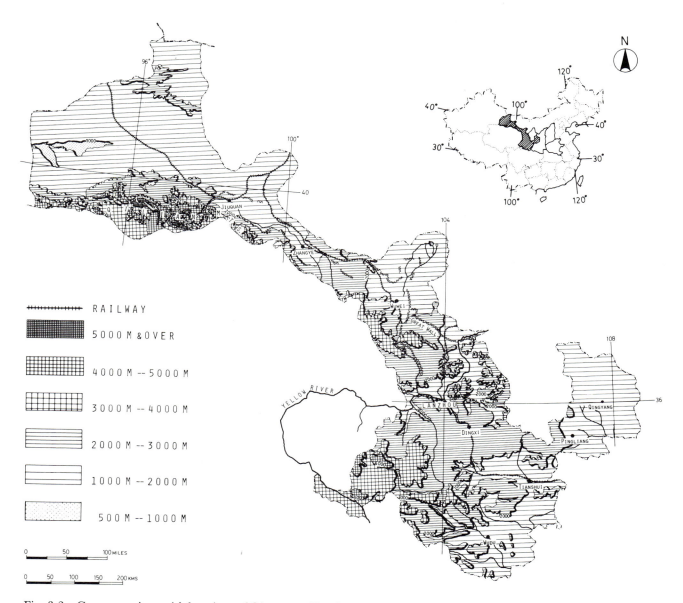

RAILWAY
5000 M & OVER
4000 M -- 5000 M
3000 M -- 4000 M
2000 M -- 3000 M
1000 M -- 2000 M
500 M -- 1000 M

0   50   100 MILES

0   50   100   150   200 KMS

Fig. 3.2   Gansu province with locations of Qingyang, Pingliang, and other towns

hilly area: soft yellow soil, also an agricultural area; and (3) the eastern mountainous area.

The Qingyang region is crossed by five important rivers and a large number of tributaries. In some cases, the rivers cut into the loess soil and create canyons as deep as 250 meters. Runoff accounts for 82.5 percent of the total precipitation, and the annual erosion of sand and soil amounts to 205,000,000 tons, or one-third of the total silt that is contributed by Gansu province to

the Yellow River (Nan Yingjing 1982a, 56). The yellow soil of the Qingyang region is composed of *ma lan* (Q4 and Q3), *li shi* (Q2), and *wu cheng* and *san men* (Q1) loess. The soft *ma lan* soil type predominates in the north. The region is generally not subject to local earthquakes but it is influenced by the seismic disturbances of adjacent areas (ibid., 57–58).

Qingyang has 1.8 million inhabitants, and in some parts of the region as many as 90 percent

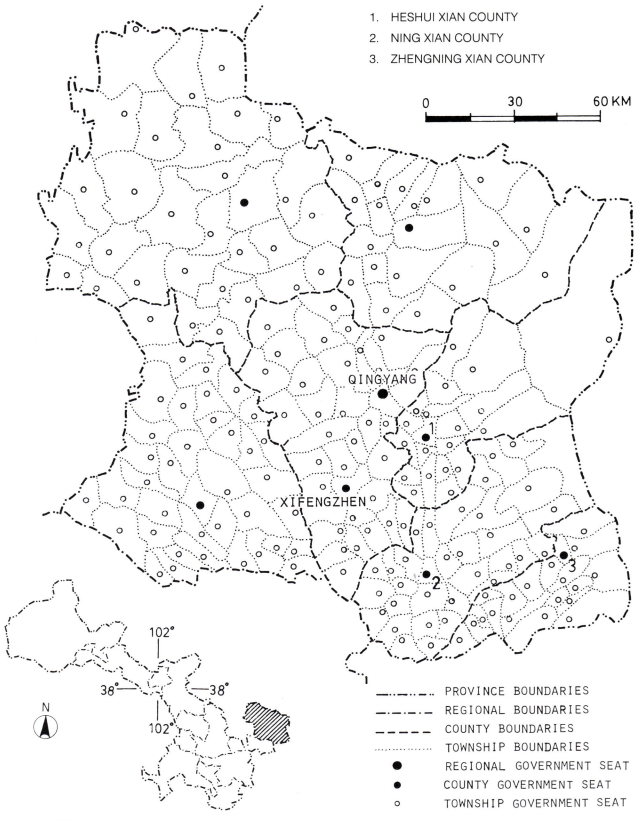

1. HESHUI XIAN COUNTY
2. NING XIAN COUNTY
3. ZHENGNING XIAN COUNTY

QINGYANG

XIFENGZHEN

N

102°

38° ——————— 38°

102°

--·--·-- PROVINCE BOUNDARIES
--·-·--·- REGIONAL BOUNDARIES
-------- COUNTY BOUNDARIES
········· TOWNSHIP BOUNDARIES
● REGIONAL GOVERNMENT SEAT
• COUNTY GOVERNMENT SEAT
○ TOWNSHIP GOVERNMENT SEAT

Fig. 3.3 Qingyang region, Gansu, where 83.4 percent of the total population is cave dwelling. The region is part of the loess plateau.

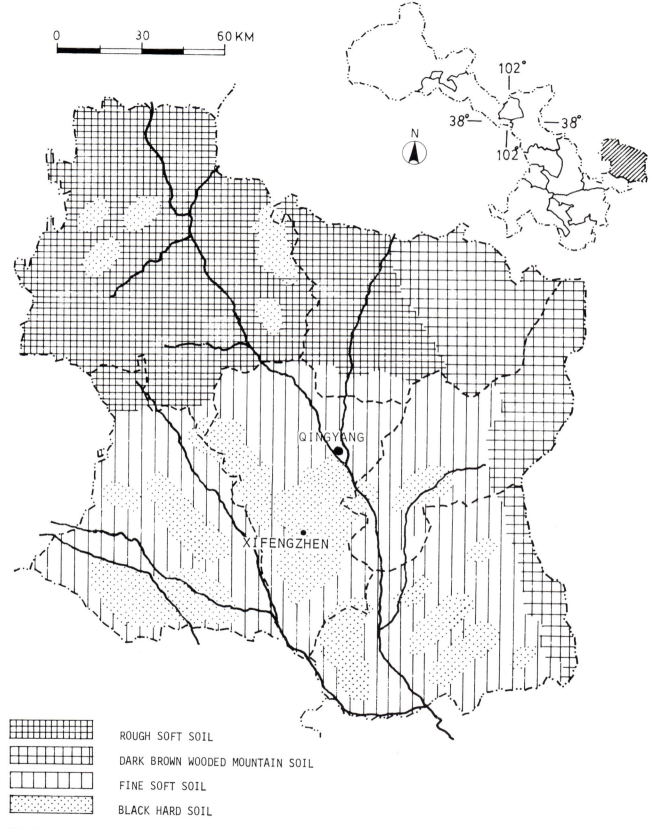

0   30   60 KM

N

102°
38°   38°
102°

QINGYANG

XIFENGZHEN

ROUGH SOFT SOIL

DARK BROWN WOODED MOUNTAIN SOIL

FINE SOFT SOIL

BLACK HARD SOIL

Fig. 3.4   Terrain of the Qingyang region

Table 3.1   Loess Layers and Cave Dwelling Distribution in Qingyang

Geological Period	Time Frame	Name of Loess Layer	Color Profile	General Distribution	Thickness	Capacity to Absorb Water	Ease of Excavation	Cave Dwelling Distribution
Holocene Q4	Formed during the last 5,000 years	Newly accumulated loess	gray-yellow, black-yellow, light brown, mixed colors	In the base of mesas, hills, or mountains	5–6 meters	Porous, absorbs a lot of water	Easy to excavate	No cave dwellings
		Old accumulated loess	black-yellow, yellow-brown, grey-black	On the lower banks of either side of a gully: Tops and slopes of mesas have a lot of dark, hard soil	8–12 meters	Average capacity to absorb water	Comparatively easy to excavate	Few cave dwellings
Late Pleistocene Q3	Formed between 100,000 and 5,000 years ago	*Ma lan* loess	light yellow, grey-yellow, white-yellow	Widely distributed in this area: Forms top part of loess mesas and hills	0–80 meters	High capacity to absorb water	Not difficult to excavate with shovel and hoe	Majority in central southern Qingyang
Middle Pleistocene Q2	Formed between 700,000 and 100,000 years ago	*Li shi* loess	deep yellow, light brown, reddish	Widely distributed in this area: Forms the middle or upper-middle parts of loess mesas and hills	120–150 meters	Usually not porous enough to absorb much water	More difficult to excavate with shovel and hoe	Some in the north
Early Pleistocene Q1	Formed between 1,200,000 and 700,000 years ago	*Wu cheng* loess	brown-yellow, brown-red	In the base of loess mesas and plateaus	0–40 meters	Does not absorb water	Difficult to excavate with shovel and hoe	Extremely few cave dwellings

Source: Ren Zhiyuan 1982. A survey on the cave dwellings in loess area in the Qingyang region of Gansu province. In *Surveys of cave dwellings in China*, 12.

reside in cave dwellings (Song Hailiang 1982, 155). Here, as in other regions, there are both pit- and cliff-type cave dwellings, exhibiting a great variety of styles. In eastern Gansu the population has been living belowground for more than one thousand years. Today most of the region's inhabitants, mainly farmers and government officials, continue to dwell in caves. In Qingyang more than 83 percent of the total population is housed belowground. In Pingliang the belowground population is 41.8 percent, while in Tianshui it is only 2.2 percent (fig. 3.5).

Three types of cave dwellings have been developed in Qingyang: cliff cave dwellings, pit cave dwellings, and a combination of the two types that generally is located on the edge of the plateau

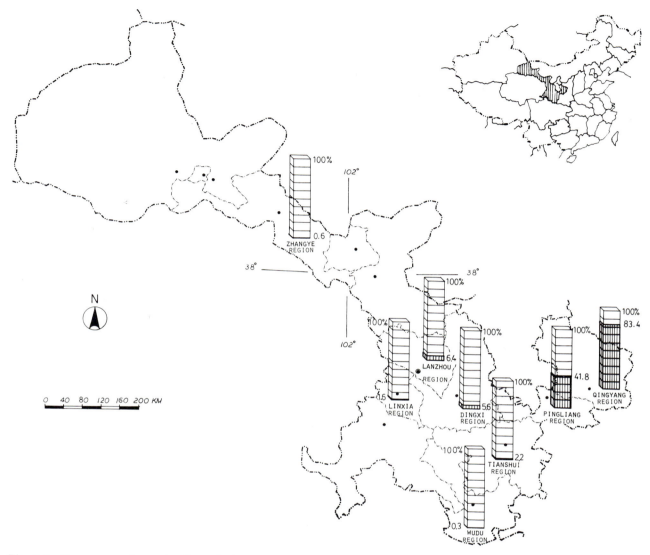

Fig. 3.5   Percentage of cave dwellers relative to total housing by administrative region, Gansu province. Note the sharp increase toward the loess plateau to the east.

overlooking the lowlands (fig. 3.6). In this region, erosion is extreme, creating gullies that range from 100 to 200 meters deep. There are also many deep ravines (fig. 3.7). Sites for cliff cave dwellings are usually located on the sides of old river courses or gullies. Semi-pit-type cave dwellings are built on the edges of gullies. Such dwellings are enclosed on three sides by the cliff walls of the gully. The dwelling itself faces a courtyard that opens onto the lowlands. Most of the true pit cave dwellings are located on the high plateau. Consequently, they are found in the soft loess soil.

According to the local inhabitants there are both vertical and horizontal layers of loess. Stone is scarce in eastern Gansu and thus it is rarely used for construction. Additionally, the shortage of wood makes it difficult to find fuel to fire bricks.

A carpenter requires five days to erect the cave front. Common forms constructed are the parabolic arch, the pointed arch, and the circular curved arch in vaulted form. The pointed arch is the form most often used in Qingyang; however, the final shape is actually selected during excavation, depending on the stability of the soil at that

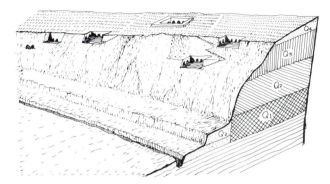

Fig. 3.6   Relationship of pit cave dwellings to soil type, Qingyang region, eastern Gansu. Note that most dwellings are located in the soft *ma lan* loess (Q4 and Q3).

Fig. 3.7   Bird's-eye view of a linear development of cliff cave dwellings along the edge of a ravine in the Qingyang region

time. The curve of the arch extends all the way to the floor of the cave. Some cave dwellers use adobe or fired bricks to line the walls and ceilings. The ratio of window size to the facade of the cave unit is 1:10. Aside from the window(s), there is also a small opening at the top of the facade (20 × 20 centimeters) for ventilation. Light enters through the windows, or through the door when it is open. Near the entrance of some units there is a

built-in heated bed, while the innermost part of the room may be used as a storage area.

There are no standard dimensions for cliff cave dwellings. On the other hand, pit cave dwellings have a standard height of four meters (13′2″), a width of three meters (9′10″) at floor level, and a length of seven meters (22′11″). The largest cave dwelling found in the entire region is the May Seventh School, which can accommodate gatherings of two hundred people. Its width is 5.4 meters, while its height is 5.7 meters, and its length 27 meters. There are a few other cave units of similar dimensions in this region that are used for habitation, storage, or oil manufacture. Cave dwelling dimensions may differ in height and length, but usually not much in width, although there are a few caves in Qingyang that are as large as six or even eight meters wide (Nan 1982a, 62–64). The pit-type cave dwelling room unit is usually a rectangle or sometimes a square. The space allowance between two cave dwelling units is three to four meters, to help ensure structural stability. In some cases, two units are connected by a tunnel that permits them both to be used by a single household. The dwelling rooms are high and wide at their entrances and are progressively lower and narrower toward the interior, maximizing the amount of light that is reflected from the brightly whitewashed walls (fig. 3.8). In general, one household may occupy two to three cave dwelling units. The floor level of the unit is usually a little higher than that of the courtyard, to prevent rainwater from entering the cave. There is also a seepage pit either in one corner or in the center of the courtyard to allow for drainage. Rainfall in eastern Gansu is meager, and therefore does not constitute a significant threat to the caves.

The life span of a cave dwelling averages one hundred years. According to the local people no major design changes have taken place in Qingyang's cave dwellings during the last two thousand years. Agricultural and economic conditions have probably remained about the same, since the region is naturally isolated and is still without a railroad. Only with recent changes in living standards have there been some improvements in the cave dwelling designs.

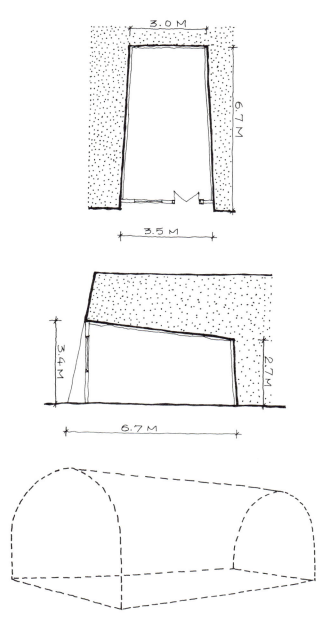

Fig. 3.8 Common cave dwelling design of the Qingyang region, eastern Gansu. The wide, high opening of the cave is intended to maximize interior penetration of sunlight.

The average size of a family farm in the Qingyang region is between one- and two-thirds of an acre, while one pit cave dwelling takes up at least one-fourth of an acre of land (2.471 acres are equal to one hectare). The amount of land approved for housing construction decreases every year. Recently, construction of new pit cave dwell-

ings was officially forbidden and currently only aboveground structures are being approved as new dwellings. As a result, many farmers of the region today are constructing aboveground earth-sheltered habitats (*yantu jianzhu*) that have a vaulted adobe brick arch covered by a tile roof. The walls are one meter thick and the inside adobe arch is a circular pointed vault form. But these dwellings are not sound under earthquake conditions. Since the construction of cave units is still cheaper and uses less land than the new type of earth-covered shelter, most of the region's farmers have come to prefer constructing cliff cave dwellings.

SHAANXI

Shaanxi province is located around the middle reaches of the Yellow River in north central China. The city of Yan'an, in the northern part of the province, is the former seat of the Chinese Communist Party Central Committee. The province covers an area of more than 190,000 square kilometers and has a population of twenty-nine million, 18.4 percent of whom live in cities. Most of these people inhabit the Wei *he* plain (the Wei River passes near Xi'an) and the Han *shui* valley (the Han River runs from west to east in the southern part of the province). The northern Shaanxi plateau occupies the center of the Chinese loess plateau. The terrain is varied, and except for scattered rocky mountains in the south, most of the plateau is covered by a deep layer of loess. The vegetation here is sparse and erosion has been extreme.

The Wei *he* plain is 30–80 kilometers wide by 300 kilometers long and is crossed by the Wei *he* and its tributaries, the Jing and the Luo rivers (Jing *he*, Luo *he*). With fertile soil, abundant farm produce, a large population, and convenient transportation, Shaanxi province is one of China's important industrial and agricultural centers. The Wei *he* carries large quantities of silt to the Yellow River, which itself creates numerous gorges as it flows southward between Shaanxi and Shanxi.

The mountainous area of southern Shaanxi features the Qin *ling* and Daba *shan* ranges with the Han *shui* valley between (fig. 3.9). Rising more

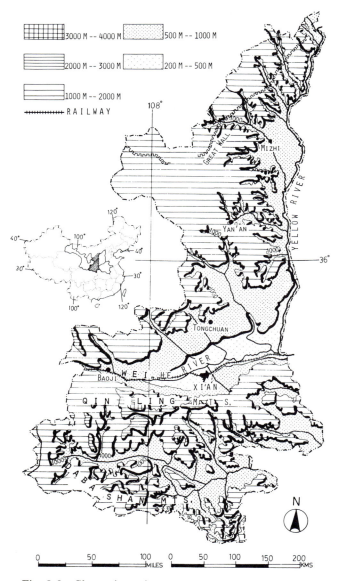

Fig. 3.9   Shaanxi province

Shaanxi has a continental climate, with great differences in temperature distinguishing the areas north and south of the Qin *ling* range. The mean annual temperature is 8–14 °C, increasing toward the south. The mean annual precipitation is 300–600 millimeters, lower in the north than in the south.

The province has a cultivated area of 3,837,889 hectares (9,483,426 acres), 32 percent of which is irrigated land. Northern Shaanxi is farm- and pastureland where millet, broom corn, and sheep are raised. The area has vast spaces that can be used for developing forestry and animal husbandry. The Wei *he* plain, with its long history of land reclamation and its highly developed agricultural activities, is one of China's best known wheat- and cotton-growing areas. Southern Shaanxi is a subtropical farming area rich in rice, maize, peas, beans, oranges, tea, bamboo, and medicinal herbs. Shaanxi has large mineral deposits and ranks fourth in the country in coal reserves, a resource found mostly in the north. Xi'an, Baoji, and Tongchuan are important urban industrial centers (China Handbook Editorial Committee 1983, 237–241).

Yan'an Cave Dwellings. The city of Yan'an (Yan'an *shi*) and its environs is an urban center full of cave dwellings. Since the destruction of the forests that, as recently as 1915, covered the Yan'an region, erosion has increased and there are now 2,847 gullies within a 2,965-square kilometer area. Transportation to the region remains difficult. Most of the cave dwellings are located in rural communities scattered along the banks of rivers and the edges of ravines. Patches of agricultural land are located on the ridges.

Yan'an *shi* is located in the northern part of Shaanxi province at the hub of the loess soil plateau. Erosion has left the area full of gullies, cliffs, mesas, and ravines. In addition to the loess soil, the underlying sandstone is also exposed near Yan'an. Along the narrow riverbanks there is aboveground construction, including that of the downtown area; however, much of the city has been built in caves and earth-sheltered habitats on the terraced slopes overlooking the river (fig. 3.10).

Yan'an is an important landmark in the recent

than 2,000 meters above sea level, the Qin *ling* range is the major watershed of the Yellow River and Yangtze River (Chang *jiang*) valleys, and an important landmark separating northern and southern China. Mount Taibai (3,767 meters above sea level) is the main peak, and Mount Hua (1,997 meters high) situated on the eastern rim is one of China's five sacred mountains. The Han *shui* valley includes many canyons and basins. One of these basins—commonly known as the Hanzhong region—is a well-known farming area.

Fig. 3.10   Partial view of Yan'an. Subterranean and semisubterranean dwellings are scattered along the acute slopes, while aboveground housing and the downtown area have developed along the narrow strip beside the river.

history of China. In October of 1935, the Red Army arrived in Yan'an at the end of its 12,000-kilometer Long March. Mao Zedong made the city his own headquarters and the headquarters of the Chinese Communist Party until 1947 (fig. 3.11). These events, along with continuous war-time air raids by Japanese bombers, accelerated the construction of belowground space. Before this period, Yan'an had only had 3,000 inhabitants. As has happened many times before in China's history, the solution to accommodating a sudden influx of new people was found by digging into the loess soil. Thirty thousand caves were dug for dwellings and offices and an extensive network of connecting tunnels was constructed. Today, many of the important caves of Yan'an are historical museums.

The Yan'an region (which includes the city proper and its thirteen surrounding counties) is inhabited by upwards of 1.6 million people. The municipality of Yan'an *shi* alone has more than one quarter of a million people. Outside the downtown area over 65 percent of the people live in cave dwellings, and 90 percent of those in suburban areas live belowground (fig. 3.12). Many of Yan'an's cave dwellings were built by cutting into the sandstone. This stone is exposed on the lower slopes of the valley and is widely distributed in the area. Some of the Yan'an structures combine features of cave dwellings and earth-sheltered habitats. A good example of this combination is provided by the Yan'an University student dormitories (fig. 3.13). The dormitories are semi-belowground terraced units that are situated on a cliff along the river facing south. The rear of the dormitories is attached to or dug within the cliff. The stone units are attached to each other and the roof is covered with earth. The student dormitories contain 240 units, housing six students per unit. There is no sewage system, and lighting, conden-

Fig. 3.11 Entrance to the former Chinese Communist Party headquarters in Yan'an, Shaanxi

Fig. 3.12 Cliff cave dwellings along the road climbing to Yan'an Pagoda in the city's suburbs

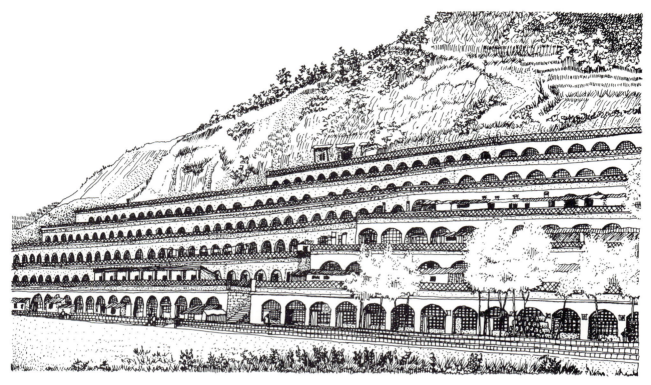

Fig. 3.13 Semi-belowground student dormitory in Yan'an. Many units are integrated with the slopes.

Fig. 3.14 Cliff cave dwelling complex at Gaomaowan *cun* Village, 12 kilometers east of Yan'an

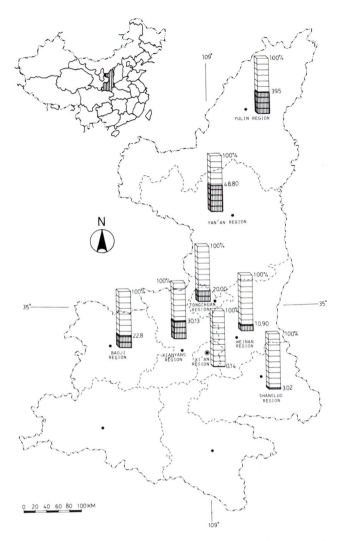

Fig. 3.15 Percentage of cave dwellers relative to total housing by administrative region, Shaanxi. Note the increase in cave dwellings toward the heavier concentration of loess soil in the northern and western parts of the province.

sation, humidity, and ventilation present continuous problems. In the Yan'an region as a whole, 70 percent of all habitats are cave dwellings and 20 percent are semi-belowground. The use of stone and brick in the interior of the caves is common, making the dwellings pleasant and attractive to the eye. Construction on the slopes is the only viable housing solution for Yan'an *shi,* and for much of the rest of this region as well (fig. 3.14).

In 1977 the average floor space per person in Yan'an *shi* was 2.8 square meters, but by the early 1980s this had increased to 3.46 square meters. One cave dwelling unit encompasses 30 square meters of floor space on the average. It costs from 1,800 to 2,000 *yuan* (60–70 *yuan* per square meter) for a brick cave to be built by the government. Private construction cuts the price by more than half (800 *yuan,* or 30 *yuan* per square meter). It is the publicized intention of city officials to emphasize and preserve the unique features of the Yan'an urban landscape, particularly its characteristic cave dwellings (Xiao Tihuan 1983).

Cave dwellings have also been constructed in many counties in the south (such as Qian *xian* and Liquan *xian*), and in the central parts of Shaanxi (fig. 3.15). Qian *xian* is located about fifty kilometers northwest of Xi'an. Its cave dwellings have heated beds, doors, and windows, whereas those in Henan province, for instance, seldom have windows and normally have only one door, even though the climate is not noticeably different.

SHANXI

Shanxi province is bounded by the north China plain to the east, the Yellow River to the west, Inner Mongolia to the north, and Henan to the south. Its area covers more than 150,000 square kilometers and the province supports a population of more than 25 million people. Only slightly fewer than four million people live in urban centers. Most of Shanxi is covered by hills and mountains, some of which rise more than 1,000 meters above sea level (fig. 3.16). The Shanxi plateau, which forms the eastern section of China's loess plateau, is covered by a thick layer of loess soil. The main farming area and economic center is the central Shanxi basin which runs from north to south through the province. The major settlements and transportation lines are located in this basin. Coalfields located in the north produce high quality ore. Other natural resources include iron, aluminum, copper, limestone, and gypsum. Shanxi also supports a textile industry (China Handbook Editorial Committee 1983, 146–150).

Shanxi's climate is continental. Because its altitude is higher than is common for regions of the same latitude on the north China plain, it has a lower temperature and drier climate. The winters are cold and summers are mild. From north to

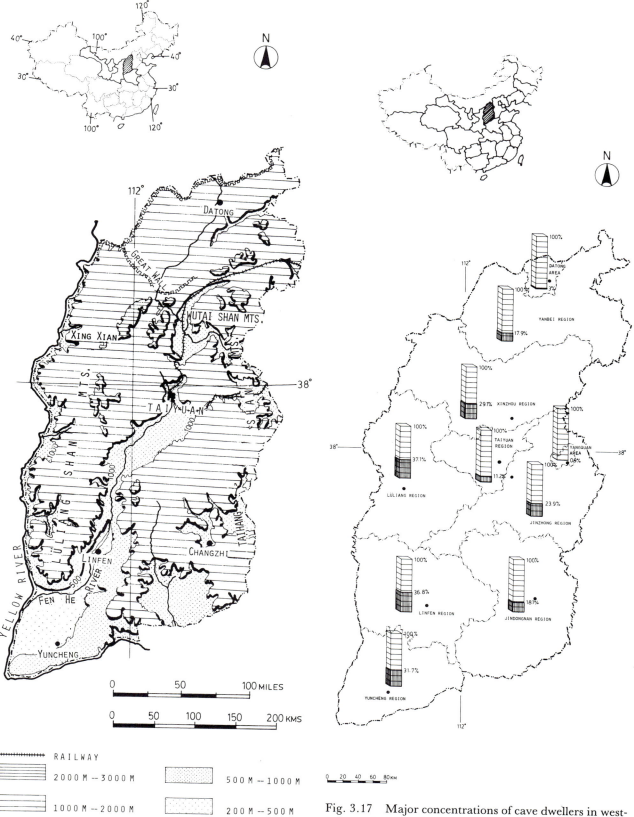

Fig. 3.16   Shanxi province

Fig. 3.17   Major concentrations of cave dwellers in western, southern, and central Shanxi. Dot indicates location of chief city in a region.

south, the mean annual temperature ranges from 8 to 14°C, and the frost-free period is three to five months long. The greater part of the province has a mean annual precipitation of 300–600 millimeters, increasing gradually from northwest to southeast.

There are an estimated 1,500,000 cave dwellings in Shanxi occupied by some five million people, or one-fifth of the total population of the province. Shanxi's cave dwellings are distributed mainly in thirty counties of the west and south, including: Pianguan *xian,* Baode *xian,* Lin *xian,* Fangshan *xian,* Lishi *xian,* Shilou *xian,* Pu *xian,*

Daning *xian,* Ji *xian,* Ruicheng *xian,* and Pinglu *xian* (fig. 3.17). Most of the cave dwellings are located on the slopes of hills and mountains, and they create a picturesque scene (fig. 3.18). There are also pit cave dwellings in the southern part of the province. In Pinglu *xian* County, there are about one hundred villages of this type that house 30,000 families and a population of more than 100,000 people (Zuo Guobao 1985a, 521). The cave dwellings in general, and the cliff cave dwellings in particular, are located in the western and southwestern parts of the province, where the loess layer is thick (fig. 3.19).

Fig. 3.18 The community of Zhoutoushan adjacent to Matousi *cun* Village, northeast of Taiyuan, capital of Shanxi province

Fig. 3.19   Cliff cave dwellings in Fushan *xian* County, east of Linfen, Shanxi

HENAN

Henan, whose name means "south of the river," is an agricultural province in the lower middle section of the Yellow River valley. One of the earliest developed regions in China, Henan became a political and cultural center in ancient times. Luoyang and Kaifeng are both former imperial capitals. In the remote past, China was divided into nine geographical regions and Henan was known as the Central Plain *(Zhong Yuan)*. The province covers an area of more than 160,000 square kilometers. Henan is one of the most densely populated of China's provinces, with more than 74 million inhabitants. Of these people, 88 percent live in rural areas.

Topographically, Henan's terrain slopes down from west to east (fig. 3.20). The province is bisected from north to south by the Beijing-Guangzhou Railway, which is flanked on the west by hills and mountains and on the east by a vast plain. Along its northwestern border is the Tai-

hang *shan* range. The western mountainous area of Henan includes the eastern extension of the Qin *ling* range. Northeast of the Waifang *shan* range is Mount Song (Song Shan), another of China's five sacred peaks, which rises 1,440 meters above sea level. The flat, low-lying Nanyang basin in the southwest has always formed a natural passageway between north and south. On the southern border is the Tongbai *shan* range, which stretches east to join the Dabie *shan*. The wide plain east of the Beijing-Guangzhou Railway is part of the north China plain and serves as the main farming area of the province. The Yellow River, which has burst its dikes and changed course often, has left broken dikes and sand dunes in the north. Mountains constitute 26 percent of the total area of Henan, while hills account for 18 percent, and plains for 56 percent.

The Yellow River and the Huai *he* River are Henan's main waterways. The Yellow River runs through the northern part of the province from west to east over a distance of 700 kilometers. The

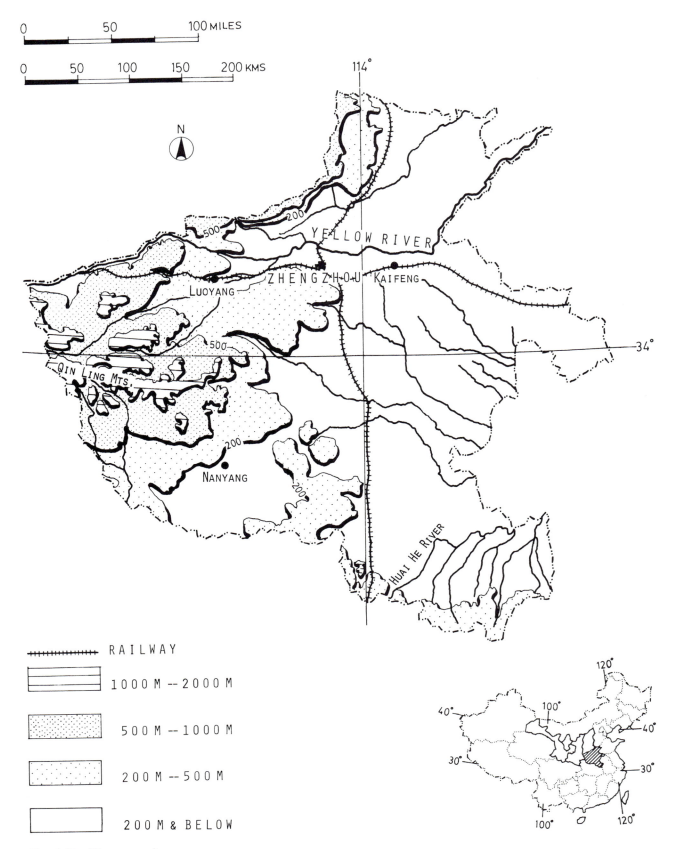

Fig. 3.20 Henan province

Huai *he* River flows from west to east through southern Henan for a distance of 300 kilometers.

Henan has the continental climate of the north temperate zone, with hot and rainy summers, dry inclement winters, and windy spring seasons. It has a mean annual temperature of 14–28 °C, increasing from north to south. The annual frost-free period lasts for two or three months. The mean annual precipitation is 600–800 millimeters and it increases from north to south. Henan prov-

ince is rich in resources such as coal, oil, gas, bauxite, gold, silver, iron, and sulphur. More than five million people are employed in resource-related industries (China Handbook Editorial Committee 1983, 196–200).

Most of the cave dwellings are distributed in the mountainous northern and northwestern parts of the province (fig. 3.21) around the suburbs of municipal Luoyang (Luoyang *shi*) (fig. 3.22). In 1984, in Mangshan, Hongshan, Sunqi-

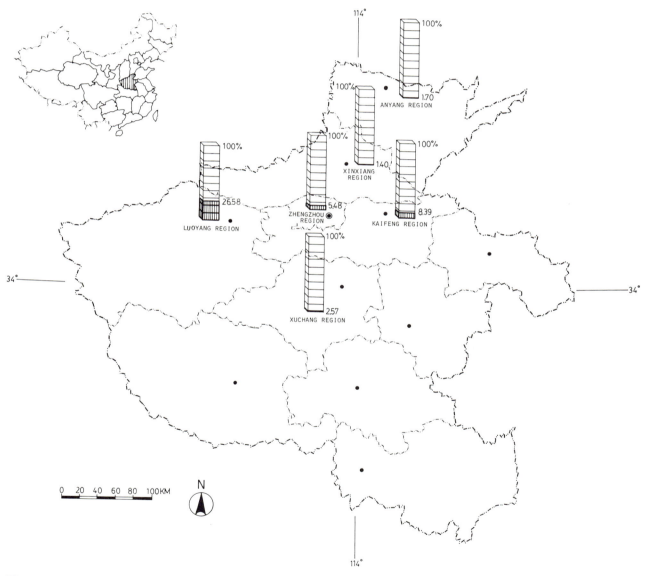

Fig. 3.21   Cave dwellers in Henan are distributed primarily throughout the northern and northwestern parts of the province. In some counties of the Luoyang region, cave dwellers constitute more than 53 percent of the total population. In some counties of the Kaifeng region they account for more than 40 percent.

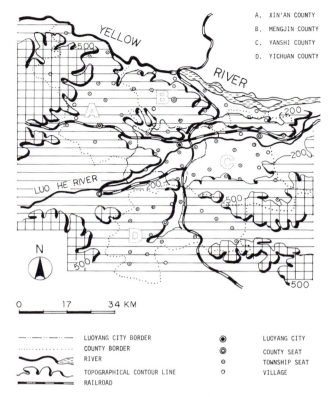

A. XIN'AN COUNTY
B. MENGJIN COUNTY
C. YANSHI COUNTY
D. YICHUAN COUNTY

0   17   34 KM

— — — — LUOYANG CITY BORDER
· · · · · · · · · · COUNTY BORDER
~~~~~ RIVER
∼∽∼ TOPOGRAPHICAL CONTOUR LINE
━━━━ RAILROAD

◉ LUOYANG CITY
◎ COUNTY SEAT
⊙ TOWNSHIP SEAT
○ VILLAGE

Fig. 3.22 Luoyang region, Henan, where more than 26 percent of the households are cave dwelling

tun, and Baimasi communes as well as Mengjin *xian,* Yichuan *xian,* and Xin'an *xian* counties, from fifty to eighty percent of the households inhabited caves (Luoyang City Cave Dwelling Investigation Group 1981, 41). Luoyang is located in hilly loess soil with a semiarid climate. The water table is low and the loess has a compact texture with good mechanical properties. The region is deeply eroded with numerous gullies and cliffs where cave dwellings have been built (fig. 3.23). The following six types of geometric arch are used in the construction of cave dwellings at Luoyang: the half-circle arch, cut-circle arch, parabola arch, ground-parabola arch, double-center circle arch, and level arch (ibid., 45).

This city was the capital of China for over 1,000 years, beginning from the Eastern Zhou dynasty (c. 770 B.C.) and continuing throughout the following nine dynasties. During the many wars and revolutions that took place over succeeding centuries, a large part of the population moved to rural areas and found refuge in caves dug into the gullies and ridges. Thus, a combination of geographical, social, historical, natural, and geological factors supported the development

Fig. 3.23 Mixed subterranean and semisubterranean terraced cliff cave dwellings in Xi *cun* Village, Gong *xian* County, Henan

of cave dwellings in the Luoyang region (fig. 3.24).

In this region, pit cave dwellers commonly plant trees in their courtyards. Trees cannot be planted above the caves, since their roots may create cracks, cavities, and other infirmities in the soil. But despite their attractiveness, these plantings produce more evapotranspiration in the courtyards during hot afternoons. This process increases the heat and humidity in both the courtyard and the cave to an uncomfortable degree. The network of tree branches also minimizes or eliminates ventilation that could help to cool the area. Of the four provinces where the majority of

Fig. 3.24   Cave dwelling of the poet Du Fu (A.D. 712-770) in Gong *xian* County, Henan

cave dwellings are located, Henan has the highest humidity, being located farthest to the southeast.

Many of the Luoyang cave dwellings are concentrated in the hilly loess area known as Mangshan in western Henan province, which forms the northern boundary of the ancient Luoyang basin lying along the right bank of the winding Yellow River. The Mangshan area, an eroded terrain with many gullies, is covered with loess. The area is 200 meters above sea level with little rainfall and high levels of evaporation. The average annual relative humidity is under 65 percent. The main earth type of the Mangshan area is *ma lan* (Q3) loess. In this layer of soil most of the Luoyang caves have been built.

In 1984, the village known as Zhongtou Brigade Eighth Team in Mangshan Commune had forty-two households housing 206 persons and about 22.66 hectares (56 acres) of land. The average annual per capita income here was 142 *yuan* in 1980 (about $60). The labor force made up one-third of the total population. There were twenty pit cave dwelling complexes with a total of 125 rooms, equalling 2,500 square meters of floor space. The cave dwelling zone made up 92 percent of the total developed area. In this entire village there were only thirty people living in aboveground homes, while 176 people (or 85 percent) occupied cave dwellings (ibid., 47).

Also in 1984, the village of Kejialing Brigade Fourth Team had forty-eight households housing 228 people, with the labor force making up 46 percent of the total population. They had 27.5 hectares (68 acres) of cultivated land and 4.65 hectares (11.5 acres) of orchards. Forty-four households lived in cliff cave dwelling complexes and four lived in aboveground houses. The total number of cave rooms was 102, making a total floorspace area of 2,856 square meters. Cave dwellings made up 84 percent of the total developed area and their households made up 92 percent of the total population.

The typical subterranean cave dwelling in Luoyang today is built with bricks and tiles for the facade. It has an open two-lane entranceway paved with bricks and four to six rooms. The total cost of a four-room complex in 1984 was 2,400 *yuan* (3 Y = $1). For a total building area measuring 151 square meters, this cost means 16 *yuan* per square meter. This is from 27 to 36 percent of the cost of an equivalent aboveground house.

Fan *xian* County is located in the northeastern part of Henan province some 300 kilometers from Luoyang *shi*. The landscape is scenic and marked by many rivers and lakes. Large numbers of cave dwellings, mostly of the cliff type, are spread over the entire county. In Luoyang *shi* and its neighboring villages, the cave dwellings are of the pit type and different from those found in the mountains of Fan *xian* (fig. 3.25). Also, in the Luoyang region most of the dwellings are constructed with fired brick walls, concrete floors, and brick facades. Still, like other cave dwellings in the loess soil region, the ones in Luoyang lack sufficient ventilation and light, and have problems with high degrees of humidity.

Fig. 3.25 Belowground alley in Gongxian (town), Henan. Note entrances to the cave dwellings at right.

NINGXIA HUI AUTONOMOUS REGION

Ningxia is located in the middle of the Yellow River valley in north China, where the ethnic group known as the Hui have long lived in compact communities. The region became autonomous in 1958. It has a total area of 60,000 square kilometers with a population of almost four million inhabitants, 21 percent of whom live in cities. About 1.16 million of these people are Hui and the rest are members of the Man, Mongolian, Tibetan, and Han ethnic groups.

Topographically, Ningxia is divided into two sections. The southern section (generally 2,000 meters in elevation), is part of the loess plateau with the Liupan *shan* mountain range being the main geographical feature (fig. 3.26). The northern section is the Ningxia, or Yinchuan, plain. This area was formed by the Yellow River's alluvial deposits, which have made it the major farming area of the region.

Ningxia has a marked continental climate with a mean annual temperature of 8–14°C and a mean annual precipitation of 200–400 millimeters. There are 897,818 hectares (2,218,509 acres) of farmland, mostly on the Ningxia plain along the Yellow River, where wheat, rice, and other crops are cultivated. Ningxia has vast pasturelands. Its argali sheep are well known for their soft hides and fine wool. The key Qingtongxia water conservancy project was built over the Yellow River in 1967. This is a large multipurpose project for irrigation, power generation, and flood control. Ningxia has large reserves of coal (China Handbook Editorial Committee, 1983, 250–252).

All the cave dwellings are located in the hilly and mountainous area to the south where the loess soil and topography support them. This region is also subject to earthquakes. The region's cave dwellings are mostly of the cliff type. The population totals nearly three million people, of whom 75 percent reside in cave dwellings.

In summary, the distribution of the cave dwellings and their dwellers is found exclusively within the confines of the loess soil region. Yet, the pattern of this distribution has been reinforced by other geographical elements. Within this area of distribution, the high-density nucleus falls within

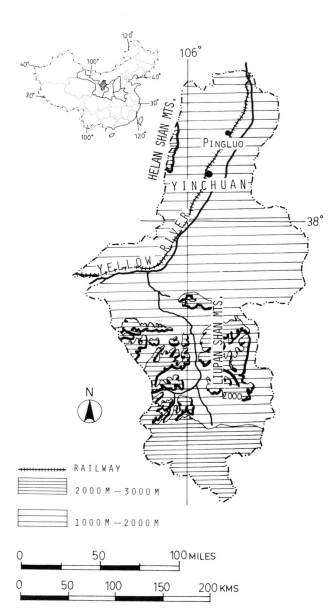

Fig. 3.26 Ningxia Hui Autonomous Region

the zone that extends from east Gansu (Qing-yang) to central Shaanxi (Yan'an) and further to Shanxi province. Beyond this zone, the distribution of cave dwellings is more sparse. Also, there have been historical and economic factors that encouraged the concentration of cave dwellings in this area. Throughout the course of Chinese history, this form of housing has responded to the recurrent need to shelter large numbers of soldiers and refugees during wars and periods of catastrophe.

Although the region has been host to several historically important cities such as Chang'an (present-day Xi'an) and Luoyang, its rural agricultural character has always been of primary importance. The focus on agriculture in this region made cave dwellings the preferred form of vernacular shelter since they enable dual land usage. Economically, they also offered the advantage of being inexpensive and easy to build during a short period of time. Their development provides an example of man's adaptation to his surroundings for the sake of survival.

In addition, the cultural characteristics of the Chinese people have contributed to the particular form of the cave dwelling and to its design. The average Chinese farmer is typified by ingenuity, pragmatism, a strong aesthetic sense, and the display of initiative. The combination of these qualities, in addition to the environmental determinants, has contributed to the innovative design and elaboration of this form of shelter. The following chapter focuses on those details of Chinese cave dwelling design through which operative social, economic, and environmental constraints are expressed.

FOUR

Design of Cave Dwellings

Types of Cave Dwellings

CHINESE cave dwellings can be grouped by form and site selection into the following three types: (1) cliff cave dwellings, constructed on the sides of cliffs; (2) pit cave dwellings, usually constructed on flat or slightly rolling land with pit patios open to the sky; and (3) adobe, stone, or brick vaulted earth-sheltered dwellings, constructed either aboveground or in a semisubterranean arrangement (fig. 4.1).

CLIFF CAVE DWELLINGS

The sides of gullies, mountain slopes, and terraces are the sites selected for cliff cave dwellings.

Cliff cave dwellings may utilize single, dual, or triple cliff walls (fig. 4.2). A courtyard enclosure is created by adding a wall. A flat cliff can be modified to create an environment similar to that of semi-pit cave dwellings (*see* figure 4.2D). Digging into the side of the cliff creates a terrace that can be used as a courtyard or to establish a wide-angled cliff, a combination half-circle with semi-square cliff, or a half-circle cliff with a divided and shared courtyard (*see* figures 4.2E, 4.2F). Another type is a combination of below- and aboveground space usage with cliff cave dwellings attached to each other, such as an aboveground house attached to the cliff and combined with rooms excavated into the cliff.

Cliff cave dwellings may sometimes be two or more stories high when built on a high cliff (fig. 4.3). It is also possible to develop cliff cave dwellings combined with pit space. This can be done by excavating the terraced courtyard at a lower level than the surrounding cave units. The cliff cave dwelling can have good cross ventilation and much sunlight if it faces south. The cliff cave can also be built as an earth-sheltered unit.

Within the category of cliff cave dwellings there are four subtypes (*see* figure 4.2). Their overall configuration is determined by the topography of the site along the cliff of a valley or gully. These sub-forms are the following: (1) terraced row arrangement; (2) L-shaped; (3) U-shaped; and (4) semicircular arrangement.

Inhabitants usually select sites facing south or southwest in order to take advantage of maximum exposure to sunlight. These dwellings are dug into the cliff and a terrace is formed from the excavated soil. A family dwelling may consist of four to six rooms used as a living room, kitchen, bedroom, storage area, and livestock pen. Often, room use is not clearly defined and one room may be used for several activities.

PIT CAVE DWELLINGS

Pit cave dwellings also come in a variety of types (fig. 4.4). There are many possible forms (such as square or rectangular) and much variety in the number of dwelling units that surround the patio. From the sociocultural point of view, the pit cave dwelling suite embodies the traditional Chinese concept of house design. It is an enclosure with a patio that provides privacy and a focal center for cohesive family interaction. Some cliff dwellings may also have a front yard enclosed by walls (fig. 4.5).

Pit cave dwellings are usually constructed on flat or slightly rolling loess land. The pit opening

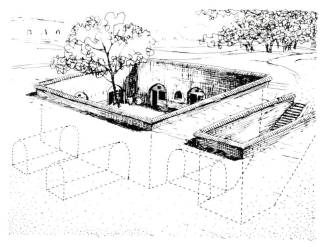

a PIT CAVE DWELLING TYPE

b CLIFF CAVE DWELLING TYPE

c EARTH-SHELTERED (ABOVEGROUND) DWELLING
CONSTRUCTED OF STONES, ADOBE, OR BRICKS, SIMILAR IN
DESIGN TO CAVE DWELLING

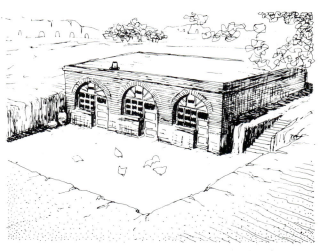

d SEMI-BELOWGROUND DWELLING FLAT SITE

e COMBINED BELOW-AND ABOVEGROUND DWELLINGS,
CLIFF SITE

Fig. 4.1   Types of cave dwellings

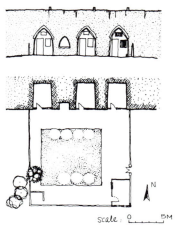

a one cliff side, dwelling no. 85 in Xifeng office lane, east Gansu

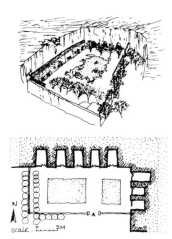

b Two cliff sides, Xihao cave dwelling, north gate, at Qingyang, east Gansu

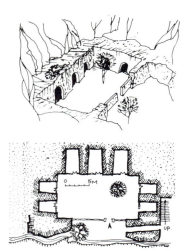

c Three cliff sides with enclosed courtyard, Shili Poll dwelling, Zaosheng Commune of 1984. Ning County, east Gansu

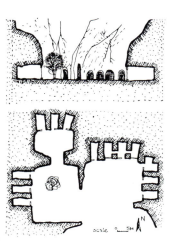

d Three cliff sides with three courtyards, Tian family cave dwelling in Xiangyang Village, Douluo, Yangqu County, Shanxi

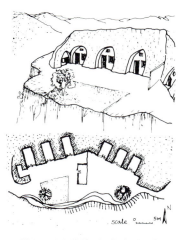

e Wide-angled cliff, Tian family dwelling, Tian Jiacheng complex, Qingyang, east Gansu

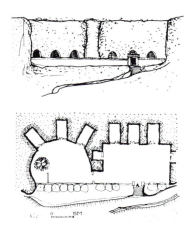

f Semicircular and three-sided cliff cuts combined, Li family dwelling, Li Jiahou Bay, Ershilipu unit, Qingyang, east Gansu

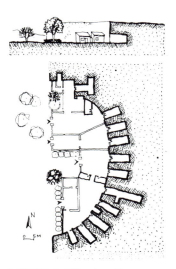

g Semicircular cliff face for multipurpose use, Zhang family dwelling, Qingyang, east Gansu

h Two-level cliff usage, Zhang family cave dwelling in Taipingtou, Linfen, Shanxi

i Three-level cliff usage, Shaanbei area, northern Shaanxi

Fig. 4.2   Design variations for cliff cave dwelling units in China

Fig. 4.3 New design for multistory cliff cave dwellings in Gong *xian* County, Henan

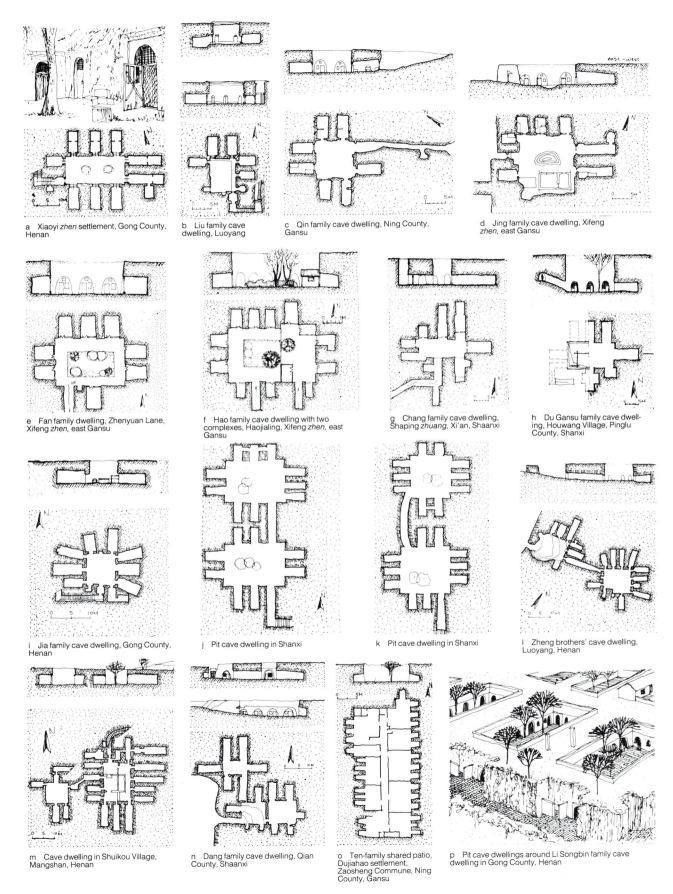

a   Xiaoyi *zhen* settlement, Gong County, Henan

b   Liu family cave dwelling, Luoyang

c   Qin family cave dwelling, Ning County, Gansu

d   Jing family cave dwelling, Xifeng *zhen*, east Gansu

e   Fan family dwelling, Zhenyuan Lane, Xifeng *zhen*, east Gansu

f   Hao family cave dwelling with two complexes, Haojialing, Xifeng *zhen*, east Gansu

g   Chang family cave dwelling, Shaping *zhuang*, Xi'an, Shaanxi

h   Du Gansu family cave dwelling, Houwang Village, Pinglu County, Shanxi

i   Jia family cave dwelling, Gong County, Henan

j   Pit cave dwelling in Shanxi

k   Pit cave dwelling in Shanxi

l   Zheng brothers' cave dwelling, Luoyang, Henan

m   Cave dwelling in Shuikou Village, Mangshan, Henan

n   Dang family cave dwelling, Qian County, Shaanxi

o   Ten-family shared patio, Dujiahao settlement, Zaosheng Commune, Ning County, Gansu

p   Pit cave dwellings around Li Songbin family cave dwelling in Gong County, Henan

Fig. 4.4   Design variations for pit cave dwelling units in China: A–I, single courtyard units in various forms; J–N, double courtyard units; O, shared family courtyard; P, aggregate of units

Fig. 4.5   Cliff cave dwellings on terraced slopes in Yan'an, Shaanxi

is a square or rectangle measuring from ten to twelve meters per side and approximately ten meters in depth. This forms a courtyard (*yuanzi*) open to the sky. Usually there are no fences around the excavation. Single-story rooms are excavated around the courtyard, with two or three rooms on each side, totaling eight to twelve living units. Each dwelling area is constructed either level with the courtyard or slightly higher (by 10–20 centimeters) in order to provide adequate drainage. Living units are usually located on the north, east, or west sides of the courtyard facing south, so as to receive maximum exposure to sunlight. The south side, facing north, is used for livestock or storage, or as the site of the main entrance.

Either one of these cave dwelling types introduces a variety of forms that are the result of a synthesis among socioeconomic, cultural, traditional, and physical environmental factors including topography and climate.

EARTH-SHELTERED HABITATS

Earth-sheltered habitats are built aboveground and covered with earth. The earth-sheltered dwelling, called *yantu jianzhu,* is a vault made of brick or stone and covered with earth. Earth-sheltered habitats, similar to cave dwellings, have a long history and the Chinese have much experience and practice in their construction. The earth-sheltered method has many advantages, yet still uses traditional forms, original architectural technology, and local materials. However, earth-sheltered dwellings, especially those built of brick or stone, amount to an imitation of cave dwelling designs with respect to their facades, vaulted arches, and dimensions. This aboveground structure is covered by a layer of earth approximately one-half meter thick (fig. 4.6).

In the village of Qinglong (Qinglong *cun*), located 25 kilometers north of Taiyuan *shi* in Shanxi, an earth-sheltered building was under construction (fig. 4.7) at the time of this research. The design of each room was the same as that of a conventional cave dwelling. It was approximately three meters wide by six meters long, three meters high to the top of the vaulted ceiling, and had a corridor between one unit and another. Built aboveground, the six units were attached to each other in a linear scheme and also to the cliff at the rear. The width of each room was 2.42 meters, the length six meters, and the height of the ceiling was 2.8 meters. There was an interior passageway between the rooms. The loess soil and the walls between the units were 75 centimeters thick and

1.65 meters high. Above this wall, sun-dried bricks were laid horizontally to a height of one meter. Above this, the curved ceiling began with sun-dried loess and straw bricks laid vertically, establishing the vault. The ceiling of the structure was whitewashed and the roof was leveled with soil; a final layer of ashes mixed with limestone was added for waterproofing. The ashes also help to keep the house warm. It takes two years for such a structure to dry thoroughly. During the first year the walls are built and when they are dry, the vault is constructed.

There has been an increase in the building of earth-sheltered units in Yan'an and the surrounding area. The dwellings are similar in both design and building materials to cave dwellings. The plan is also similar to that of a typical cave dwelling with respect to the design of the arch, window, door, low half-wall, and ceiling height. The ceil-

Fig. 4.6   Earth-sheltered dwelling with four room-units under construction east of Yan'an

ing is curved in a vaulted form nearly identical to the arch at the front, and the inside dimensions are also similar to those of other cave dwellings.

An earth-sheltered dwelling located at the eastern end of Yan'an was being constructed aboveground at this time; it was covered with soil, and had grass planted on top to prevent deflation by wind. In front of this building there were four huge fishponds. The dwelling consisted of four room units. First a stone wall had been built to a height of one and one-half meters. Then a temporary arch made of wood and stone was formed and above it, bricks and mortar had been placed. The "rings" of brick were also laid. Limestone mortar had been put above the bricks and covered with one and one-half meters of soil topped with grass. The limestone was to prevent water and moisture penetration. There were two chimneys in each unit. The total size of the four rooms was

150 square meters. The soil covering the building was to insulate the rooms and save energy, especially in winter when the temperatures would be low. Each of the side walls was 1.50 meters thick and the rear wall was 0.60 meters thick. The house faced south. One of the units was almost finished at the time of this research and the brick ceiling was already visible. When finished, the soil would be cleared away from all sides of the building. This was a private building and the land had been given to the homeowner by the government. Using the cave dwelling design idea the inhabitants had created an earth-sheltered habitat.

OTHERS

Another type of cave dwelling is a combination of underground cave dwelling and aboveground house. This type is the most promising for Chi-

Fig. 4.7   Earth-sheltered dwelling under construction in Qinglong *cun* Village, 25 kilometers north of Taiyuan, Shanxi

na's future housing needs. The aboveground structure compensates for the deficiencies of the cave dwelling and vice versa. This type of habitat is becoming the fashion in China today (Ren Zhenying 1985a, 322).

Site Selection Criteria

Site selection is a vital phase in the construction process and involves the consideration of many factors related to the future safety of a cave dwelling. The cave dwellers first choose a site and then suit the design of the dwelling to it, as determined by the topography and the composition of the soil. The semi–cave dwelling also results from taking this approach.

Soil type consideration is a prime factor in the site selection process and the local people's observations can be important here. The most common loess, and the main component of the loess plateau and hills, is *ma lan* (Q3) or *li shi* (Q2). Accordingly, most of the cave dwellings have been developed in this type of soil, although the best is hard soil of the Q or Q1 Quaternary periods that has been uncovered through erosion. Soil in horizontal layers is more desirable than that with vertical sedimentation layers.

Each cave dwelling unit should support the earth load associated with it. This load capacity is usually determined by the soil quality, the design of the arch, the selection of proper relative dimensions, and the facade angle. The following soil criteria are considered important by the villagers: (1) hard and dense; (2) dry; (3) horizontal deposit; (4) allowing at least 3.5 meters of thickness above the cave dwelling; and (5) southern exposure. The dimensions of the cave dwelling cannot be too large especially in those parts of the cave's structure that are subject to shearing stress. The dimensions must be designed relative to each other.

Several concerns are considered when selecting a site and constructing a cave dwelling. Interviews with cave dwellers revealed that they were most often concerned that the cave be located on a slope with southern orientation and adequate drainage away from the site. Orientation depends on topography. A southern orientation is pre-

ferred because it permits maximum exposure to available sunlight. Cave dwellers will select another orientation only when a site facing south is not available. In order of preference, the remaining orientations are: east, west, or north.

For strength, the vertical depth should be at least ten meters from the surface of the ground to the cave floor. If the height from floor to ceiling is four meters, six meters of earth are left above. This thickness offers better resistance to earthquakes. A horizontal width of at least nine meters is necessary to make two adjacent rooms. Since the width of each room is around three meters, this leaves only three meters of earth between the rooms. The depth from the surface ground level to the cave floor should be about ten meters to provide adequate insulation. Also, the thicker the soil, the more durable the cave dwelling. According to the local people, solid loess is the best soil for cave dwelling construction since it allows the dwellings to be cut more easily from the cliff and permits the structures to be more uniform.

The development of cliff type cave dwellings is complex in contrast to the simplicity of constructing pit dwellings where the topography is almost uniform. Site selection for cliff dwellings depends on the geomorphological configuration and most sites range from the vertical (90 degrees) to the relatively gentler slope (45 degrees). Many of the dwellings are constructed on terraced cliffs where each terrace has been enlarged by the soil excavated to form the courtyard. In other cases, the courtyard may be partially enclosed by walls and cliffs. In some cases, the basic cliff dwelling units facing the lowland are indented and flanked on each side by others. This latter form, with the courtyard wall on the fourth side, conforms to the traditional Chinese house style where the dwelling units surround an enclosed courtyard.

Construction Process

Chinese cave dwelling construction involves self-help labor. Not much is required in the way of equipment, building materials, or financial investment. Tools are simple and those used are commonly available farming implements such as the hoe, shovel, wheelbarrow, and bamboo baskets (fig. 4.8). The disappearance of ancient forests and the resulting shortage of wood for use as a building material brought about an increase in the development of subterranean dwellings. Building materials used in construction are primarily natural ones. The cave dwellings themselves are simply cut from the soil, and brick or stone facing is often unnecessary, whereas aboveground houses are made of brick and stone, with roofs of tile and wood. Thus, the cave dwelling requires almost no prefabricated material.

Slow excavation of the cave is best for stability since it allows the soil to lose its moisture. In regions where the moisture content of the soil is

Fig. 4.8   Tools used for digging are made locally

high, cave dwelling excavation requires periodic interruptions to allow the soil to dry. The cave may be excavated during the summer, including intervals for drying, and then tested in the fall. However, in the eastern part of the loess zone where rainfall is higher, it may take from one to three years before a dwelling is entirely ready for occupancy.

In the case of pit cave dwellings, the first stage is carried out gradually with the excavation of a trench three or four meters wide around the perimeter of the designed courtyard and down to the full depth of the future courtyard (fig. 4.9). In this way the courtyard walls are given a longer time to dry out. The length of this drying period depends on the amount of moisture in the soil and may last from one to four months. The excavated soil is removed to the surrounding area.

The next stage involves digging the cave rooms around the courtyard. This is not a continuous process, but is rather carried out at intervals allowing the units to dry. When excavation of the cave is finally complete, smoothing of the surfaces begins. All the while the moisture in the soil is gradually being reduced. The removal of the soil from the courtyard area, and the enlargement of the patio and the cave units themselves, constitute the third and fourth stages in the construction process.

The final stage consists of covering the facade with some finishing material such as brick, wood, or stone. The cave's interior walls and ceilings are also finished in this way or they are mortared with a layer of fine soil sometimes mixed with straw. Another method is to apply a whitewash made of burned limestone. Sometimes a space is left between the front wall and the ceiling to accelerate the drying process. Such a space will be closed in two or three years.

Pit cave dwellings have a graded tunnel entranceway leading from the outside surface level down into the courtyard. Most of the tunnel is below ground with the entrance covered to shield it from rainfall. There may be a door either at the upper level or at the courtyard entrance.

There are also similar major stages in constructing cliff cave dwellings (fig. 4.10). First, the cliff is cut to an angle of 80 or 85 degrees. In some

STAGE 1.   PATIO, BEGINNING WITH THE PERIMETER

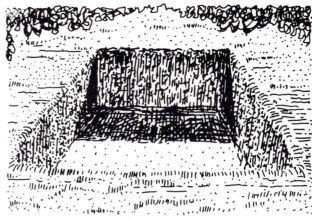

STAGE 2.   ENLARGEMENT

STAGE 3.   BEGINNING A ROOM

STAGE 4.   ROOM ENLARGEMENT

STAGE 5.   ROOM FACADE

STAGE 6.   LAYING THE BRICKS

Fig. 4.9   Process of digging pit cave dwellings

STAGE 1.   CUTTING THE CLIFF

STAGE 2.   PATIO TERRACING AND LEVELING

STAGE 3.   BEGINNING THE ROOMS

STAGE 4.   ROOM ENLARGEMENT

STAGE 5.   CONFINED ENCLOSURE

STAGE 6.   ROOM FACADE

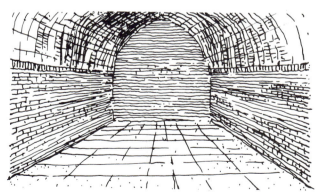

STAGE 7.   BRICK INTERIOR

STAGE 8.   MULTI-STORY CLIFF DWELLINGS

Fig. 4.10   Process of digging cliff cave dwellings

cases it is necessary to terrace the cliff above an eight- to ten-meter height in order to prevent future landslides. Next, the patio is terraced and leveled. Terracing also continues when new soil is excavated for the cave's rooms. Excavation of the rooms is the third stage. This can be a lengthy process since it is necessary to occasionally interrupt excavation in order to enable the rooms to dry. During stage four, each room is enlarged to its final vaulted shape, height, and length. The earth removed during the enlarging process is used to level and terrace the courtyard. The fence surrounding the courtyard and a gate are built in the fifth stage. The average height is two to 2.5 meters. The wall is built of loess soil and is usually wide at the base (around 0.75 meters) and narrower at the top (around 0.5 meters). The sixth stage is construction of the room facades including doors and windows. Contemporary facades are usually covered with burned brick, stone, or blocks. Older facades are usually made of rammed earth and mortared with soil mixed with straw. As the final stage, another terraced cliff cave dwelling layer is developed above or below the first.

Soil excavated from the new cliff dwelling can be used to construct the terrace and the enclosure wall, to fill in depressions and grade the surface to permit proper drainage and improve environmental quality, to build additional aboveground units, to construct the facade of the dwelling, to make adobe bricks, for agriculture, or for road repair.

In any case, the Chinese design tradition is very strong in defining the patio and creating an enclosure as an expression of the desire for privacy.

Removing the excavated soil from the site is a difficult task. The cave dweller/farmer may use some of the soil to make bricks. An alternative is to dig the cliff cave perhaps a meter higher from ground level and deposit the earth in front of the cave to level the patio with the rooms. This elevates the patio and prevents flooding during heavy rain. Winter is the best season to excavate a cave dwelling because the soil is warmer and the water volume is lower, making the cave structure more resistant to cracking.

CONSTRUCTION COSTS

Cave dwelling construction costs at least 50 percent less than construction of an equivalent size dwelling above ground (fig. 4.11). Maintenance also costs less and is comparatively easier than that required by an aboveground structure. The few required building materials are usually available locally. The highest costs are those required for labor to finish the walls, doors, and windows.

According to a report based on research conducted in Gong xian, Henan, "the costs of building each square meter of an unlined loess cave is about four yuan, which is only one-tenth of the cost of simple ground-based structures" (ibid., 321). Interviews with residents of the twelve researched cave dwellings confirm that the total construction costs are significantly less than those required for the same size aboveground units.

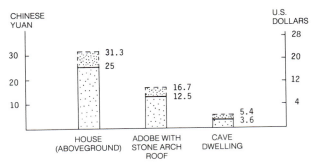

a   AVERAGE PRICE RANGE PER SQUARE METER FOR THREE DIFFERENT LIVING UNITS

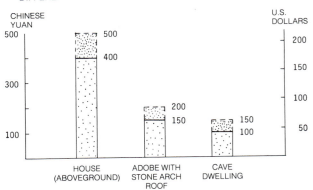

b   AVERAGE PRICE RANGE OF ONE ROOM (3.2 X 5 M) FOR THREE DIFFERENT LIVING UNITS

Fig. 4.11 Minimum (solid line) and maximum (broken line) construction costs for cave dwellings compared to other dwellings in 1981. (One U.S. dollar was equal to 2.3 Chinese yuan.)

For example, in Henan the initial cost of a cave dwelling with a brick facade is only 17 to 20 percent of the price of an equivalent above-ground dwelling built of wood and brick (Li Jinle, Zhang Congrong, and Li Liangsheng 1985, 207–208). Cost estimates differ from region to region, but are still always less expensive for a dwelling built belowground. In the Linfen region of Shanxi province, for example, it costs 1,000 *yuan* to build an earth-sheltered habitat above-ground while a cave dwelling built entirely below-ground costs 600 *yuan*. (One U.S. dollar equaled 2.30 *yuan* at the time of the interview with the farmer/builder).

In addition to the wood used in doors and window frames, bricks and labor are the two other main expenses involved in the construction of cave dwellings. The Chinese national standard for brick dimensions is 24 x 12 x 6 centimeters. In Taiyuan a single brick costs 3.5 Chinese cents, or 35 *yuan* for one thousand bricks. The price of bricks also depends on the degree to which and length of time they are fired. The designations of 100, 75, and 50 are commonly used to rate both the quality of the bricks and the number of kilograms per centimeter of pressure they can withstand. The most expensive Chinese bricks are the 100-quality standard. Builders may also use sun-dried bricks to construct cave dwellings. These are less expensive than fired bricks since they can be made with soil excavated in the building process and require only the cost of labor to make. In one cave dwelling unit measuring 3.5 meters wide, seven meters long, and 3.5 meters high, ten thousand bricks were required to cover the walls of the cave's vault.

Traditionally, Chinese farmers did not use bricks to cover the interior vault or facades of their cave dwellings. It has only been since recent improvements in the farmers' standard of living that brick use has become more common. Sun-dried bricks are clearly cheaper than fired bricks. Although the use of bricks in general increases the cost of cave dwelling construction, the cost is still much less than that of an equivalent aboveground dwelling.

Usually, four people are involved in the excavation of each room of a cave dwelling. Two people are occupied in digging out the cave while the other two remove the excavated soil. Often, members of the family that will live in the dwelling help with this process. Two workers can excavate an area 3.3 meters deep, four meters long, and 3.10 meters wide in one eight-hour day. It costs approximately eighteen *yuan* to excavate 21.8 cubic meters. In Liquan *xian* County, Shaanxi province, one cave dwelling (3.45 m wide x 12.25 m long x 3.10 m high) took four days to complete and cost two hundred *yuan*.

In Qinglong *cun* Village, Shanxi province, the builder of an earth-sheltered dwelling reported that each room of the dwelling cost five hundred *yuan*. Since the builder used sun-dried rather than fired bricks, most of his construction costs took the form of wages for labor, with each laborer earning three to five *yuan* for an eight- to ten-hour workday. Another earth-sheltered dwelling in Yan'an cost 1,000 *yuan* per room to build with each laborer receiving two *yuan* per day.

There are three or four villages near Taiyuan *shi* City, Shanxi province, that use cave dwellings. The largest among them, like Zhenzhumao *cun* Village, has six hundred residents—70 percent of whom live in cave dwellings, while the remaining 30 percent live in earth-sheltered dwellings. In this village, one room in a cave dwelling represents an investment of four hundred *yuan* while a similar room in an aboveground earth-sheltered dwelling costs one thousand *yuan*. Sixty percent of the cost in the case of the earth-sheltered dwelling is spent for labor, with each laborer earning four to five *yuan* per eight-hour workday. Families hire laborers from outside their village to build and finish their dwellings since most of their time is taken up by their subsistence agriculture.

Impact of Environment on Design

Although most Chinese cave dwellings are similar in their design principles, the environmental forces that contribute to their detailed articulation differ from one region to another within the loess zone. The topography, temperature, and precipitation change gradually from west to east in northern China. The topography changes from higher to lower; the temperature, precipitation, and humidity change from lower to higher; and the thickness of the loess soil changes from thicker to thinner. Naturally, changes in cave dwelling design result from these differences in the natural environment. For the purpose of examining the impact of the loess geographical region on cave dwelling design, four areas were selected for analysis by Ren Zhiyuan, of the Architectural Society of Gansu (fig. 4.12) (Ren Zhiyuan 1985a, 333–334).

Among all the environmental factors influencing cave dwelling design, the vital one is precipitation. Because of the impact of water penetration into the soil and the effect of moisture and erosion, the height, width, supporting walls, and especially the ceiling-to-surface soil thickness are all critical factors. Also, since precipitation increases from west to east, the consideration of these factors has become a type of "building code" resulting from inhabitants' knowledge of

traditional construction practices. Basically, space dimensions increase from west to east. This is more readily applicable to pit than to cliff cave dwellings.

Although many factors have contributed to determining the dimensions of cave dwellings, the dominant one has been the structure and composition of the loess soil. The structural stability of cave dwellings and their resistance to water penetration depends entirely on the quality of the loess soil. Other factors, such as sunlight, ventilation, and storage and comfort needs, must also be considered by the builders. The standard dimensions were developed by the villagers over many centuries of experience and familiarity with loess soil behavior under different environmental conditions. Although the environmental conditions (rain, wind, humidity in the air, soil moisture, and temperature) differ somewhat from one region to another within the loess soil zone, the

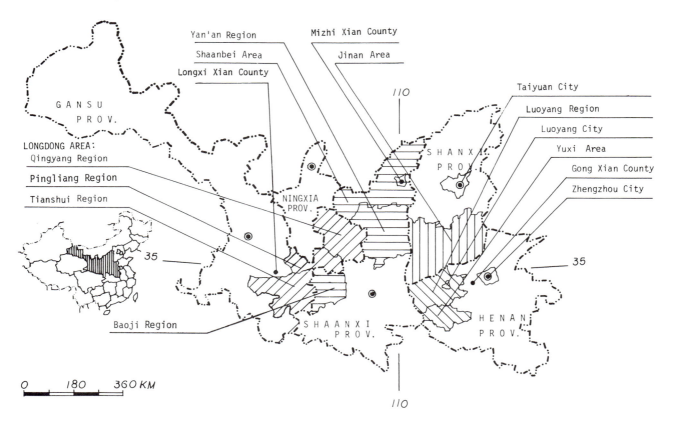

Fig. 4.12   Impact of the environment on cave dwelling design changes from west to east. This map indicates the regions of the four provinces with significant cave dwelling distributions researched by Ren Zhiyuan.

inherited dimensions remain almost identical. Moreover, a change in these dimensions, such as the ratio between height and width, may cause the collapse of the cave dwelling unit.

CEILING TO SURFACE THICKNESS

The amount of water penetration and moisture in the soil are important determinants of ceiling thickness. A minimum amount of thickness is required between the ceiling of the cave and the surface of the ground above to avoid potential leaks caused by normal amounts of rain or moisture. Traditional experience demonstrates that in hard loess soil a ceiling to surface thickness of three to 3.5 meters is reasonable. In the case of rain that continues over several days without intervals of sunshine, this may not be thick enough, particularly if no special waterproofing has been implemented. During periods of heavy rain, such as those common in the eastern loess region, dwellers may prefer to live in temporary aboveground structures because of the risk of possible collapse of their cave dwellings. This soil cover dimension is commonly accepted for the pit cave dwellings and affects the efficiency of the seasonal temperature time-lag and the soil's thermal performance. The dimensions also determine the overall total depth of the pit patio. On the other hand, cliff cave dwellings may have a much greater ceiling to surface thickness.

The thickness of the soil layer above the cave dwelling is an important element to consider. The saying in China is that this earth cover should be equal to the height of the cave dwelling itself. In Gansu, however, the following various measurements occur: in Longdong, eastern Gansu, the average thickness is three to six meters; in the Longxi, western Gansu area, it is five to sixteen meters, with a minimum of three meters; in Qingyang it is usually three to six meters, equal to 0.7 to 1.5 times the width of the cave.

In the Baoji area of Shaanxi, the thickness of the earth is generally greater than five meters and in Mizhi *xian* County, Shaanxi, it is five to eight meters. The thickness is five to seven meters in the Taiyuan area, Shanxi, and in Henan province. Thickness measures from three to six meters in Jinnan, southern Shanxi, more than five meters in Gong *xian* County, and over three meters in Luoyang and Zhengzhou (ibid., 337–338).

RATIO OF HEIGHT TO WIDTH

Both width and height are correlated. In case of no supporting brick or cement wall, traditional Chinese practice indicates that the width of one cave room unit should not exceed the height of the cave vault for structural reasons and cannot be greater than 3.5 meters. The rules regarding thickness of earth cover are commonly accepted by the society that made them. In some cases, they are enforced by the county, especially when dwellings do not have interior supporting structures and no waterproofing materials are used. While the width may not exceed 3.5 meters, in certain cases the height of the dwellings does not conform to the standard average of 3.5 meters. The ceiling toward the front entrance may be higher by one-half to one meter than the slanted rear portion. This slanted ceiling design allows maximum sunlight penetration into the cave's interior and is more common in areas with higher amounts of rainfall.

To meet structural limitations the average room width does not normally exceed 3.5 meters. The ratio of height to width is usually expressed as 1:1. The length is often determined by the optimization of sunlight penetration. The average dimensions of fifteen bedrooms among six cliff cave dwellings were 7 × 3.2 meters, and the average dimensions of twenty-two bedrooms among six pit cave dwellings were 5.9 × 2.9 meters. The average of the two types of cave dwellings was 6.4 × 2.9 meters.

The two interrelated factors, the ratio of height to width, depend upon the quality of the soil composition, the degree of moisture, and soil stability. The ratio of height to width (H:W) is 0.94:1.1 in the Longxi, western Gansu, whereas in the Qingyang region of the same province, H:W is 1.0:1.3. In Baoji area, Shaanxi, the ratio is 0.8:1.21, while in the Yan'an region it was found to be 1.0:1.3 and in the Mizhi *xian* County, 0.71:1.15. In Jinnan, southern Shanxi, the ratio is 0.9:1.3, in Luoyang (Henan) it is 0.9:1.3, and in the Gong *xian* area of Henan, the ratio is 1.0:1.1.

Height. The tradition of the 11-foot-high cave (three to four meters) is followed in Longdong, eastern Gansu, although some caves are built to a maximum height of 6.7 meters. In the Shaanbei area, northern Shaanxi, cave height is generally three to 4.2 meters, and in Jinnan and Taiyuan (Shanxi) it is usually 3.2 to four meters. In Ruicheng *xian* County, Shanxi, cave height may reach seven meters. In Luoyang (Henan) cave heights have been measured from 3.4 to four meters, while in Gong *xian* County (also in Henan) heights range from 2.5 to 3.6 meters.

Width. The average cave width in the Longdong area is 3.33 meters, known as the "10-foot-wide cave." Ren's survey of 114 caves in this district indicates that the general width is 2.7 to 3.4 meters with a maximum width of 4.2 meters. On the other hand, in the Qingyang region further north, the usual width is from three to four meters. Normally caves in Shaanbei are also ten feet wide, being between 2.4 and 3.8 meters for civilian use; those larger than thirteen feet are for non-civilian use (ibid., 336). In Henan province, caves are traditionally built in three sizes: the " '8.5 foot cave,' 2.8 meters wide, the '9.5 foot cave,' 3.2 meters wide, and the '10.5 foot cave,' 3.5 meters wide." Ren's report on 225 caves surveyed in Gong *xian,* Henan, indicates that 78 percent of them were 2.5 to 3.5 meters wide with one exception having a width of 4.2 meters (ibid.).

Length. The length of cave dwellings is flexible and not determined by structural needs or humidity. The main factors to consider are available sunlight penetration and lighting needs. The Chinese practice is that the average length of a cave unit is around six to seven meters. In some cases when the length exceeded this average figure, the height of the dwelling was five or more meters. In the Qingyang region, Gansu, there is a cave twenty-seven meters long. Such a cave can accommodate 250 people for a meeting (Ren Zhiyuan 1982b, 15). There are many cases where the length of cave dwellings far exceeds the average of six to seven meters, even to as much as fifteen meters or more. In cases such as these, the cave

was usually divided into two rooms with a connecting doorway, with the inner part being used as a storage room. In other cases, a "food well" had been dug deep into the floor of the inner room to take advantage of the cool temperature for storage. In one village near Taiyuan, a secret tunnel had been dug from the inner room to a lower underground space perhaps to enable residents to hide or escape from the village in times of political tension. The length of the cave unit is especially great in the cliffside type. It may be that the amount of available sunlight influences this. If the unit is wider toward the back the height increases, and if the cave is narrow toward the rear the height usually decreases.

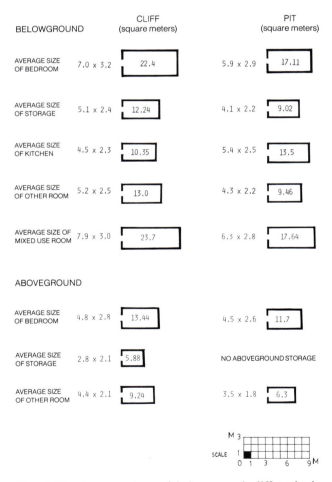

Fig. 4.13 Average sizes of belowground cliff and pit dwelling rooms compared with aboveground. Based on twelve cave dwelling complexes researched by the author in different geographical regions of the loess zone.

The findings of a pilot study of twelve cave dwellings point out that the average length and width of the bedrooms was 6.4 × 2.9 meters. The cliff bedroom averaged larger (7 × 3.2 meters) than the pit bedroom (5.9 × 2.9 meters) and similar averages were common in storage rooms and mixed-function room units (fig. 4.13). However, the kitchen of the pit cave dwellings was larger (an average of 5.4 × 2.5 meters) than that of the cliff dwellings (4.5 × 2.3 meters).

The length of the cave units in the Longdong area, eastern Gansu, is generally five to nine meters, with the maximum being twenty-seven meters. In Shaanbei, northern Shaanxi, it is generally 7.9 to 9.9 meters, with a maximum of more than twenty meters. In Shanxi province the length is seven to eight meters and is referred to as the "20-foot-deep cave," with the largest, found in Ruicheng *xian,* being more than thirty meters deep. In Luoyang, Henan, the length is usually from four to eight meters and in the Gong *xian* County, from six to twelve meters.

SUPPORTING WALLS AND SPACING

The supporting walls are those which line both sides of the length of the cave units. Such walls may divide two cave units and they may also be bisected by connecting tunnels. These walls give the most support and stability to the cave structure. In Longdong, the supporting wall is usually around three meters thick and in Shaanxi and Shanxi, the thickness is 1.5 to three meters.

The basic minimum requirement for spacing between the room units is primarily for structural reasons in order to support the mass of earth above the cave. A minimum of 3.5 meters of earth is normally required between cave room units. In some cases corridors are built between adjacent units to connect all the units together (fig. 4.14). There are very few Chinese cave dwellings built on two levels. In the few cases that were found, the second floor was much smaller in height, width, and length than the first floor and was used mostly for storage or as a hiding place. The dimensions of earth-sheltered dwellings (aboveground) are similar for the single unit. However, the thickness of the wall between two adjacent units is much less than 3.5 meters (fig. 4.15).

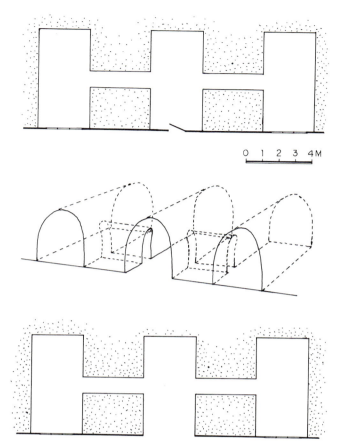

Fig. 4.14   Plans and perspective of interior connections between three-room cave dwellings in a village near Tai-yuan, Shanxi. The center unit in each of the two dwellings shown is covered with earth. They differ in that one is used as an open passageway, or as a sort of patio, while the other has a door and is used as a room.

Here the wall is constructed to support the ceiling and the roof.

The average number of rooms was 8.3 per cave complex. However, this average was lower (7.3 rooms) among the six cliff dwellings than among the six pit dwellings (9.3 rooms). The average number of rooms per person in the cliff dwellings was 1.21 versus the average in the pit dwellings of 1.09. The maximum number of rooms was eleven in both cliff and pit cave dwellings and the minimum was four rooms for the cliff cave dwellings and six for the pit dwellings. The room average in square meters was 16.9, with the cliff dwelling average (17.3 square meters) being higher than that of the pit (16.6 square meters). Similarly, the

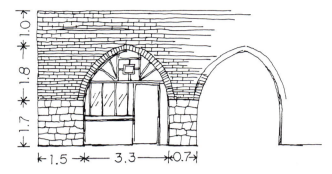

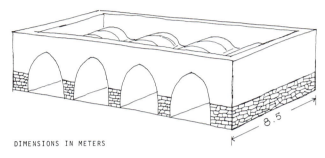

DIMENSIONS IN METERS

Fig. 4.15 Design plan and dimensions of an earth-sheltered dwelling

total average floor area of the cliff (508 square meters) was much higher than that of the pit dwelling (309 square meters).

The average total of earth excavated in construction of the twelve researched cave dwellings was 1,531 cubic meters. The average amount of the six cliff cave dwellings exceeded (1,698 cubic meters) the amount of the six pit dwellings (1,365 cubic meters).

Cliff cave dwellings have a higher average number of aboveground rooms (3.3 rooms) per dwelling complex than the pit cave dwellings (1.5 rooms). Although the cliff type usually has aboveground structures for storage while the pit type does not, the total average square meters of aboveground floor space is lower in the cliff type (26.6 square meters) than in the pit type (30.3 square meters). In conclusion, cliff cave dwellings use land that could not have been used for agriculture, but require more excavation than do pit cave dwellings.

Cave dwelling population density is much lower than that of urban housing. Research find-ings point out that the twelve cave dwelling complexes averaged 2.3 families each. This average is lower in the cliff type (two families) than in the pit cave dwellings (2.6 families). The total average number of residents for one complex was 6.6, with averages of six for the cliff type and 8.5 for the pit type. The average total floor area belowground was 408 square meters, with an average of 508 square meters for the cliff type and 309 square meters for the pit type. Cliff dwellings have more belowground space, on the average, than do pit dwellings because there are limitless possibilities for excavation and expansion. This is also the reason the average aboveground floor area is less for cliff type dwellings than it is for the pit type.

CLIFF CAVE DWELLING DESIGN

In Longdong, eastern Gansu province, the trapezoidal form prevails, wider in the front and narrower in the rear, deep, but with few inner cave units. In Shaanxi and Shanxi to the east, cave dwellings have the same width or span from front to rear and generally are not very deep. In the Yuxi area, western Henan province, they are trapezoidal: small and narrow at the front but wider and larger inside, with infrequent cases of "turned and tailed" inner caves. In Gong *xian* County, Henan, 95 percent of the cave dwellings with a southern orientation have no inner partition wall; the outer part of the unit serves as a living room and is separated by a curtain from the inner part, which serves as the bedroom.

PIT CAVE DWELLING DESIGN

In the Longdong area, the facade usually includes one door, one lateral window, and one high window (the latter is used for ventilation). Generally, caves have good lighting when oriented toward the south. The shape of the arch depends on the quality of the loess soil. The facade wall is often made of adobe brick with simple decorations. Occasionally the interior also has a brick facing. Wooden supporting beams may be installed inside. In the Shaanbei area, northern Shaanxi province, large doors and windows allow maximum exposure to available sunlight. The arch is semicircular and covered with brick. In the Jin-

nan area, southern Shanxi province, cave dwellings generally have one door, one lateral window,
and one high window, good lighting conditions,
and brick on both sides of the facade wall. In
Yuxi, western Henan, cave dwellings often have
one door and the outward appearance may not
resemble an arched cave; or they may have only a
small door and one window with poor lighting.
Most have brick on the inside of the facade.

Cave Dwelling Architecture

Cave dwelling architecture differs from that of
other types of habitats in the sense that it does not
have an external form. Its architectural identity is
found primarily in its internal form. The architectural vitality of belowground space is derived

from its passive integration with the natural environment.

The reciprocal interaction between structure
and space in belowground dwellings differs from
that of conventional aboveground habitats (Jing
Qimin and Anthony Vacchione 1985, 173). In the
belowground pit cave dwelling, the central courtyard begins at the edge of its walls. This courtyard space is the center of family activities and the
intermediate link to all other parts of the dwelling.
In the conventional aboveground dwelling, the
edge of the walls is the point where outside space
starts. In this sense, belowground pit cave dwellings are in keeping with the Chinese traditions of
privacy and intimacy of family life (fig. 4.16)
(Ren Zhiyuan 1983, 76).

Many of the Chinese pit cave dwellings display

Fig. 4.16   Pit cave dwelling in Beitai *cun* Village, Henan. This type of cave dwelling is usually found in flat or rolling
topography. Very few pit cave dwellings in China are surrounded by a fence.

Fig. 4.17   Basic design concepts of the pit cave dwelling above, and the cliff cave dwelling below, for a one-family complex

this concept of space as a transition by degrees and levels of intimacy between the outer world and inner household world. Pit cave dwellings can have more than one courtyard with the view of the entrance blocked by a wall, a curving stairway, or another indirect approach. The screening wall may be inside or outside the entrance to the patio with a setback of about two meters.

In most cases, pit cave dwellings have two or three room units on each side of the courtyard. In general, the rooms that face south and receive the maximum amount of available sunlight are used by parents and grandparents (fig. 4.17). The children are located on the west side, the kitchen and storehouse are on the east side, and the privy, pigsty, and other livestock are located on the south side. There is usually a well and/or cistern in the

patio. Room use is not as clearly defined as it is in the west, and often a single room will serve a variety of functions.

The development of a second story in Chinese cave dwellings is very limited because of the risk of water penetration, which can cause the collapse of the dwelling. A second floor reduces the ceiling to surface thickness of the soil above the cave vault, weakening its stability and distorting temperature performance. During field research some caves with upper floors were located. Most of these two-story complexes were built many decades ago and are deep in the ground. They were used for defense, hiding, or storage. The second floor normally has much smaller dimensions than the first and entrance is gained from inside the first floor or from the outside front via a ladder.

The Li Zhimin family cave dwelling in Bei *cun* Village, Liquan *xian,* Shaanxi, consists of two long rooms, one opening into the other (fig. 4.18). Above these is another small room where, according to the dwellers, the inhabitants were able to hide from the military (before the Cultural Revolution) or to protect their valuables from thieves. The large room is paved with stone and the walls are mortared with a mixture of straw and loess. The Li Zhimin family home is large compared to the standard Chinese cave dwelling. The general layout of the house is a long, narrow trapezoid (fig. 4.18, A1, B1). The width in front is six meters narrowing to 3.3 meters in the rear. The total length is 18.3 meters. The home is divided into two sections—the innermost part is used for storage and the front section is used as a combination living/bedroom. The height at the front of the dwelling is 6.5 meters and it tapers to 3.75 meters in the rear (fig. 4.18, B2). The other cave room on the second floor, which was built primarily for storage, is accessed by a ladder outside the cave's front. The width of this room is 2.75 meters, becoming narrower toward the inner part of the room's interior. Its length is three meters. This small room helps to decrease the load on the lower cave (fig. 4.18, B1, B2). The cave dwelling faces south and, because of the sloping ceiling, it receives a generous amount of sunlight.

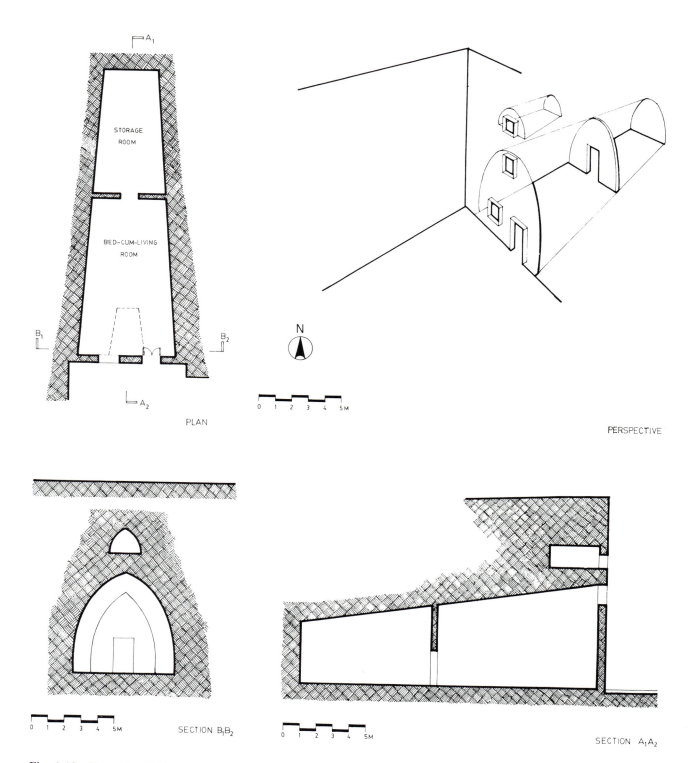

PLAN

STORAGE
ROOM

BED-CUM-LIVING
ROOM

N

0 1 2 3 4 5M

PERSPECTIVE

0 1 2 3 4 5M

SECTION B₁B₂

0 1 2 3 4 5M

SECTION A₁A₂

Fig. 4.18   Exceptionally large two-story cave dwelling built early in this century. Li Zhimin family dwelling in Bei *cun* Village, Liquan *xian* County, Shaanxi. Note the slanted ceiling and the window that allows light to penetrate.

VAULT FORM

Through experience in using loess soil for structures, the Chinese have found the tunnel or barrel form of vault to be highly stable. This vault form is easy to design and excavate and is extendible without limitation. Also, the curve of the vault itself can be varied slightly (fig. 4.19). This vault form differs from one region to another as determined by soil strength and moisture content. There are several vault styles used in Chinese cave dwellings including the parabolic arch, pointed arch, circular arch, and half circle arch.

In the traditional cave dwelling unit, the soil is not supported by brick, stone, or other types of building materials. If the soil is dry it will hold firmly in place; however, with an increase in soil

moisture there is a risk to the stability of the structure. Many cave dwellers paste newspapers to the surface of the vault to prevent dust from falling. Recently, with increases in economic prosperity and improvements in their standard of living, many families cover the vault surface with brick.

Beyond its basic design, the topography and location determine—to a great extent—the vault form of the cave dwelling (fig. 4.20). Within the cave complex a single cave unit alone has limited flexibility of form because of the obligatory vault form. Yet, some minor diversions are possible (fig. 4.21).

In a few cases, a semi-combined vault is used to connect one room to another. The connecting passage also takes the form of a vault and is lower than the arch of the room. The connection occurs

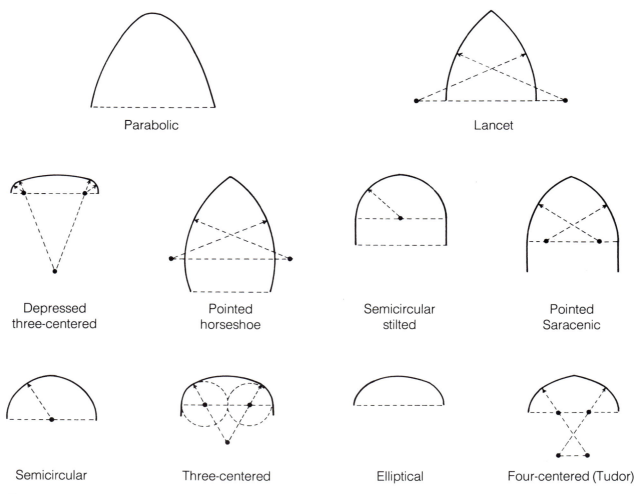

Fig. 4.19   Some vault form variations used in Chinese cave dwellings

TYPE	SITE	PRIME CHARACTER	PERSPECTIVE	CROSS SECTION	PLAN
CLIFF	a GULLIES	TERRACE, NO PATIO			
	b EDGE OF THE SLOPE, WITH THREE SIDES ON THE CLIFF	THREE CLIFF WITH PATIO			
	c EDGE OF THE SLOPE WITH TWO SIDES ON THE CLIFF	WITH TERRACED PATIO			
	d MIDDLE OF THE SLOPE	WITH TERRACED PATIO			
PIT	FLAT OR ROLLING SITE	WITH SQUARE, RECTANGLE OR OTHER FORM OF PATIO			

Fig. 4.20   Schematic forms of Chinese cave dwellings are determined by the topography

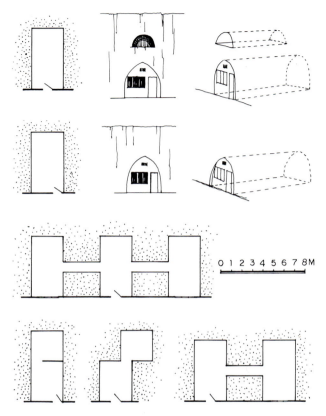

Fig. 4.21 Possible design forms of the single room in a family cave dwelling complex

0 1 2 3 4 5 6 7 8M

tion of arch type. Curved and parabolic arches are used in good-quality soil. In poor-quality soil, dwellers select the pointed arch as optimal for structural support (Ren Zhiyuan 1982b, 33).

In the Longdong area, Gansu, the vaults of cliff cave dwellings are wedge-shaped in the sense that the floor to ceiling measurement is higher at the entrance in the cave's front and lower at the rear of the dwelling. Larger caves can be two stories high since they usually have wooden garrets. In the Shaanbei area, northern Shaanxi province, the cave dwelling vaults are generally higher, while those in Yuxi, western Henan, are lower at the entrance and higher toward the rear.

ORIENTATION

A southern orientation has been applied consistently throughout the history of Chinese urban and house design. The rooms of pit cave dwellings usually surround the patio on all four sides. The rooms on the side facing north are used for storage, for housing livestock, and for the stairway or ramp to the patio. Rooms that face east and west receive less sunlight than those facing south; however, all are used as living areas. Typically, rooms facing south are occupied by senior family members while the children occupy rooms that face east and west.

In the case of pit cave dwellings an increase in courtyard depth detracts from the quantity of sunlight penetration. The average length of a cave dwelling is five to six meters, with an average floor-to-ceiling height of 3.5 meters. If the depth of the patio floor is ten meters and the soil above the dwelling is around four to five meters deep, it is then expected that the sun will penetrate deeply (about six meters) into the unit in the winter (fig. 4.22). A deeper patio floor would result in less sunlight penetration. Many rooms have higher ceilings in front than in the rear. This slanted ceiling design improves the amount of sunlight penetration into the cave's interior.

Cliff dwellings that face north have serious problems with dampness and moisture. A southern orientation guarantees maximum exposure to available sunlight. This is essential to the cave dwellers not only for the sake of the quantity of natural light it provides but also for the warmth from the sun that helps to keep the loess soil dry.

at the wall level and not at the ceiling. Basically, the fully connected diagonal or perpendicular vault connection can weaken the room and may be subject to collapse under earthquake conditions.

The Chinese have found the vault to be an earthquake resistant form, given the nature of loess soil. The general form of the vault itself has some variations which, through practice, were found suitable for different types of loess. The standard form is determined by structural needs. The selection of type depends on the soil's texture and its degree of stability, which is directly related to the type and degree of dryness of the loess. Accordingly, the arch may be parabolic, pointed, curved, or semicircular.

The dwellers/builders have learned through experience: first they try the curved arch and if the top collapses, they select the parabolic; if this too collapses, they use the pointed arch. Experience has led them to relate soil quality to the selec-

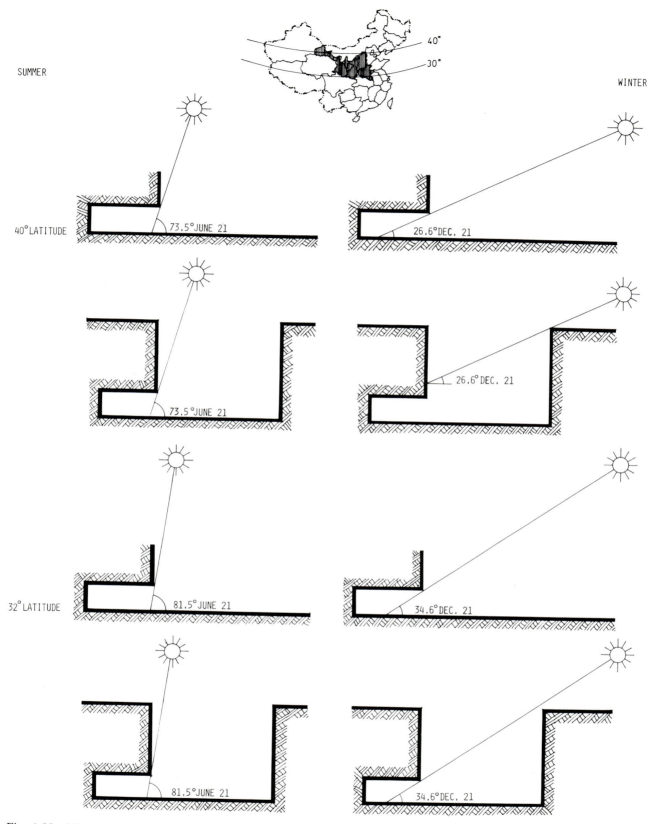

SUMMER

WINTER

40°LATITUDE

73.5°JUNE 21

26.6°DEC, 21

73.5°JUNE 21

26.6°DEC, 21

32°LATITUDE

81.5°JUNE 21

34.6°DEC, 21

81.5°JUNE 21

34.6°DEC, 21

40°

30°

Fig. 4.22   Maximum possible winter sunlight penetration in a cave unit facing south. Calculated for 40 degrees north latitude, with a cave unit 3.5 meters high, 6 meters long, and 10 meters deep from the surface to the patio floor. A higher ceiling would enable more sunlight penetration and permit an increase in the dwelling's length.

a   Entranceway to pit cave dwelling descending in two flights, Luoyang region, Henan

b   Entrance to cliff dwelling, Xifengzhen, east Gansu

c   Entrance to cliff cave dwelling on the same level as patio, screened by a wall for privacy, Qian County, Shaanxi

d   Descending entrance to pit cave dwelling, Qingyang region, east Gansu

e   First flight of descending stairway, pit cave dwelling, Zhongtou Village near Luoyang, Henan

f   Entrance descending from a higher terrace to a cliff cave dwelling complex, Qingyang region, east Gansu

Fig. 4.23   Cave dwelling entrances in different regions

ENTRANCES

Entrances to cave dwelling complexes or to single rooms take a variety of forms. The determining factors for the entrance can be the topography, available building materials, practical considerations, and aesthetics.

Cliff cave dwellings can be approached from a higher level terrace (fig. 4.23A) or they can have an entrance to the courtyard from an alley or terraced road (fig. 4.23B). In many cases, the view from the road into the courtyard is blocked by a single wall standing a short distance from the entrance situated either in the inner patio or at the outer front part of the courtyard (fig. 4.23C).

Pit cave dwelling entrances take many forms. Graded entrances can lead directly to the courtyard by way of a stairway (fig. 4.23D) or have a right-angled turn at the bottom (fig. 4.23E and F). A graded entrance may have a staircase and also a paved ramp for use by animals (fig. 4.24). In some cases, the road, pedestrian alley, and entrance are all level with the courtyard. In one instance, the alley was seven to ten meters below ground level and open to the sky. The entrance to the courtyard was roofed with a mass of earth covered with brick (fig. 4.25).

In the settlements of Changwu (Shaanxi) and Qingyang and Pingliang (eastern Gansu), the entrances are simple, without special structures. In Luoyang and Gong *xian* (Henan), the entrances are often inlaid with brick or stone. In others, the path is divided into two lanes, one with a stairway for pedestrians and the other with a ramp for carts and livestock (fig. 4.23E). Entrances to pit cave dwellings of this type usually have a curve at the bottom before arriving in the courtyard (fig. 4.24).

Fig. 4.24   Entrance to a pit cave dwelling, Luoyang region, Henan

Fig. 4.25   Entrance to a pit cave dwelling from a below-ground alley level with the patio. Li Songbin family cave dwelling, Gongxian, Henan.

The entrance to a single cave dwelling unit also has a different design style which stems from both practicality and aesthetics (fig. 4.26). The location of the entrance (whether on the left, in the middle, or on the right-hand side) is primarily determined by the interior arrangement of the furniture (fig. 4.26A). The large heated bed is an important fixture in cave dwellings (especially under the harsh climatic conditions of the north) and takes up much of the width of each cave. The location of entrances is also planned to maximize sunlight penetration into the cave's rooms.

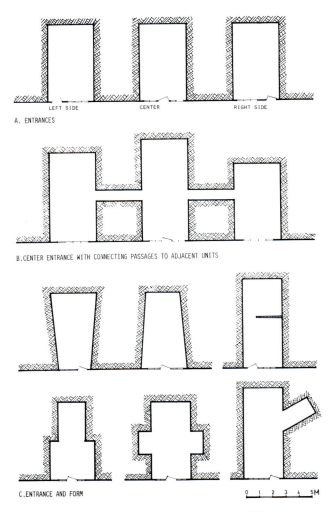

A. ENTRANCES
LEFT SIDE   CENTER   RIGHT SIDE

B. CENTER ENTRANCE WITH CONNECTING PASSAGES TO ADJACENT UNITS

C. ENTRANCE AND FORM

0 1 2 3 4 5M

Fig. 4.26 Entrances to single units of different cave dwellings. The variations in form and height are partially related to differences in climate. Narrow openings are used in cold and dry climates, while wide openings are used in warm and humid climates. Variations in the wall plans are attributable to design innovations and storage needs and are not related to climate.

COURTYARDS

Cave dwelling courtyards are structured in accordance with Chinese tradition. Courtyard size and form are determined by diverse social, economic, and topographical conditions. Tradition dictates that the courtyard should be a physically confined space for privacy, safety, and as an expression of the family's social identity. The courtyard is the geographical and social center of family activities, the place where the food storage well is often located, and the place where occasional cooking and limited agricultural production is carried out. The forms of most courtyards are strongly prescribed (fig. 4.27).

Pit cave dwelling courtyards can be square (fig. 4.27C). They may also be L-shaped, elliptical, or triangular. They are usually excavated to a depth of more than seven meters. Rain drains to a cistern or large hole in the center (fig. 4.28).

Cliff cave dwelling courtyards are most commonly terraced and leveled at the front of the cave and surrounded by retaining walls built up of the loess soil. They are confined by one, two, or three cliff sides (fig. 4.27D and E). The form, however, is determined by topographical conditions. Drainage does not constitute a problem. In most cases they are integrated with the cliff, using the excavated soil for terracing, and they offer attractive views of the lowland (fig. 4.29).

Very large courtyards, both cliff and pit, are often divided by walls built of loess soil and may have separate entrances to accommodate the needs of two or more families who live in the complex (fig. 4.30). In the pit-type cave dwelling, privacy is limited to some extent due to the absence of fences around the courtyard openings.

Based on pilot surveys, the cliff courtyards' average dimensions (23 × 19.8 meters) far exceed those of pit cave dwellings (13.3 × 8.7 meters). The cliff courtyard is mostly terraced on site with the soil excavated from the caves, while the pit type requires the excavation and removal of large quantities of soil. Also, almost all the cliff courtyards have some aboveground structures within them while the pit courtyards usually do not. The average cliff courtyard is much deeper (10.5 meters) than the pit (7.6 meters). The total average floor area of the cliff courtyard (381 square

a   Square pit patio: Tian Lu family dwelling, Xingyang County, Henan. Note depth of patio.

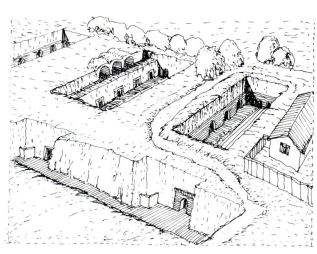

b   Rectangular pit patio: Li Songbin family dwelling, Gong County, Henan. Note second floor earth-sheltered units and belowground alley level with entrance and patio.

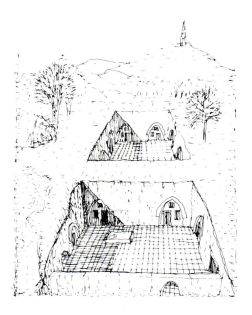

c   Double pit patio: Bai Lesheng family dwelling, Qian County, Shaanxi

d   Cliff patio: Cao Yiren family dwelling, Gaolan County, Gansu. Note aboveground structures in patio.

e   Cliff patio: Zhao Qingyu family dwelling, Yangqu County, Shanxi

f   Cliff patio: Zhang Yinfu family dwelling, Gaomaowan Village, Yan'an region, Shaanxi

Fig. 4.27   Pit and cliff cave dwelling courtyards in different regions

Fig. 4.28   Facing view of a rectangular pit patio typical of Luoyang region, Henan

Fig. 4.29   Bird's-eye view of a patio integrated with the cliff. Zhenzhumao *cun* Village in the mountains east of Taiyuan, Shanxi.

Fig. 4.30 Divided patio in a cliff dwelling complex shared by several families in the town of Xifengzhen, Qingyang region, eastern Gansu

meters) is more than three times that of the pit courtyard (115.71 square meters). The total average cubic meters of earth excavated from the cliff courtyard (1,456 cubic meters) is more than two times that of the pit courtyard (879.3 cubic meters).

As is usual, each of the six researched cliff cave dwellings had only one courtyard, while among the researched pit cave dwellings, one had three courtyards and two had two courtyards each, or

an average of 1.5 courtyards. Also, the cliff courtyards ranged from 85 square meters to 728 square meters. Among the six pit courtyards, the smallest was 58 square meters and the largest was 319 square meters. The latter was made up of three large courtyards and two smaller ones. Dimensions of the courtyards differ from place to place. The twelve cave dwellings that were surveyed are representative of the courtyard dimensions typical of Chinese cave dwellings.

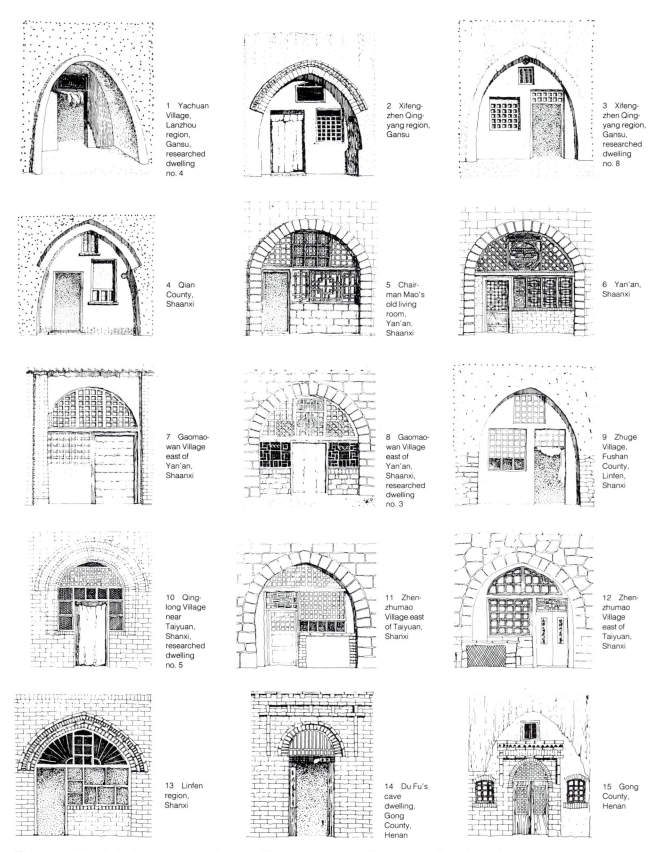

1 Yachuan Village, Lanzhou region, Gansu, researched dwelling no. 4

2 Xifengzhen Qingyang region, Gansu

3 Xifengzhen Qingyang region, Gansu, researched dwelling no. 8

4 Qian County, Shaanxi

5 Chairman Mao's old living room, Yan'an, Shaanxi

6 Yan'an, Shaanxi

7 Gaomaowan Village east of Yan'an, Shaanxi

8 Gaomaowan Village east of Yan'an, Shaanxi, researched dwelling no. 3

9 Zhuge Village, Fushan County, Linfen, Shanxi

10 Qinglong Village near Taiyuan, Shanxi, researched dwelling no. 5

11 Zhenzhumao Village east of Taiyuan, Shanxi

12 Zhenzhumao Village east of Taiyuan, Shanxi

13 Linfen region, Shanxi

14 Du Fu's cave dwelling, Gong County, Henan

15 Gong County, Henan

Fig. 4.31   Facade design of cave dwellings in different regions. All facades introduce the arch or the vault as representative of the cave dwelling's interior form.

FACADES

By implementing the "cut-and-use" method, the cave dwelling is the only architecturally created space built without consuming building materials. However, the facade requires an earth-constructed wall and wood materials for the door and window. Facade design is largely dependent upon the need for sunlight penetration into the dwelling's interior and the availability of building materials. The overall facade form is determined by the vault shape of the cave and includes a door and windows. It is sometimes decorated with stone, which emphasizes its shape. Limited design options within the cave encourage the dweller to express creativity through the facade form. The facade design is meant to offer protection against rain, heat loss, and heat gain, and to enable maximum light to enter the dwelling.

Older styles of facades commonly consisted of one wall with a door, window openings, and a small opening for ventilation at the top. The base wall, one-half meter thick and approximately one meter high, was usually built of loess soil and sometimes had a stone front. The upper part, not as thick, was mortared with loess mud. More recent styles of facades are quite different with respect to materials used and overall design. The use of wood in grid and radial window frames became common only in this century (fig. 4.31). This facade design still includes a central or side-located door and an openable window, as well as a smaller window at the top for air circulation.

The quality of the materials and the design of the facade reveal the interests of the inhabitants and their standard of living. Some cave dwellers now combine the loess soil with brick or adobe. In some cases, brick covers the entire wall including both sides and the upper parts (fig. 4.32). Such brick construction prevents the deterioration of

Fig. 4.32   Facade view of Zhao Qingyu family dwelling, Qinglong *cun* Village near Taiyuan, Shanxi. The central unit is connected to the two adjacent rooms. Design of the doors and windows is unique. Note sunflower crop above.

Fig. 4.33   View of earth-sheltered dwelling facade. The window woodwork shows originality in design, intended to maximize sunlight penetration. Note similarity of the overall design to that of a cave dwelling, including stone wall and sunflower crop on the roof. Zhang Yanfu family dwelling, Gaomaowan *cun* Village east of Yan'an, Shaanxi.

the front due to changes in weather. In Yan'an *shi* City, the walls are built with local stone (fig. 4.33). The angle of the facade ranges from ten to fifteen degrees. The gradient at the top of the unit is usually 5 percent to help keep the doorway clear of rain runoff.

DOORS AND WINDOWS

The doors and window frames of all the cave dwellings are custom-made of rough wood although wood has been, and still is, quite expensive in China. More recently doors and windows, while still made to order, are nicely designed and consequently more elegant (fig. 4.34). Still they do not have quite the same quality as those enjoyed by urban dwellers.

In general, most cave dwellings have one window installed on the side parallel to the door and another small square or round opening at the top of the facade. The window size is usually about ninety × sixty centimeters. Doors are usually 2.1–2.5 meters high and 0.9–1.2 meters wide. Windows are covered with a transparent milky paper that lets in light (fig. 4.35). The design is flexible, allowing a variety of forms including square, rectangular, and radial patterns.

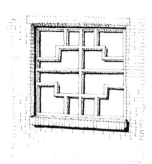

a Zhenyuan County, Qingyang region, Gansu

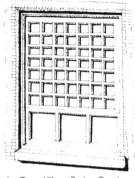

b Zhuge Village, Fushan County, Shanxi

c Xifengzhen, Qingyang region, Gansu

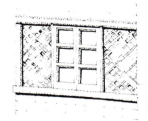

d Gaomaowan Village, Yan'an region, Shaanxi

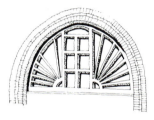

e Yangshui Village, Linfen region, Shanxi

f Author's cave dwelling design near Linfen, Shanxi

Fig. 4.34   Local variants in window design

Fig. 4.35 Windows facing a courtyard, Fushan *xian* County east of Linfen, Shanxi

HEATED BEDS

The heated bed, called *kang,* is commonly used in the traditional Chinese cave dwelling, especially in the cold, dry regions. The bed tends to be very large and can accommodate more than two people (fig. 4.36). The heated bed is used for sleeping in the winter and as a dining platform in the summer.

The overall construction material is loess soil, dried flat bricks, and fired bricks with some wood used around the edges. The bed's surface rests on a framework of four brick walls, and is about eighty centimeters high. The surface is made of large flat bricks and is supported by columns within the framework. It is heated by the embers of a slow-burning charcoal fire taken from the stove, which is usually attached to it. The embers are placed beneath the bed's surface within the framework. Smoke from the attached stove escapes through a chimney located in the facade wall.

The location of the bed differs from place to place. The bed is a built-in structure usually located along the wall near the entrance to the

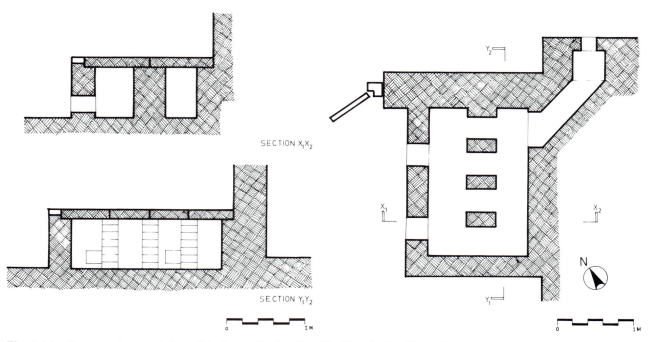

SECTION X₁X₂

SECTION Y₁Y₂

N

0   1 M

0   1 M

Fig. 4.36   Cross sections and plan of the heated bed in Gao Kexi family dwelling, Liquan *xian* County, Shaanxi

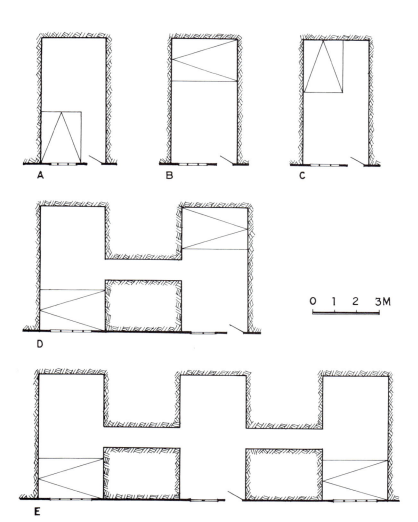

A   B   C

D

0 1 2 3M

Fig. 4.37   Variant locations of built-in heated beds

E

Fig. 4.38　Built-in heated bed near dwelling's entrance, positioned along the length of the room. Newspaper is pasted to the wall to prevent dust from falling.

Fig. 4.39　This heated bed spans the width of the room.

unit, or in some cases at the intersection of two rooms (fig. 4.37). The bed may also be situated along the front wall near the window of the facade, along the length of the room unit or crosswise (figs. 4.38 and 4.39). Bed dimensions are usually large (2.80 × 1.60 meters).

INTERIOR ARRANGEMENT

In spite of all the advantages of the loess soil for cave dwelling development, it does impose certain restrictions on design dimensions. These dimensions, in turn, impose limits on the type and scale of furniture which can be accommodated within the cave's interior space. Traditionally, furnishings were very simple: a stove for cooking or heating, a heated bed, a small table and chair, a sewing machine and sometimes a closet, a sofa; more recently radios and even televisions. There are some families with urban-style furniture and others with the simple rural agricultural type.

Most of the Chinese cave dwellings have a stove for cooking usually adjoining the heated bed. They also commonly have a portable charcoal-burning stove, not unlike a Russian samovar, that can be used to warm the area as well as to heat kettles of water (fig. 4.40). This stove's chimney extends to the outside and terminates at either the top or the bottom of the front of the unit (fig. 4.41). The portable stove may be disconnected

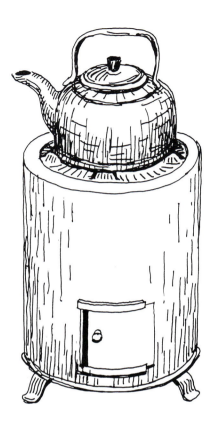

Fig. 4.40   Portable charcoal cookstove

Fig. 4.41   Chimney designs

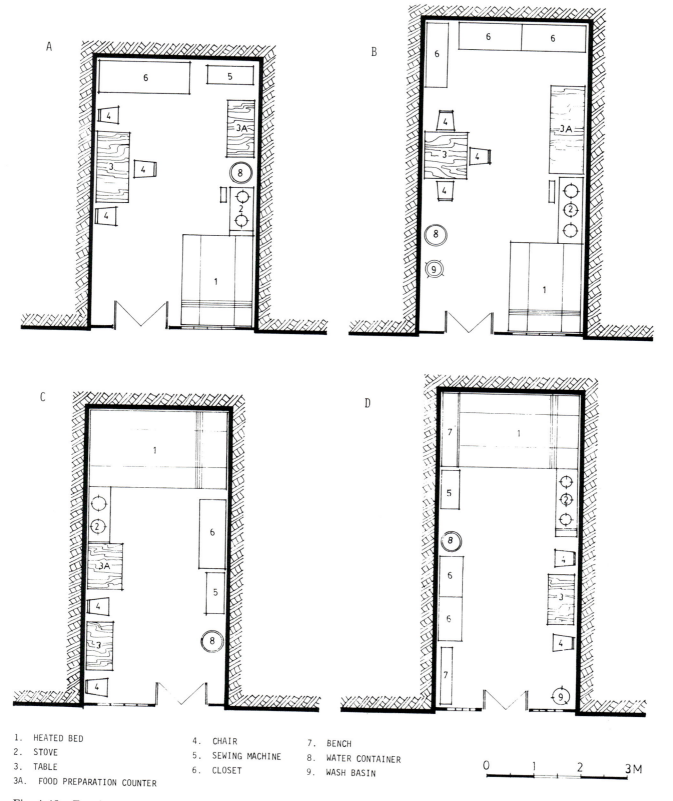

1. HEATED BED	4. CHAIR	7. BENCH
2. STOVE	5. SEWING MACHINE	8. WATER CONTAINER
3. TABLE	6. CLOSET	9. WASH BASIN
3A. FOOD PREPARATION COUNTER		

Fig. 4.42 Furniture arrangements in the cave dwelling unit. Cave rooms are limited to a maximum width of 3.5 meters because of constraints imposed by the stability of the soil. The length is limited only by sunlight penetration. These limits determine the room's form and furniture arrangement.

from the chimney and moved outside in the summer.

Arrangement of furniture is constrained by the linear form of the dwelling (fig. 4.42). In the Chinese style, especially among rural people, a room's functions are mixed and not always as well defined as in the West. Thus, a room may be used for living, sleeping, cooking, dining, and working, and can have simultaneous multifunctions.

CLIFF CAVE DWELLING DECORATION

In general, cave decoration, both indoors and outdoors, is more primitive in the west and becomes finer and more distinctive toward the eastern section of the loess plateau.

In the Longdong area of eastern Gansu, the cliff facade is of earth and the inner part is plastered with lime. Dwellings in Shanxi, the Shaanbei area (northern Shaanxi), and the Yuxi area (western Henan) feature a more advanced decoration with facades of brick and interiors plastered with a straw, mud, and lime mixture. In Yuxi and Jinnan (southern Shanxi) the dwellings have brick facades and a decorative treatment of the eaves. The pit cave dwellings in Yuxi generally have sloping entrance pathways paved with brick or a ramp of "beaten hard and serrated" earth (Ren Zhiyuan 1985a, 335).

NEIGHBORHOOD DESIGN PATTERNS

The design of the neighborhood is simple in the Longdong area of Gansu. The cliff cave dwelling type usually has single cave units in horizontal rows; however, the pattern is determined by the topographical configuration and may take a curved shape, an L shape with a right angle, or a double L shape. In Shanxi, two or three adjacent cliff cave dwelling units are connected by underground tunnels. The most common type consists of three parallel caves connected by tunnels for a one-family dwelling. Family units, however, are not connected with each other.

As for vertical construction, there are two-story caves, called *gaoyaozi* or "high cave" in the Longdong area, and *tian yao* or "sky cave" in Henan province. Some are constructed one above the other, connected by steps or a wooden ladder, and accessed from either the inside or the outside.

Others are built on alternating axes. Usually the upper floor is small.

VILLAGE DESIGN

The design of a cave dwelling village can be concentrated with a large number of families, or it can be dispersed with twenty to fifty families. A predominately pit cave dwelling village is hardly noticeable until one is very close to it. In some villages, the road is cut deep into the ground, creating an alley open to the sky at the same level as the cave entrances and courtyards. In this case, the inhabitants move within an environment of loess walls formed either by man or by erosion. The village surroundings are integrated with the environment with minimum change.

Most of the existing cave dwelling complexes, especially the cliff cave dwellings, are the result of spontaneous, unplanned development. Consequently, they are dispersed, occupying large tracts of land. Cave dwelling villages are usually supervised by a local governing authority.

The pit cave dwelling villages, such as those in the Luoyang region, are arranged in a more orderly manner with an attempt to save space and develop a compact pattern. Basically a pit cave dwelling village occupies more land than an aboveground village, because each pit cave dwelling requires more land than an equivalent aboveground house.

The overall vista of a cliff settlement is very appealing and attractive. Good examples of this are the cave neighborhoods of Yan'an *shi* City (fig. 4.43A, C, D, F, L, and N). Such settlements normally have good ventilation, an attractive view over the lowland, a good drainage system, adequate sunlight penetration into the dwellings, a thick earth cover above the cave units, the potential for expansion into the mountain, and the added value of special landscape architecture. Mountain cliff cave dwellings are commonly found in the hilly areas of the Longdong, Gansu; the Shaanbei, Shaanxi; the Yuxi, Henan; and in Hejia *cun* Village of the Chengguan Commune of 1984 in Loufan *xian* County, Taiyuan area, Shanxi.

On the other hand, a settlement located on flat or rolling land does not, by its very nature, share

a Cliff cave dwelling neighborhood on the way to Yan'an Pagoda east of Yan'an, Shaanxi

b Zhoutoushan community near Matousi Village, north of Taiyuan, Shanxi

c Cliff neighborhood east of Yan'an on the way to Yan'an Pagoda, Shaanxi

d Wangjia terrace neighborhood west of Yan'an, Shaanxi

e Village on the edge of the loess plateau, Qingyang region, east Gansu

f Terraced neighborhood east of Yan'an, Shaanxi

g Zhongtou Village, Mangshan township, near Luoyang, Henan

h Xi Village, Gong County, Henan

i Xi Village in Gong County, Henan

j Weixia Village, Pinglu County, Shaanxi

k Town of Guxian, Gong County, Henan

l Yan'an

m Shemadao Village, Qian County, Shaanxi

n Student dormitories, Yan'an University, Yan'an

o Gaojiadui Village (1984), Liquan County, Shaanxi

Fig. 4.43   Cave dwelling complexes in rural and urban communities

in all the advantages of a mountain settlement, but pit cave dwellings do have other advantages. The overall design is likely to be a grid system of pit openings almost equidistant from one another (fig. 4.43G, H, J, and K). Pit cave dwelling villages where preconceived overall planning has been experimented with are located in the southern part of the Qingyang region (Gansu), in the areas of Changwu *xian,* Bin *xian,* and Tongguan *xian* (Shaanxi), in the southern part of the Yuncheng region (Shanxi), and in the areas of Lingbao *xian,* Sanmenxia *shi* City, Luoyang, and Gong *xian* (Henan). Recently some counties have begun to discourage the construction of pit cave dwellings.

In conclusion, the discussion in this chapter dwells broadly and deeply on the details of design. Chinese cave dwelling designs offer a stimulating example of indigenous housing solutions and they are the product of combined environmental and cultural forces. They are both innovative and pragmatic in design solutions that meet daily needs. The Chinese example is based on historical layers of accomplishment that have been passed from one generation to another. Cave dwellings are one of the most enlightening historical examples of indigenous ingenuity in the world. These dwellings require the use of very few, if any, building materials, demand only low levels of technology, and are far cheaper to build than equivalent aboveground units. Awareness of environmental design constraints should lead architects and urban designers to improve on these housing and settlement forms in order to meet modern needs and standards of living.

FIVE

Structural and Environmental Constraints

DURING the chaos of the Cultural Revolution there was much confusion in China about the role of planners and architects, particularly in rural planning and design. Some felt that peasants were capable of doing their own design and construction and that there was no need for modern theory and technology. For an architect to design earth structures in rural communities was considered a serious underutilization of his skills. But professionals did not foresee the rapid changes that were to take place—the increase in income, and the demand for improvements in the standard of living (Xu Sishu n.d., 51). Such developments necessitated changes in housing design and especially in the design of cave dwellings. Although cave dwellings do not yet utilize advanced technology or prefabricated products, they do require a new design to accommodate modern furniture and fixtures. Functionally designed spaces such as kitchens, dining areas, living rooms, and bedrooms as well as problems of ventilation, lighting, and moisture control all require serious consideration and planning. The Architectural Society of China has become aware of these deficiencies only recently and is now making an attempt to confront the needs of the millions of people living in *yao dong,* or cave dwellings.

Environmental Constraints

Cave dwelling safety requires continuous maintenance of the immediate environment. The construction of cave dwellings does minimum damage to the environment and may actually preserve it. First, the underground space is constructed from the same materials as the environment, the

loess soil. The new form thus integrates itself harmoniously with the natural surroundings. Second, the construction of the cave dwelling alters the natural landscape of the site only slightly, and thus preserves the equilibrium of the ecosystem.

The Chinese cave dwellings are located primarily in the middle layers of loess soil of the Pleistocene epoch. Most of them are constructed in Q3 loess areas. In general the upper part of the soil is yellow ochre and the lower part is dark brown in color. Traces of calcium strip layers can be observed on the sides of steep hills. Usually stronger than the surrounding soil, these layers are selected as the ceilings of the dwellings. In the lower part of the layer there is also a thin buried strip of soil that is light red in color. The surface of the soil is covered with sparse vegetation, often wild jujube bushes (Li Jinle, Zhang Congrong, and Li Liangsheng 1985, 202). The part of the loess soil used for cave dwellings has a soft to medium density. Very few, if any, building materials are used in construction and the cave dwelling form is adjusted to suit the characteristics of the soil.

The plan and height of cave units slightly differ from one region to another. This is attributed to the noticeable climatic differences within the overall area of loess soil distribution. The northwest is arid, cold and dry in winter, and warm with little or no precipitation in the summer. The diurnal differentiation of temperature is great. The southeast is semi-arid to semi-humid, cold with little precipitation or snow in winter, and warm and humid in summer.

The lack of chimneys, tunnels, or windows for cross ventilation almost totally impedes the circulation of air in the cave dwellings. Gully sites are shielded from the cold winds of winter, while those on the mountain slopes are not. Although this makes cliff caves in gully sites warmer in the winter, they lack ventilation, making them warm and humid in the summer. Also, a narrow gully site obstructs the residents' views of the outdoors. However, airflow does occur when there is a noticeable difference in temperature between two spaces. In the summer this process occurs between the cave's rooms and the overheated patio if a circulation system is established.

With the lack of air exchange, the effects of air pollution are greater than in aboveground habitats. Air pollution, in the form of carbon dioxide, carbon monoxide, and sulphur dioxide, is a result of the charcoal stoves used for cooking in summer and cooking and heating in winter. Also, there is a certain amount of dust created by particles falling from the walls and vault, especially when they are not covered by newspaper. The floors are not tiled or bricked. In general, it can be assumed that the highest concentration of pollutants occurs in the cave's farthest interior with a consequent negative impact on the health of its residents. In addition, closed structures without ventilation show higher levels of radioactive radon gas. Radon is produced by the decomposition of uranium in the soil and can be harmful to health and may shorten the life span (Qian Fuyuan and Su Yu 1985, 301).

In terms of acoustics, the cave dwelling is a good sound insulator because of the thick layers of soil surrounding it. However, because of this insulation and the lack of windows, any noise generated inside reverberates within the cave. Only some of this sound will be diffused to the front and sides. Noise levels inside a cave dwelling were measured at about 1 to 8 decibels (dB) higher than those in a similar type of aboveground structure (ibid., 302).

In existing cave dwelling design, natural light can enter only through the cave's front door and any windows that may be used for ventilation purposes. The degree of exposure to natural sunlight can be affected by the cave's orientation, color, reflective qualities, and the depth of the unit, as well as by the height and angle of the vaulted ceiling in relation to the patio, the dimen-

sions of the pit courtyard, and the existence of trees or other obstacles in the courtyard. Natural illumination within cave dwelling units decreases as the depth increases. However, at 40 degrees latitude it is possible for winter sunlight to penetrate directly into the cave at a depth of seven meters provided the cave has a southern orientation and the height of the ceiling at the entrance is five meters. Both light and ventilation can be significantly improved with a rear corridor, an air shaft, skylight openings or, in certain cases, the installation of rear windows.

Cave dwellings do have an advantage over aboveground houses in that they are warmer in winter, consuming less fuel, and cooler in summer. The difference in temperature between the inside and the outside of the cave is always considerable. One resident even asserted that this was the major "mistake" in cave dwellings, making it easy for people to catch cold or become sick as they go back and forth from the indoors to the outdoors.

Many residents consider cave room ceilings to be too low and find the units themselves too small. They feel that aboveground houses are both nicer looking and more comfortable. Older cave dwellings tend to be limited in size because of structural considerations and cannot accommodate new, more modern furnishings. Maximum width of the cave in the loess soil usually cannot exceed 3.5 meters, although residents would prefer that their caves were wider. Room dimensions are determined relative to height and soil structure, and greater width can cause collapse of the ceiling. To prevent dust from falling from the ceiling, the residents of one cave dwelling made a bamboo drop ceiling in a grid form that was quite beautiful as well as efficient.

In areas of heavy rainfall, inhabitants were concerned about the safety of their cave dwellings. Every time there was a storm they were afraid the structures would collapse. They felt that the high humidity weakened the dwellings and damaged their furnishings as well. In the case of one cave dwelling near a road, the residents felt that there could be problems resulting from vibrations caused by the vehicles, even though the soil thickness above this cave was 5 meters.

As is the case in many developing countries,

public institutions have given a certain priority to the development of basic utilities. Of these, water and electricity have become essential for Chinese cave dwellers and have been supplied to many of the existing dwellings. However, water is often supplied without an adequate sewage system and this has created serious sanitation problems. Some cave dwellers attempt to solve this problem by digging a hole in the center of the cave's patio to absorb sewage. Inhabitants sometimes use the sewage to water their plants, which are cultivated as a means of solving the disposal problem.

Plumbing and water facilities in Chinese cave dwellings are primitive by Western standards. The dwellings lack modern conveniences such as showers, lavatories, and adequate toilet facilities. Human waste is often simply buried and used later as compost for crops. Where plumbing does exist, it is usually simple in design: a drainage pipe leading to an open sewage outlet from a covered hole dug in the floor of one of the cave's rooms. A faucet with running water or a hose nearby the hole is used to flush away both wash water and waste. Obviously, in a cave dwelling without sufficient drainage and ventilation, facilities of this type can cause serious health and sanitation problems.

In recent years, a rapid increase in cave dwellers' incomes due to economic reforms has changed both their lifestyles and the diversity of their cave furnishings. Many of the cave dwellings now have electricity, although some inhabitants still use batteries to operate radios and televisions. The accelerating use of electrical appliances has increased the demand for the supply of electricity to the cave dwellings. Inhabitants want to bring modern items such as televisions, refrigerators, and washing machines into their dwellings. Consequently, a re-evaluation of cave dwelling design is required to meet the changing needs of the residents.

SEISMIC IMPACT

Northern China, where the research for this book was mainly undertaken, is especially subject to earthquakes. Geologically, the region is characterized by foldbelts, uplifts, faults, or thrust faults that surround its central platform and basin (fig. 5.1). These foldbelts include the Nan *shan* in the

west, extending northwest to southeast; the Qin *ling* in the south, dividing China into its northern arid and southern humid zones; and the Yuhua in the southeast. The Ala *shan* Stable Block in the north, the Yin *shan* Uplift in the northeast, and the North China Basins in the east also bound the area of research. Most important are the many faults north of Ningxia and Shanxi and the bulk of thrust faults south of Shaanxi and west of Henan provinces, especially those associated with the Qin *ling* foldbelt. The region forms a geological and pedological unit with the Ordos Basin at its hub. It is subject to seismic activity that affects the cave dwellings' stability and the well-being of their inhabitants.

According to an estimate, 45 percent of the cave dwellings of China are located where earthquake intensity registers above 7 on the Richter scale. There are 60 million square meters of cave dwelling settlements in this area (Luo Wenbao 1985, 233). The bulk of the cave dwellings are located in central and northern Shaanxi, southern and western Shanxi, western and northwestern Henan, the eastern part of Gansu, and the southern part of Ningxia Hui Autonomous Region.

The following four areas are the most seismically active: the deep fracture zone before the Taihang *shan* mountains, the collapse zone of the upwarping region of Shanxi province, the deep fracture belt on the east side of the Liupan mountains, and the northern reaches of the Tianshui-Wudu-Wenxian zone. The Taihang *shan* constitute a deep fracture zone with a series of grabens and fault blocks. The area concentrates earthcrust stress and has produced nine major earthquakes. Upper Shanxi province is the region where the most intense seismic activity has occured with 87 earthquakes recorded, three of which registered 8 on the Richter scale. The Liupan *shan* have a deep fracture belt on the eastern side. Here, seven destructive earthquakes took place between the years 1117 and 1920, including one in 1920 in Haiyuan *xian* County, Ningxia, that registered 8.5 on the Richter scale. The Tianshui-Wudu-Wenxian zone is an earthquake belt that has experienced 57 earthquakes, one of which, in 1964, registered 7.5 on the Richter scale.

Cave dwelling design requires special attention and study in relation to seismic activity. However,

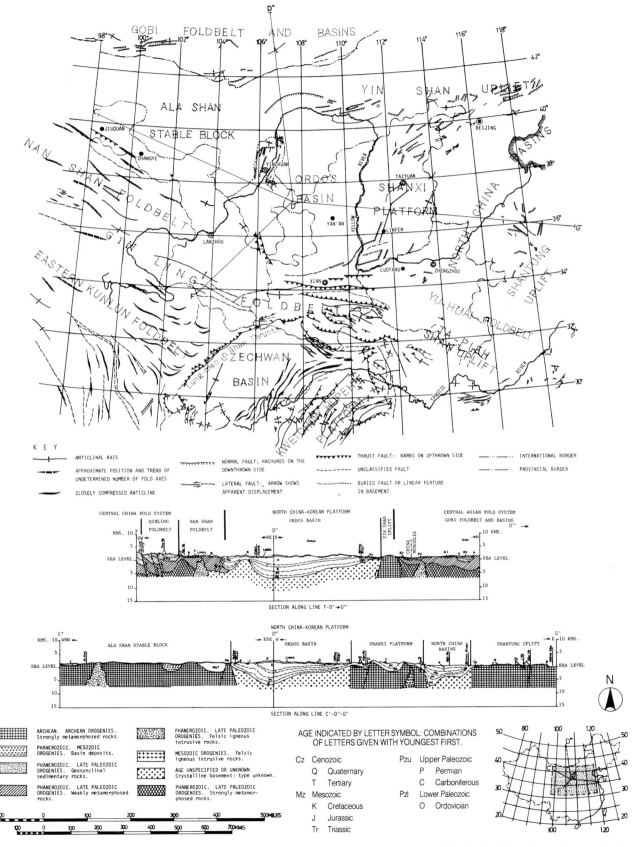

Fig. 5.1 Tectonic features of the cave dwelling region. Note high concentration of faults in Shanxi province and the Qinling Mountains. This is one of China's most earthquake-sensitive zones and cave dwellings here require special design and construction considerations.

for most of the past earthquake disasters, detailed records and of course scientific analyses are lacking (ibid., 234).

Earthquakes in China have caused great loss of life. During the 1920 Haiyuan disaster more than 230,000 people died (Yang Yuecheng and Yang Liu 1985, 453). In 1815, an earthquake occurred in Pinglu County, Shanxi, that measured 6.7 on the Richter scale. Houses and cave dwellings collapsed and many people were killed (Luo Wenbao 1985, 233). In Hebei province there are many belowground buildings, especially in the northern part, where it is very cold in winter. According to local witnesses, the 1976 earthquake that took place in the Tangshan area, Hebei, and in the mountains near the city of Beijing, did a great deal of damage to aboveground buildings while the subterranean dwellings survived (Zhao Dajian, personal communication, University Park, Pa., spring 1982). It is worth noting that most of the caves were constructed in recent wind-deposited Q3 loess, such as *ma lan*, and in older Q2 *li shi* loess, both of which are relatively soft. Q1, the oldest loess, is difficult to excavate and contains few dwellings (Hou Xueyuan and Sun Yiming 1985, 125).

The southern part of Ningxia Hui Autonomous Region is covered with Q4 Holocene loess. This stratum covers older loess layers with depths ranging from 10 to 200 meters, the thickest part being located in the mountains of the Guyuan area, south of Ningxia (Bai Mingxue 1985, 55). Ningxia is seismically sensitive, with faults and grabens. Since 1949, seven earthquakes measuring more than 5 on the Richter scale have been registered in this region. The earthquake of 1970, with an epicentral intensity of 7, caused 64 percent of the cave dwellings and vaulted earth-sheltered habitats made with mud bricks (*fa la*) to collapse in Xiji County, while 18 percent of the single-story aboveground houses with flat roofs collapsed as well. In Haiyuan County, an earthquake in 1982 registered 5.7 on the Richter scale with 7 measured as the epicentral intensity. This earthquake caused the collapse of 46 percent of the cave dwellings and vaulted earth-sheltered structures built with sun-dried bricks. It also caused the collapse of 14 percent of the flat-roofed houses (Huo Fuguo and Cao Shaokang 1985, 117). Many of the affected cave dwellings were located at the foot of loess valleys. Under earthquake conditions the landslides intensified along the slopes and piled up at the doors of the caves themselves. Locations such as these require safety measures such as terracing to control landslides on the slopes.

If the workmanship of the rammed earth-bearing walls is poor in earth-sheltered houses, the walls deteriorate over time because of alkali and rain. During earthquakes the walls are forced out of shape, causing the vault to collapse. In one instance, the vault had been built with sun-dried bricks without centering and thus the top of the vault split open longitudinally. Also, the vault and the front and back walls may have been constructed with different materials at different times. Thus these parts collided with each other and caused the collapse of the house (ibid., 118).

The force of an earthquake intensifies the downward landslide on the slopes (fig. 5.2). The steeper the gradient of the slope, the greater the intensity of the slide. This process changes the landform. It is also influenced by the granular

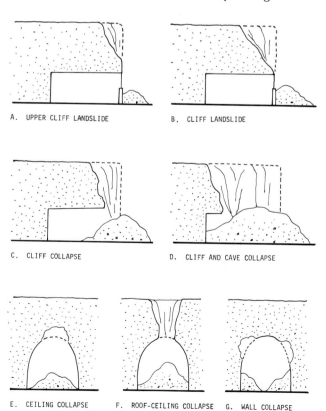

A. UPPER CLIFF LANDSLIDE   B. CLIFF LANDSLIDE

C. CLIFF COLLAPSE   D. CLIFF AND CAVE COLLAPSE

E. CEILING COLLAPSE   F. ROOF-CEILING COLLAPSE   G. WALL COLLAPSE

Fig. 5.2 Examples of possible cave dwelling collapse

composition of the soil and its density—soft, medium, or hard. According to Bai Mingxue, who researched the impact of earthquakes on the loess soil of southern Ningxia, "when the inclination angle of the slope changed from 10 to 45, its horizontal vibration would increase 2.5-fold" (Bai 1985, 58). When seismic activity reaches 6 on the Richter scale, slope collapse and landslides take place. Under such circumstances, residential areas or cave dwellings located at the foot of a slope, gully, or gorge are damaged by the accumulation of loose earth.

In 1982, an earthquake in southern Ningxia (7 on the Richter scale) severely damaged both pit and cliff cave dwellings that were located at the foot of a hill; however, only slight damage was caused to earth-wood houses (ibid.). Cave vaults split, producing longitudinal fissures, and there was heavy damage to the lateral walls, causing the collapse of the arches. According to Bai, "about 46 to 64 percent of earth cave dwellings would collapse under the pressure of a magnitude 7 earthquake" (ibid., 59). Some of the damaged cliff cave dwellings had been excavated from layers of earth that had accumulated from former landslides. It is now known that it is important to remove these accumulations before excavating new cave dwellings. In the Yan'an region, some of the inhabitants reinforced the cave vaults with layers of brick or stone or added wooden beams to prevent collapse (fig. 5.3). Near the city of Luoyang in Henan, cave dwellers used the hard layer of loess, rich in calcium, as support for the upper part of the vault.

The earthquake survey shows that damage was extremely heavy due to landslides. The front wall or facade, already suffering from climatic changes, erosion, wind, and rain, was the first to slide. This action could block the cave entrance and lead to the suffocation of the inhabitants.

Fig. 5.3 Supporting beam in ceiling as protection against earthquakes, Yan'an region

STRUCTURAL STABILITY

Cave dwelling stability is related to many factors including loess soil composition and density, which determine soil behavior under stress; degree of moisture in the loess and especially in those parts that form the ceiling/roof and walls; and the design and form of the cave.

A major weakness in cave dwelling structures is the tendency for cracks to appear in the ceiling of the vault or in the walls including the front wall. The ceiling crack, short at first, usually appears longitudinally along the central axis. In both cases, cracks may appear in the very early stages of excavation. In that case, digging must be stopped to allow for observation (Hou and Sun 1985, 124–125).

Moisture is also a factor that needs to be considered during the excavation process. The structural stability of the cave is improved by allowing the soil to dry out gradually, during a construction process of two or more steps, before the vault is completed. The moisture content of loess soil is usually 15 to 20 percent before excavation. The drying process reduces this moisture content to 10 percent or more below its plastic limit when completed (ibid., 125). Many cave dwellers let their caves dry for a year or more before occupying them.

To keep the cave dwelling dry throughout the four seasons, the Chinese select sites that face south. This allows the cave to receive maximum sunlight penetration and improves ventilation when an effective air circulation system is used. Such a system is essential during the rainy summer season in the eastern and central parts of the loess region. Unfortunately, the majority of Chinese cave dwellings do not have any ventilation systems for air circulation. Although some have small windows at the top of their facades, their effectiveness is limited.

Cave dwellings with roof thicknesses of 10 meters or more were usually very dry and safe. Surveyed caves that were three hundred years old were found to be in reasonably good condition. In short, mechanics, pedology, and geology should be evaluated jointly when considering the structural stability of cave dwellings.

Design Problems

The following are serious problems present in Chinese cave dwellings that require special design treatments: land consumption, ventilation, humidity, drainage, moisture, and waterproofing.

LAND CONSUMPTION

The arable land per capita in China is .26 acres, only about one-fourth of the world acreage per capita of .91 acres (one hectare is equal to 2.471 acres) (Ren Zhenying 1985a, 321). The development of cave dwellings or other types of below-ground space use should in theory leave much of the land's surface free for agriculture, recreation, and other purposes.

Cliff cave dwellings occupy much less land, and such slopes as they do occupy are generally unsuitable for farming (fig. 5.4). Cliff caves are developed according to the given topography. To construct them in an aggregate compact form instead of the present scattered form would require extensive earth removal, grading, and terracing.

A pilot survey of twelve dwellings located in four provinces of the cave dwelling region indicated that the average lot size of the six cliff cave dwellings was 638 square meters. The average lot size of the six pit cave dwellings was 1,116 square meters for the same size family. The average square meters per resident of a cliff dwelling lot was 98, while for a pit cave dwelling lot it was 138. Moreover, the dimensions of each type were different. In the cliff type the average lot dimensions were 29 by 22 meters. In the pit cave dwelling the average lot dimensions were 36 by 31 meters (fig. 5.5).

Pit cave dwellings use up much more arable land than do cliff cave dwellings. The average amount of land used in one pit cave dwelling complex is .41 acres, with the smallest pit cave occupying only .25 acres while some large complexes cover .49 to .66 acres. In 1982, the Hao brothers' family complex in Houguanzhai Commune in the Qingyang region of eastern Gansu used much of its land for dwellings. This production unit had 59.85 hectares (147.90 acres) of land with a population of 242. The 42 dwellings occupied 5.66 hec-

ture difference between the outdoor air and the slightly cooler air of the shaft itself. Also, a self-rotating air catcher, in the form of a half-dome, helps air to penetrate the shaft. The second factor is the vacuum created within the patio. The increase in temperature between 2:00 and 4:00 P.M. in the patio causes air to be drawn out from the cave units (if the shaft and the windows facing the patio are open) and thereby establishes air circulation. During the experiments, the highest wind velocity occurred at 2:00 P.M. The difference between the highest wind velocity outdoors and the lowest indoors did not exceed 20 percent. On the other hand, it is theoretically possible for the air flow to circulate in the opposite direction (from the window and/or door to the shaft and upwards). This will not occur in a pit patio (where air can accumulate), but it is possible in a cliff cave dwelling where a closed patio does not exist and the air currents flow up the face of the cliff. Otherwise, the air flow will circulate in the described pattern. Another result of this experiment was a reduction of relative humidity within the cave dwelling by evaporative cooling (Golany 1990, chap. 4).

The experiments in existing cave dwellings near Taiyuan *shi,* Shanxi, showed that the air flowed from the chimney through the room and then to the patio, and not vice versa. The tendency of the heated patio air to rise caused cooler air to be drawn from adjacent areas. This air circulation was increased by opening the chimney. Basically, the cooler air of the cave room moved toward the warmer rising air of the patio. Outside warm air, when funneled through the earth-sheltered and shaded passageway of the chimney, became cooler and therefore moved downward into the cave room. In any case, no air-conditioning was required in the cave dwelling. In the winter, the newly constructed chimney was closed and air movement was eliminated in order to minimize heat loss. The door was also kept closed most of the time to keep the room warm. Some heating may be needed in the rooms during winter since cold air sinks and stagnates in the patio when temperatures reach their lowest point late at night. In both seasons, however, energy consumption is minimal (ibid.).

HUMIDITY

The cliff dwelling is preferable to the pit dwelling when the patio itself is the drainage base. In one case, three cliff cave units were built thirty centimeters higher than the patio, with the patio slightly higher than the adjacent road. Consequently, the drainage base of the caves' massive walls was lowered, excess water drained off, and humidity was reduced.

It is the usual practice of the dwellers to allow the cave units, once constructed, to dry out for as long as two years before occupying them. The layer of earth above the room units of a cave dwelling complex must be thick enough to prevent water penetration. In one cliff cave dwelling studied, the covering earth layer measured only 1.8 to two meters thick and was not substantial enough to prevent this problem.

A variety of methods can be used to ventilate belowground units and reduce summer humidity (fig. 6.4). An experiment to remove moisture from cave walls was undertaken in Shanxi province and reported by Mr. Zuo Guobao of the Architectural Scientific Academy in Taiyuan, Shanxi. In this experiment, bricks were set in place at a height of 1.5 meters around the walls of a cave unit measuring nine meters long by four meters high. Above the bricks, paper was installed at a distance of five centimeters away from the ceiling and the vault (fig. 6.4G). It was expected that moisture would be removed from the ceiling by air circulating from the small front shaft or upper window opening through the space created, and directed up and out the chimney. The residents felt that the treatment had been somewhat effective because the unit in question seemed dryer while an adjacent dwelling, lacking this treatment, was covered with moisture.

Terraced cave dwellings, constructed on either side of a gully with a southern orientation, were less damp than those facing north. Inhabitants of caves with a northern orientation suffered from humidity, moisture on their walls and ceilings, and lack of sunlight. An overhang along the front of the cave dwelling, built to prevent rain from entering the cave, also eliminates moisture on the

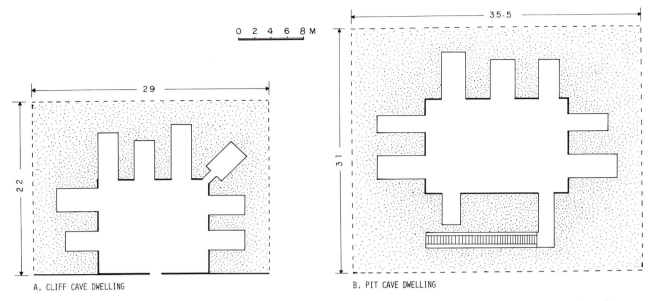

Fig. 5.4 Pit cave dwellings use a large amount of arable land while cliff cave dwellings, with the same number of rooms and a larger courtyard, use very little if any. The twelve surveyed cave dwellings indicate an average lot size of 1,116 square meters for pit cave dwellings and 638 square meters for cliff cave dwellings.

tares (14 acres)—only five residential complexes were not of the pit type. Thus, each pit cave dwelling occupied about .36 acres or .06 acres per person (253 square meters per person). Recently the local government in eastern Gansu province prohibited the building of additional pit cave dwellings. Accordingly, since 1980 no more have been constructed and in time they may disappear from this area (Nan Yingjing 1982b, 111). In any case, most of the pit cave dwellers do not use the land above the dwellings for agriculture.

The interior space of a pit cave dwelling measuring 3.5 meters wide by six meters long is equal to twenty-one square meters. The two dividing walls measuring three meters wide by six meters long are equal to thirty-six square meters. The total of the interior space plus the walls is equal to fifty-seven square meters, which is the total land required for one pit cave unit. This size is necessary only in the case of the pit cave dwellings, since the cliff dwellings are built on non-arable slopes. If eight cave units are allowed per rural family, then the total land consumption for one pit cave dwelling complex would be 456 square meters (plus 100 square meters for a ten-foot-square courtyard) or a total of 556 square meters.

This does not include the land required for bordering setback lines of at least one meter that must be allowed between neighboring cave dwelling complexes. The land consumed by the pit caves is 4.5 times greater than that consumed by the courtyard. In addition, the land used by the entrance pathway must also be considered.

The land surface required above a cave for its stability is equal to the size of the cave opening plus the thickness of its supporting walls. Moreover, in the case of the pit cave dwelling type, the stability of the cave dwelling (especially in the rear) is maintained by a larger area than the actual usable space within the cave itself or in an equivalent aboveground house. This area is two or three times larger than the cave courtyard. Consequently, the pit dwelling consumes more land than any other type. In theory, the land above the pit caves can be used for agriculture. In practice, this is not feasible because of the possible risk of water penetration and development of cavities that can threaten the caves' structural stability. Throughout the lifetime of a cave dwelling there will be a need for renewal: cutting away the eroded or damaged front part and extending the length of the rooms deeper, a process which neces-

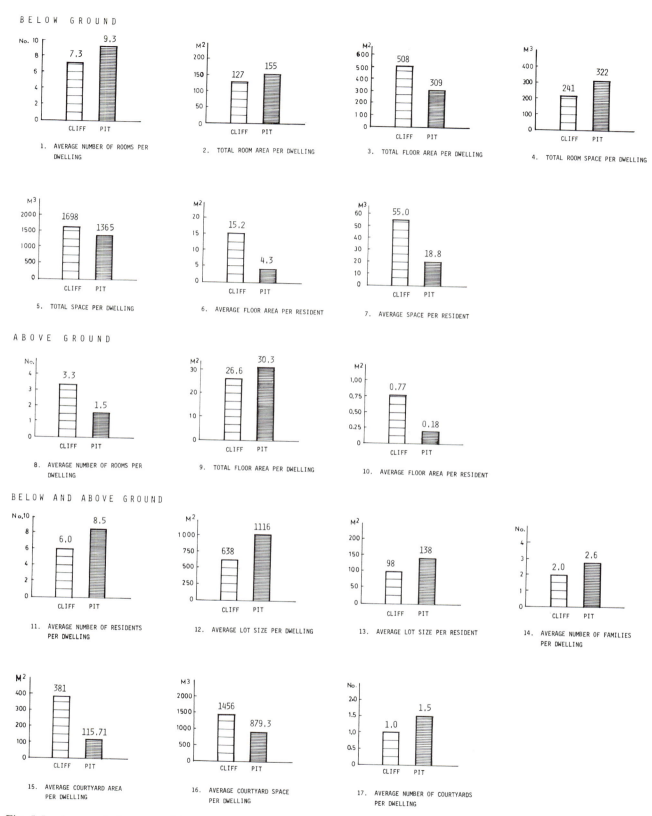

Fig. 5.5   Average belowground dwelling unit dimensions compared with aboveground sections of the same unit. Based on 12 cave dwelling complexes researched by the author in different regions of the loess zone.

sitates the use of additional land. In conclusion, the pit cave dwellings do not save land, but waste it. Population growth in China and the needs of agricultural production make arable land ever more precious and make conservation even more necessary.

VENTILATION

Cave dwellings are not free from serious problems resulting from improper design. Among these are a lack of ventilation and air circulation within the rooms and, in many cases, within the pit cave patios. Improper design also contributes to a shortage of natural sunlight exposure, high relative humidity within the pit patios and rooms, water penetration, and inadequate space for modern needs. Only a few cave dwellings have been designed to provide air circulation throughout the units. Lack of air circulation makes cave dwellings very humid during the rainy periods of July and August, and they become very uncomfortable to live in. The lack of an air shaft in Chinese cave dwellings may have resulted from a need for security, the threat of erosion around the shaft, a need to minimize the number of openings in the cave during lengthy, cold, dry winters, or a combination of all of these. However, almost every cave dwelling has a small round or square window at the top of the facade. This opening stimulates a limited amount of circulation if the air within the cave space is heated and therefore rises. However, it does not provide enough air circulation or reduce the high summer humidity. One interim solution for increasing ventilation is to enlarge this small window to allow for more air flow. Ventilation in the cave dwellings is also essential because of potentially high levels of radon (radioactivity caused by the decomposition of uranium), which can be a risk in any earth-enclosed space. Also, the increase in humidity in the caves during the summer season can cause decomposition of the loess particles and consequent weakening of the ceiling and walls.

During the period of field research for this book, residents did not complain about or even mention the potential hazard of radon from the loess soil where their cave dwellings are con-

structed. Similarly, at the time of this writing, radon was not mentioned as a threat to cave dwellers in any of the Chinese or English language literature that was reviewed. According to Huo Yan, "results of investigations have not disclosed cases of cancer or radiation sickness caused by cave dwellings" (Huo Yan 1986, 173).

HUMIDITY

Some of the inconveniences associated with living in cave homes, whether of the pit or cliff type, are pointed out by the residents themselves. The main problems are dampness, moisture, and condensation, especially inside dwellings located in regions where there is relatively heavy summer rainfall, such as Henan province. These problems are aggravated by the lack of ventilation and poor air circulation through the rooms and patios of the cave dwellings. Without ventilation, the ambient humidity combined with high summer temperatures makes living conditions very uncomfortable. Such conditions cause some residents to feel that they would prefer aboveground housing during the summer season. This combination of rain and high summer temperatures poses problems that do not exist in the pit cave dwellings of arid Tunisia, for example, and they consequently require special solutions (Gideon S. Golany 1988b, 26–30, 83–108).

An accumulation of rainwater in the center of the cave dwelling's patio also adds to the humid conditions and creates drainage problems. In one dwelling, for example, green mold was observed covering the floor and walls around the courtyard. In another cave complex, the owner built two aboveground rooms within the patio itself, thus compounding the lack of ventilation and accumulation of moisture. It would have been preferable to build additional subterranean room units above the existing cave complex rather than within the patio.

Within the cave dwellings, relative humidity is comfortably low in the winter but higher than that of the outdoors in the summer due to condensation and high summer humidity (fig. 5.6). In the winter, air entering the cave from outside has a lower relative humidity which combines with

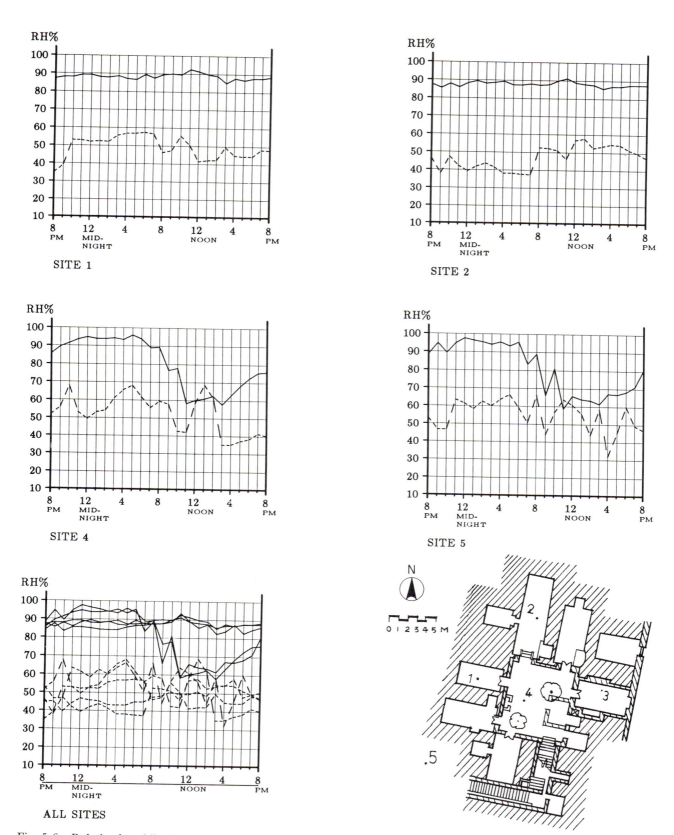

Fig. 5.6 Relative humidity for summer (solid line) and winter (broken line) in a pit cave dwelling. Yin Xinyin family dwelling, Xi *cun* Village, Gong *xian* County, Henan.

higher temperatures indoors. In the summer, air entering the cave from outside has a higher relative humidity while the indoor temperatures are lower. Condensation occurs when air temperature decreases to a certain level and adds to the high perspiration of the dwelling. This is the main reason for the greater degree of dampness inside the caves in the summer. Added to this is the vapor produced by the inhabitants themselves. Occasionally, the interior walls of the units are covered with moisture. Under such conditions, the development of ventilation and air circulation systems becomes essential.

DRAINAGE, MOISTURE, AND WATERPROOFING

Most damage to cave dwellings is caused by water. Other damage is caused by wind, by heating and cooling, and by burrows created by mice, insects, or other vermin. Small burrows can easily develop into cavities, which may lead to intense erosion and threaten the safety of the caves. One form of protection is to place shallow-rooted vegetation at the facade wall in order to prevent the soil from sliding. Another is to cover the front with a brick or stone facing.

Loess soil erodes vertically. This process creates cavities and tunnels when water penetrates the soil. Although loess soil is hard when dry, moisture constitutes a serious threat to the structural stability of cave dwellings during the heavy rains of July and August. Since the cave dwelling region has an arid to semi-arid climate, these rains—although brief—can be torrential and turbulent. This often causes flash flooding, which, coupled with a lack of vegetation cover, intensifies the erosion process.

Drainage is more of a problem in the pit-type cave dwellings than in the cliff type. In almost every pit cave dwelling there is a seepage well in the middle of the courtyard. This is especially true in Henan province, where summer precipitation is higher than in other loess soil regions.

Ancient Chinese cave dwellers used to "bake" their dwellings with fire to make the inner wall surfaces harder and therefore waterproof—a lesson learned from the process of manufacturing pottery. According to Deng Qisheng, the Chinese

learned during the Xia dynasty (21st–16th centuries B.C.) that beating the earth walls of their caves with wooden clubs increased the ability of the soil to resist water and moisture. During the Western Zhou dynasty (ca. 1095 B.C.) air-dried clay bricks were used as the primary building material, and a mixture of sand, lime, and loess was used to construct the walls. The addition of lime to the soil greatly improved its waterproofing capacity. Such materials are still in use in rural areas (Deng Qisheng 1985, 65).

Provisions for drainage of water from the walls and courtyard are essential to keep the cave dwelling dry, especially in the case of the pit type. Cracks that appear in the front wall are primarily the result of exposure to weather. The uniformly porous loess soil is subject to water penetration and the development of cavities and cracks. A reduction in the amount of moisture content of the soil is necessary; it should not exceed 15 to 20 percent.

Waterproofing of the cave dwelling is a special process differing from the conventional one in that it is aimed at achieving different results: to avoid water penetration, which is liable to cause collapse, to avoid indoor dampness and high humidity, and to make possible the use of the soil above the cave for agriculture. However, the argument of gaining land for agriculture is questionable indeed because of the porosity of the soil. In general, we can state that water tables are low in the loess soil zone, where rain is not plentiful. Yet, when the soil is saturated after heavy rains, the threat of collapse or landslides is very real.

Moisture dispersion can be achieved by effective active or passive ventilation systems. Raising the room temperature for moisture dispersion is not applicable here because dampness in the Chinese cave dwellings occurs primarily during the summer, when the temperature is already high.

When outdoor vapor pressure becomes higher than the humidity in the cave, dampness starts accumulating (fig. 5.7). Thus, relative humidity indoors will be higher than that outdoors. The cave walls themselves are a source of dampness as well. Also, in the rainy summer season, the colder indoor air contracts, causes condensation, and increases the relative humidity while the warmer

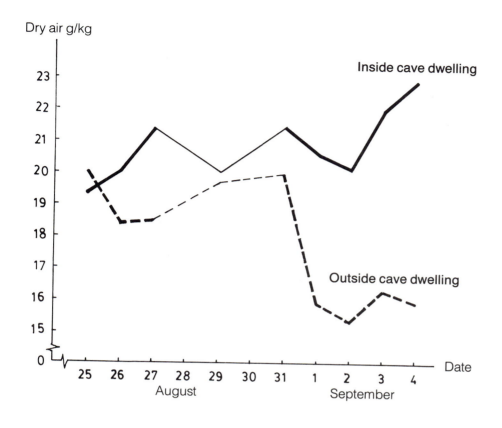

Fig. 5.7   Humidity inside and outside a cave dwelling. Measured between 7:00 and 10:00 A.M., 25 August and 4 September 1983.

outdoor air expands and decreases the relative humidity in the air. In July and August, with the increase in rainfall, the relative humidity rises, increasing the indoor moisture level. Another important factor contributing to the increase in relative humidity is the evapotranspiration process produced by the wide-leaved plants found within the courtyards of the pit cave dwellings.

The pit-type cave dwelling courtyards have serious ventilation and humidity problems, especially during the rainy summer season, and this creates very uncomfortable living conditions. Due to limited air circulation in the rooms of below-ground caves and their usual depth of six to nine meters, there is a serious lack of essential ventilation in the patios. In the summer, when high humidity is combined with high heat, the courtyard temperature rises to a peak during the middle hours of the afternoon, becoming much higher than that of the outside space. Unless a ventilation system is established for the courtyard, humid air and high heat prevail in the patios. The

pit courtyard presents another problem during the second half of winter nights. During these hours, cold air sinks into the confined enclosure of the pit. The low temperatures that develop make the pit dwelling uncomfortably cold and a heating system becomes a necessity.

The need to utilize all available land for agricultural production leads many cave dwellers to plant gardens in their patios. These gardens frequently contain banana and other fruit trees that have thick branches and dense foliage. Although these trees shade the patio, they tend to increase humidity, because evapotranspiration through their leaves is intense. They also interfere with air movement and increase the heat in the patio, because the foliage obstructs the prevailing winds and air currents (fig. 5.8). Although the trees may absorb the rain water that becomes trapped in the patios, they combine with the patio's lack of ventilation, the summer rain, and high heat to cause the humidity and ambient temperature of the patios to rise even higher.

a Pit patio without plants facilitates air movement and ventilation; however summer heat increases with lack of shade.

b Plants with dense foliage and short trunks provide shade but cut off ventilation and increase ambient discomfort and summer humidity by evapotranspiration.

c Tall bare trunks and sparse foliage provide the pit patio with shade and allow for air movement throughout the summer.

Fig. 5.8 Plantings in the pit patio: impact on residents' comfort

Maintenance

Chinese cave dwellings require constant maintenance to prevent deterioration. Local experience demonstrates that an empty cave deteriorates ten times more quickly than an inhabited one. Humidity and water are the most destructive forces. Human inhabitants help to ventilate the dwellings in the summer and increase the heat in the winter, thus these seasonal activities keep the dwellings dryer and therefore more stable. Routine maintenance requires filling cracks and smoothing the wall surfaces; eliminating insects, snakes, and mice; and removing loosened soil and replacing it. Special seasonal maintenance is required to prevent erosion at the entrance, the ventilation hole, the front wall, and similar sites.

Vibrations (especially from earthquakes) and weather changes cause deterioration of the facade. This is especially true when the wall is not faced with brick or stone, and when it is not sloped properly. An angle greater than 75 to 80 degrees can lead to landslides during the rainy season. To protect the wall, some dwellers extend the cave dwelling base forward outside the cave's entrance by three to four meters and upward to a height of 1.2 to 1.4 meters (Ren Zhiyuan 1982b, 33).

One popular method of cave unit renewal is to cut away the front part of the cave and, in compensation, dig the unit deeper into the earth. Such a major change may extend two to five meters on each side and is done only every fifty to one hundred years. The maintenance of cave dwellings is rather easy compared to that of aboveground houses since changes in the weather do not affect them as drastically.

In the east and southeast, where many of the pit cave dwellings are located, rain can be torrential in the summer. This requires that the dwellings be designed with large window openings to promote air circulation. The openings of the pit dwellings are lined with brick to prevent rapid deterioration of the pit walls. Cave dwellings with slanted ceilings that are higher in front than in back have better ventilation than those with level ceilings, because the slope of the ceiling allows for a greater degree of air circulation.

Because exposure to sunlight can help to allevi-ate dampness in cave dwellings, orientation becomes even more important toward the eastern part of the loess soil zone, where precipitation increases in the summer. Dampness in the cave dwelling units in Henan province, for example, is most common in the summer. Lacking a ventilation system, the caves become very uncomfortable to live in. The stability of the caves can also be weakened under these conditions, making them a threat to the health and safety of the occupants.

Thermal Performance

The optimal functioning of belowground habitats occurs in stressful climates—e.g., cold and dry (such as Siberia or northern Canada) or hot and dry (such as the Sahara or northern China). One of the basic considerations in building a shelter belowground is the fact that summer heat and winter cold affect the soil very slowly, yet steadily, to a depth of about ten meters. A wave of temperature is created which moves downward, reaching the indoor environment a season later through a time-lag process. The seasonal time lag thus provides cool temperatures below ground in the summer and warm temperatures in the winter. The thermal principle to be understood is twofold: first, that the soil functions as an excellent insulator; and second, that the soil is an efficient heat retainer.

At a depth of around ten meters, indoor temperatures will be diurnally and seasonally stable with minimal fluctuation. This creates an environment that is comfortably warm in winter and cool in summer. The Chinese have recognized through experience that it is at this depth that temperature fluctuation becomes minimal and ambient temperature within the subterranean space remains comfortable.

Arid regions have extremely high summer temperatures during the afternoons between 2:00 and 4:00 P.M. The lack of air circulation in Chinese pit cave dwellings accentuates the extreme afternoon heat in the courtyards (fig. 5.9). Late at night and in the winter, the temperature drops to a very low point as a result of the inversion caused by stagnant cold air sinking down into the courtyard (Golany 1990, chap. 2).

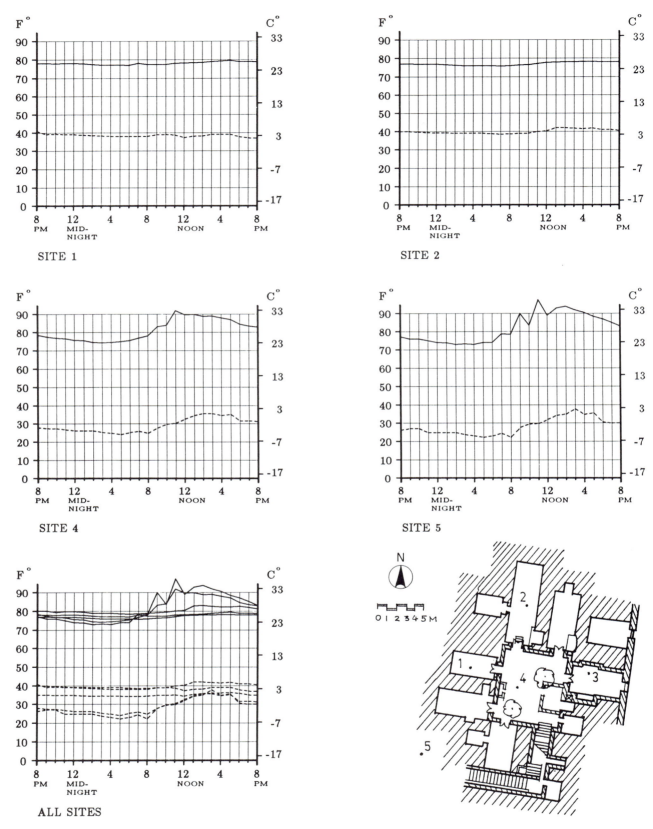

Fig. 5.9   Dry-bulb temperatures for summer (solid line) and winter (broken line) in a pit cave dwelling. Yin Xinyin family dwelling, Xi *cun* Village, Gong *xian* County, Henan. Site five is the open area outside the complex.

The ambient indoor temperature of cave dwellings is diurnally stable. The indoor summer temperature is comfortable, especially when compared with the outdoor temperature of the patio or surrounding environment. Rooms indoors do not require an active cooling system that would consume energy. Winter indoor temperatures, although stable, are not within the range normally desired for personal comfort, and an active heating system is required to bring the temperature up to an acceptable level. The number of days that heat is needed are fewer than would be necessary for an equivalent-sized aboveground dwelling. Where there are two stories in a cave dwelling complex, the upper floor obviously leaves less soil thickness overhead and temperatures on the upper level are much less stable than on the lower floor.

Human Health Issues

Human health depends primarily on conditions affecting personal physiology and on the quality of the environment. Human comfort in cave dwellings is a result of two characteristics: stable diurnal ambient temperature and relative humidity, both in contrast to the seasonal outdoors.

The earth surrounding the cave is both an insulator and a retainer of heat. The stable ambient temperature in winter is a consequence of the heat wave being processed through the earth from the previous summer season. Thus, the summer outdoor air temperature is retained within the soil so as to reach, slowly and steadily, the cave's inner walls by wintertime. Likewise the winter's cooler air reaches the inner cave walls by summertime. This movement of heat or cold down through the earth usually stops at a depth of about ten meters. Out of the practical experience and knowledge gained through generations of cave dwelling, the Chinese have excavated their patios to approximately this depth. Under these conditions the diurnal temperature fluctuation is minimal. The indoor ambient temperature differentiation between winter and summer ranges from 10 to 20 °C.

The process of ambient humidity is different. In general, the soil itself during the dry season may have a relative humidity of 30 to 40 percent, which can offer a certain amount of comfort to the dwellers. Yet the outdoor relative humidity, such as in the patio during the rainy summer season, can be around 70 or 80 percent. Normally, the "physiological comfort threshold" or comfortable ambient temperature is 18 to 22 °C with relative humidity of 30 to 75 percent. The diurnal stability of ambient temperature and relative humidity has a positive effect on the physiological functions of temperature regulation and metabolism, while sudden changes in temperature and humidity of the outdoor natural environment can have a less positive effect on the body.

Several physiological advantages associated with living in cave dwellings are cited: "it can reduce the incidence of upper respiratory tract infection . . . rheumatism . . . bleeding and infection of nasal mucosa and other troubles; . . . makes the skin smooth and tender, especially those exposed parts more resistant to infections; . . . helps to avoid the harm and irritations caused by noise acting on the human body; . . . reduces the direct harmful effects of some radioactive substances on the human body; . . . and ensures good health and longevity" (Huo Yan 1985, 137–140). The statistical data compiled during the last twenty years also suggest that the Chinese cave dwellers live long lives with no particular diseases to be found among them (ibid., 140).

In research conducted by the author in a belowground hospital in Shanghai, doctors claimed that external surgical wounds heal 20 to 25 percent faster in belowground recovery areas than in those above ground. The time savings and improvement in the quality of healing are due to the stability of the ambient temperature and relative humidity. In contrast, the author's research on belowground housing in southern Tunisia, on the edge of the Sahara, suggests that inhabitants tend to catch colds when they move from indoors to outdoors. Apparently this is due to extreme differences in ambient temperature and relative humidity between the indoor and outdoor environments (Golany 1988b, 83–108).

In conclusion, the environmental constraints of the loess soil region where cave dwellings have evolved have always been a serious issue of concern. In spite of limited accomplishments in technology and resources, the cave dwellers have been able to overcome some of the environmental constraints. Throughout history, the cave dwellers have been able to ease the impact of some problems, such as those relating to seismic activity as well as others related to water penetration. Through experience they have developed design norms to cope with these problems. Still, the major challenge to the modern designer of Chinese cave dwellings is to synthesize the traditional, historical experience with contemporary needs in order to improve the environment of the cave dwellings. In any case, to implement any new design, the economic conditions of the cave dwellers and the affordability of their dwellings should be considered. While the solutions should be comprehensive in nature, they should also attend to pressing problems such as site selection criteria, ventilation, lighting, humidity, and seismic activity.

SIX

Conclusions

THIS chapter introduces solutions to the design problems posed by Chinese cave dwellings and explores the lessons to be gained for modern urban design norms. The previous chapters have described a specific, unique type of vernacular dwelling. The object of this book is not only to document this unique phenomenon, but also to highlight the lessons to be learned from the Chinese cave dwellings in order to bring their contributions to bear on modern urban design applications. The following is an outline of these lessons:

(1) The thermal performance of the loess soil and the time-lag temperature transformation process have an optimal effect on indoor ambient temperatures in both summer and winter.

(2) Passive heating and cooling systems, when designed properly, can replace conventional active systems and will conserve energy and reduce costs.

(3) The negative view of belowground dwellings can be considerably changed through a comprehensive approach to high-quality modern design. It is advisable that the newly emerging movement toward the use of residential belowground space in developed countries should emphasize the use of such space in nonresidential buildings before introducing the concept in residential structures, so as to educate and inform the public through tangible examples.

(4) It is recommended that modern belowground dwellings should not be located on flat sites but rather on slope sites, that the dwelling should be accessed by an ascending rather than descending entrance, and that there be direct eye contact between the indoor and outdoor environment.

(5) Studying and understanding the geological structure of the area when selecting a site can cut costs and provide a comfortable environment. Some geological layers can provide cut-and-use conditions where the soil will firmly retain its shape.

(6) Belowground space construction may not require sophisticated building techniques and can respond to the needs of some communities that have limited access to technology and skilled labor.

(7) Modern design of dwellings on a cliff or slope site can provide maximum exposure to available sunlight and compete respectably with conventional aboveground housing.

(8) The use of belowground space can allow positive response to needs for expansion and therefore solve acute problems of space shortage.

(9) The use of belowground space, especially in the center of a city where land prices are exorbitant, increases the amount of usable space and reduces the expenditure for land.

(10) Belowground space design permits reduced consumption of all types of urban services and utilities, keeps land uses in proximity to one another, and facilitates heightened social interaction.

The Chinese cave dwellings have evolved during millennia of accumulated experience. Their contemporary development represents an evolutionary synthesis of environmental, physical, and cultural forces. As such, the dwellings are an excellent resource for research and study. In concluding the volume it would be desirable to outline for Chinese designers some solutions relevant to the problems associated with cave dwellings. In doing so, the following principles should be considered: (1) solutions should be economically affordable for Chinese consumers; (2) they should adopt the standard of technology available in the region; (3) dwellings should utilize local building materials; (4) construction should be in accordance with the basic Chinese requirement of saving land for agriculture; and (5) any solution should focus primarily on an innovative design for the management of space. Solutions should respond to existing design deficiencies and introduce ways to meet the challenge of new and expected changes in standards of living, as represented by the need to accommodate modern furniture, electrical appliances, and also social gatherings beyond the family size.

Advantages and Disadvantages

The pragmatism of the Chinese people has been the basic principle in the development of their cave dwellings. Some of the advantages of the Chinese cave dwellings may be summarized as follows:

Skills. The use of skilled labor for construction is not essential; cave dwelling construction follows a self-help method with no special training involved.

Low technology. Cave dwellings are easy to construct with the simple tools already in daily use by the farmer/builder.

Savings in materials. There is almost no need for building materials such as wood, stone, or brick.

Cost. The cost of construction is far lower than that of an equivalent aboveground house.

Expandable. Cave dwellings, especially of the cliff type, are potentially easy to expand by excavating more rooms and passageways deeper into the interior.

Energy savings. There is a savings in energy not only in the building process but also for maintenance. Cave dwellings are cool in summer and warm in winter and require little, if any, fuel. The dwellings respond adequately to the stressful climatic conditions of their arid region. Also, they offer the possibility of food storage by natural refrigeration without decay or consumption of energy.

Maintenance. They require a minimum amount of maintenance during their lifetime as compared with aboveground dwellings. They can also be more durable than an aboveground structure if an adequate site is selected and proper design is implemented.

Land use economy. The cliff-type dwellings in particular preserve level land for agricultural purposes and permit dual land use.

Earth recycling. Earth excavated from the caves can be reused in a variety of ways: for building terraced courtyards or for constructing the courtyard wall in front of the cliff cave dwellings; for building dividing walls within the dwelling; for building the fireplace, chimney, or heated beds; for constructing chicken coops and beehives; for adding aboveground structures; for leveling the land; for making adobe or bricks; and for building roads or pedestrian pathways.

Health considerations. Living in cave dwellings provides a healthy environment because of the stable diurnal temperature and relative humidity, especially when the dwellings are properly designed.

Environmental preservation. The construction of caves has less impact on the surrounding environment than does that of aboveground structures. In the loess soil zone, where land erosion is extreme, maintaining the environmental balance is crucial.

Safety: Cave dwellings are fire resistant.

There are still deficiencies in the design and development of Chinese cave dwellings. Some disadvantages associated with them are:

Negative image. In the past, cave dwellings were

associated with poverty. "Don't live in a cave if you are rich," say the people of Gansu province.

Design deficiencies. Traditional cave dwelling design is deficient in the following areas: amount of exposure to available sunlight; air circulation and ventilation; size limitations; high levels of humidity, moisture, and condensation combined with high temperatures; erosion; susceptibility to damage by earthquakes and vibrations; inadequate waste disposal and drainage; and (in the case of pit cave dwellings) wasteful use of valuable agricultural land.

Under the present Chinese circumstances—population growth, scarcity of land, acute housing needs, limited financial subsidies for housing, and shortage of construction materials—adequately designed cave dwellings seem an ideal solution for many rural and some urban dwellers within the loess zone. However, new and innovative design models should be introduced to keep up with recent socioeconomic changes.

Solutions for Indigenous Design

SITE SELECTION

A variety of factors has traditionally influenced the site selection for Chinese cave dwellings. Above all, the capacity of loess soil to support and maintain its own shape after excavation, proximity of the selected site to important resources (water, arable land suitable for agriculture, and transportation), and orientation to the south have been of primary importance. In many cases, especially for cliff cave dwellings, sites were selected because of their unsuitability for agricultural use.

Cave dwellings require sufficient soil above the vault for safety. Moreover, the excavated soil should be used to build the terrace or the courtyard without blocking the dwellings or the natural drainage system. Cave dwellings should be oriented toward the south to permit maximum exposure to available sunlight and to help keep them dry. A southern orientation exposes the cave front to sun, rain, wind, frost, and other climatic conditions that cause contraction and expansion and

may result in cracks, weathering, and landslides. Consequently, to protect the cave structure, it is recommended that the facade and interior vault be covered with bricks. Land that is subject to collapse, landslides, and faults, or sites where the soil is too soft should not be selected. Also, a site with underground water or cavities that are hard to discover should be avoided. Loess soil is characterized by vertical erosion and it develops underground drainage, so it should be investigated carefully prior to construction.

According to Chinese researchers, the pit cave dwelling should be at least eight meters deep to the patio floor for stability, when the room ceiling height is three meters (Ren Zhiyuan 1982b, 11). The site should be above the water table and moisture in the soil should be less than 20 percent. The soil should be graded to provide good drainage and the site should be far from an area where flooding or landslides may occur. Sites having a high water table or disturbed drainage should not be chosen. The site should not be on the lowland or flatland, and should not utilize land that is suitable for agriculture. In addition, the cave dwelling should be located away from main highways to avoid frequent vibrations from traffic.

Cliff cave dwellings, by virtue of their location, have good drainage. The land above the caves should not be planted with deep-rooted trees that would create cracks and cavities or increase the moisture in the soil. However, the land can be used for smaller shrubs or for threshing grain. Perennial creeping plants should be grown to protect the soil from erosion and disintegration. In any case, this land should not be cultivated. There are four circumstances where conditions may cause cave dwelling collapse—during digging and construction, during periods of heavy rain, at times of melting and freezing, and during earthquakes. Early danger signs are falling granular particles, cracks in the walls or vault, and landslides (Wang Fu 1985, 406–409).

Basically, between the two traditional Chinese cave dwelling sites, the cliff and the pit, the cliff-type dwelling offers the most advantages. It uses a minimum of land suitable for agriculture, is better ventilated, receives more sunshine, is extendable, has views to the lowland, usually retains much soil above it (thereby minimizing the threat of erosion and collapse), is drier since it is well above the water table, has more privacy, can integrate below- and aboveground structures, is safer under earthquake conditions if the front is adequately protected, and offers the possibility of recycling the excavated soil for terracing the patio, building the fence or wall, or making bricks. Cliff dwellings should be given preference when considering belowground construction and pit cave dwellings should no longer be constructed in most areas.

DRAINAGE, MOISTURE, AND WATERPROOFING

The soil's upper level is the gas-absorbent water zone, while the lower level is saturated with water. In most instances, cave dwellings are located in the upper zone. Although leaking sewage or water supply networks can be sources of moisture, most of the water comes from precipitation and surface runoff, and requires certain control measures. The treatment of waterproofing here is different from that for the earth-sheltered unit (Wang Zuoyuan and Tong Linxu 1985, 421). The following two steps should be taken: effective site drainage and waterproofing. Site drainage can be accomplished simply by elevating the soil above the cave dwelling site and grading the earth downward toward the sides. Another method is to construct drainage trenches (fig. 6.1). Waterproofing can be accomplished by compacting the soil and thereby decreasing its permeability; by constructing a properly sloped concrete layer above or below the soil's surface; or by placing a concrete layer thirty centimeters below the soil's surface (fig. 6.2A). Another method of waterproofing cave dwellings is to place a layer of plastic sheeting forty centimeters beneath the surface with a layer of pebbles above it to serve as a water filter (fig. 6.2B) (Xia Yun and Hou Jiyao 1985, 436). If treated properly, the soil above the cave can then be used for agriculture.

An effective drainage system can be helpful in reducing dampness. Dampness is also caused by the capillary system, water vapor migration, high humidity in the air, and an absence of sunlight. In addition, high indoor relative humidity can create condensation on walls and ceilings, especially

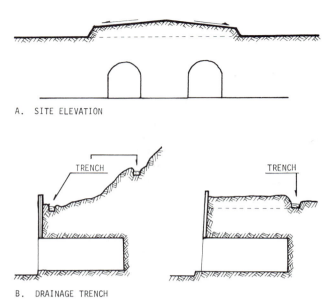

A. SITE ELEVATION

B. DRAINAGE TRENCH

Fig. 6.1 Suggested site drainage systems for cave dwellings

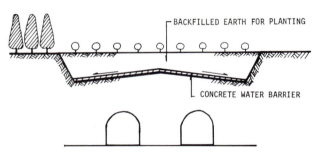

A. CONCRETE WATER BARRIER

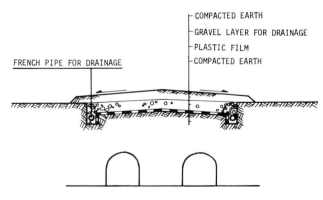

B. PLASTIC FILM WATER BARRIER

Fig. 6.2 Waterproofing with a layer of concrete or plastic film. A compacted base course is laid with a slope for drainage and then the barrier is spread.

when air circulation is inadequate. To minimize dampness, moistureproofing or moisture dispersion is suggested (Wang and Tong 1985, 424). Moistureproofing involves constructing a wall or barrier of brick or concrete that insulates the cave with a bituminous layer between the wall and the earth. A film of plastic may also be added if an air circulation system is provided.

One way of preventing moisture from coming out of the walls is to seal them with a spray coating of hydrophilic, asphaltic, or plastic material. Another method (experimented with by the Chinese), is to hang a layer of moisture absorbing paper a few centimeters away from the ceiling. When air circulation is established above the paper, theoretically the humidity should evaporate. However, in the author's opinion, this method has not proven effective. A passive ventilation system, something that is lacking in the majority of Chinese cave dwellings, is essential for improving these dwellings.

VENTILATION

Some attempts have been made to utilize new methods for improving ventilation. An experiment was carried out in Shikusi Primary School, located in Gong *xian,* Henan province, by constructing a ventilation chimney that resulted in

improved ventilation, reduced humidity and dew formation, and disappearance of the musty smell and mildew associated with unventilated space (Jin Oubo 1983, 69).

The most effective ventilation solution to promote air circulation is to construct a vertical shaft, one meter across, that leads from about five meters above the surface of the earth (over the cave dwelling) and extends down behind the cave unit to end in a 1 × 2-meter opening at the innermost part of the room close to the floor. An experiment conducted by the author during the summer months in an existing cave dwelling near Taiyuan *shi,* Shanxi province, proved that passive air circulation is an effective tool for decreasing air temperature and, most important, for reducing high relative humidity and the resulting condensation.

Intense heat within the cave's patio causes the air there to rise and be replaced by air from adjacent rooms. When a shaft like the one described above is installed in the cave air travels from the opening at the top down into the cave dwelling. The air then leaves the room via an open window, passes through the patio, and rises away from the dwelling (fig. 6.3). Two factors promote this direction of air flow. The first is that warm air is forced to enter the shaft because of the tempera-

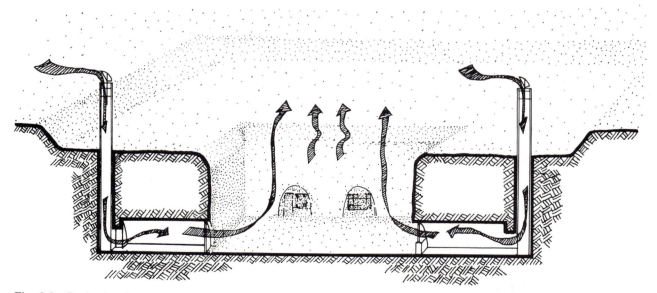

Fig. 6.3 Basic plan for air circulation in pit cave dwellings

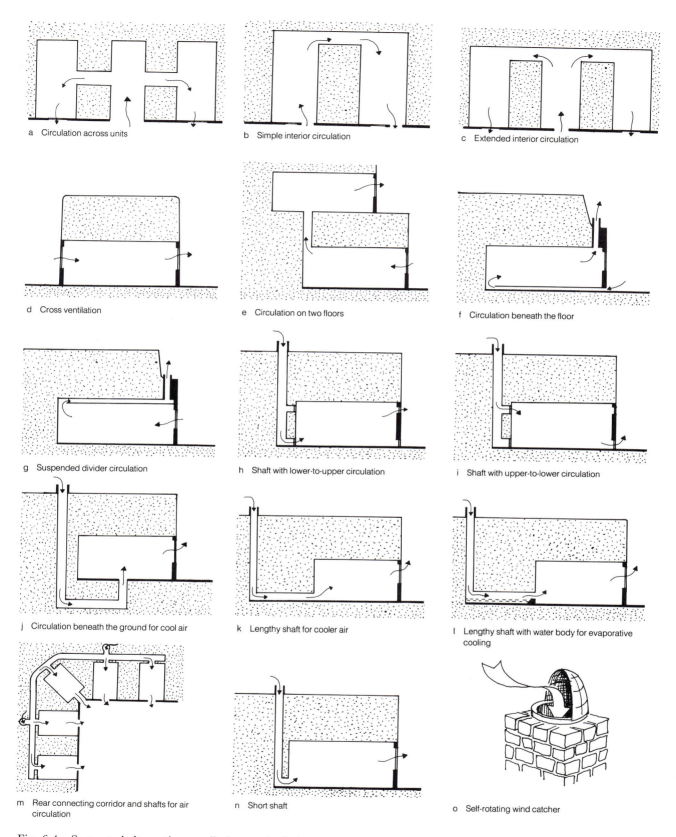

a   Circulation across units

b   Simple interior circulation

c   Extended interior circulation

d   Cross ventilation

e   Circulation on two floors

f   Circulation beneath the floor

g   Suspended divider circulation

h   Shaft with lower-to-upper circulation

i   Shaft with upper-to-lower circulation

j   Circulation beneath the ground for cool air

k   Lengthy shaft for cooler air

l   Lengthy shaft with water body for evaporative cooling

m   Rear connecting corridor and shafts for air circulation

n   Short shaft

o   Self-rotating wind catcher

Fig. 6.4   Suggested alternative ventilation methods for cave dwellings—*a, b, c,* and *m* are plans, *o* is a perspective, and all others are cross sections.

front wall of the cave. This style can also give a homey feeling to the cave's design.

It should be possible to landscape such dwellings using trees with tall, slender trunks and high, sparse foliage. Trees of this type, grown taller than the eight to ten meters of the courtyard's depth, would shade the patio but keep the leafy sources of evapotranspiration above the enclosure. This would enable air to flow into and through the patio. Furthermore, trees with shallow root systems can be planted directly atop the cave, where evapotranspiration would help to reduce the moisture levels in the soil. Rainwater accumulation in the patios should be discouraged.

In some cave dwelling complexes of this region, the roofs of the dwellings are used as worksites for the processing of wheat after the harvest. The soil is graded and packed down, becoming quite hard, and this helps protect the cave from water penetration. Of course the soil can no longer be used for agriculture under these circumstances.

LIGHTING

The psychological aspects of life in earth-sheltered dwellings combine a variety of related elements that should concern the designer. These include: acoustics, lighting, color, the need for direct eye contact with the larger outdoor environment, a potential feeling of confinement, and special requirements for wall treatment. Lack of adequate natural light inside cave dwelling units is a serious problem.

To achieve improved sunlight penetration, the following factors should be considered:

Latitude of the site. The latitude of the site makes a difference in the maximum and minimum amount of sunlight penetration in summer and winter. The loess soil zone, where the cave dwellings are distributed, falls within the boundaries of approximately thirty-three to forty degrees north latitude. Within this zone, there are fewer hours of daylight during the winter and more hours of daylight during the summer. Both the number of hours of daylight and the angle of the sunlight are influenced by latitude, which therefore has an impact on the amount of sunlight penetration into the cave dwellings.

Depth of the courtyard. The deeper and narrower the dimensions of the courtyard or pit patio, the less light will penetrate into the cave dwelling's room units. The shallower and larger the dimensions, the greater the amount of sunlight the rooms will receive.

Cave dwelling orientation. Eastern orientation provides the most sunlight in the morning while western orientation provides the most sunlight in the late afternoon. A southern orientation provides the maximum amount of sunlight throughout the day.

Arch height. The height of the front part of the arch determines the extent of sunlight penetration into the dwelling (fig. 6.5).

There is a variety of possible ways to achieve direct, natural lighting (fig. 6.6). Ideally, the length of the cave should not exceed eight meters because of sunlight penetration requirements.

A cliff cave dwelling that was designed by the author and constructed near Linfen *shi*, Shanxi, had more than the average number of windows and the ceilings were 4.5 meters high. This design allowed sunlight to enter the windows to a depth of six meters on January 21, at thirty-seven degrees north latitude (fig. 6.12). The typical ceiling height of most traditional caves is 2.5 meters, with a small window opening at the top of the facade, which aids somewhat in sunlight penetration and ventilation.

Light penetration can be increased through improved designs, including: (1) a horizontal window in the upper part of the facade; (2) an overhang to provide shade from the summer sun at noon; (3) a slanted ceiling with the front higher than the back by at least one meter; and (4) thick bricks made of transparent plastic or glass (colored or clear). The angle of the ceiling should be the same as the sun's angle in the winter.

If additional sunlight is required, a large glass window can be installed at the top of the facade. Another way to increase sunlight penetration is to increase the height of the arch to five meters or more and slant the ceiling more acutely toward the rear of the cave. Such a design is possible in a

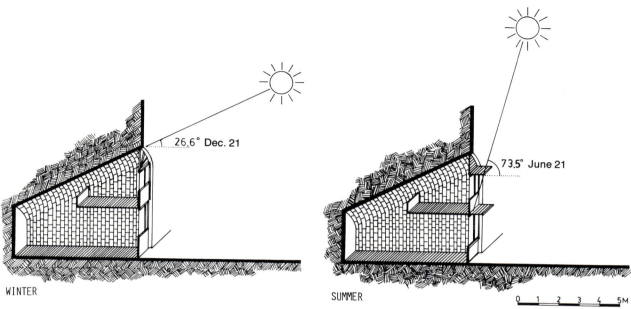

Fig. 6.5 Angle of sun penetration in summer and winter. The sun's angle in Beijing during winter matches the angle of the cave ceiling; thus the cave receives maximum sunlight in winter. During summer the overhang prevents sunlight penetration. The building faces south. Depth of the dwelling is 6 meters and the front ceiling height is 5.5 meters. Walls are arched, covered with bricks, and whitewashed.

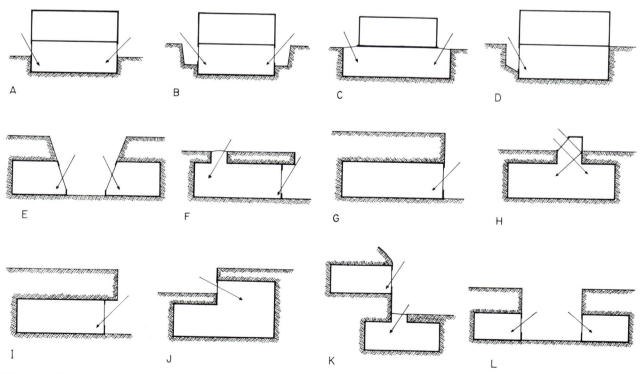

Fig. 6.6 Possible window locations and designs for lighting in cave dwellings and earth-sheltered habitats. *D* is the Roman type found in Bulla Regia, northern Tunisia.

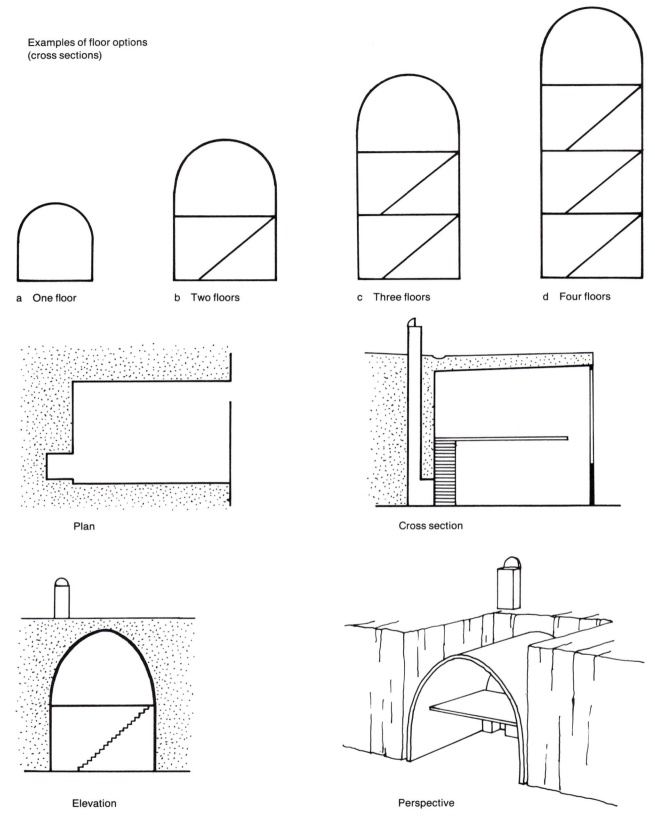

Examples of floor options
(cross sections)

a One floor

b Two floors

c Three floors

d Four floors

Plan

Cross section

Elevation

Perspective

Fig. 6.7 Design of cliff cave dwelling unit to increase space and sunlight penetration, especially in winter. Note the slanted ceiling, two floors, and long window. Designed by the author and constructed near Linfen, Shanxi.

two-story structure like the dwelling constructed near Linfen. This design also provides increased air circulation (fig. 6.7).

HEALTH

Human physiological comfort is a reflection of the ambient environmental conditions provided by temperature, relative humidity, intensity of evaporation, and most important, the diurnal stability of all these. Human health conditions are affected by these factors both diurnally and seasonally. It is commonly accepted that a stable temperature of between 18 and 20 °C is considered a healthy ambient microclimate in most cultural contexts when combined with a comparatively stable relative humidity of around 50 to 70 percent. This combination of seasonal and diurnal stable temperature and relative humidity is provided in both summer and winter within cave dwellings—in contrast to the outdoor ambient conditions that prevail during these seasons. But although relative humidity is kept nearly stable, it is higher than desirable on some days during the summer. Still, this condition can be alleviated.

Human beings, through interaction with their environment, lose or gain heat through respiration. Human heat dissipation and gain take place through conduction, convection, radiation, and evaporation. When the ambient temperature rises above 30 °C, heat dissipates from the body through evaporation. When body temperature falls below 30 °C, dissipation takes place through conduction, convection, and radiation. When the temperature is below 10 °C and the relative humidity rises above 90 percent (as happens during the rainy season in some areas of the cave dwelling zone), body heat dissipation is stopped or slowed and the effect is very uncomfortable for most people. Also, when the temperature is below 10 °C and the relative humidity falls below 25 percent the skin becomes very dry and causes discomfort.

The ambient environment of combined stable temperature and relative humidity found within cave dwellings is favorable to the temperature regulation of the human body, helping to maintain a balance between heat gain and loss. Thus, this environment not only supports physiological functions, but also regulates the nervous system, reduces the possibility of bacterial infection, strengthens resistance to disease, reduces the incidence of rheumatism, smooths the skin, and generally promotes overall health (Huo Yan 1986, 172–173).

In Dayang cun Village located in Linfen xian, Shanxi province, a group of researched cave dwellings was popularly known as the "Immortals' Caves." According to Huo Yan, among four families living in the old cave dwellings, three people were more than eighty years old and one was over ninety. All the family members were in good health. Huo's survey of Chinese cave dwellings shows that the residents enjoyed greater longevity than residents of non–cave dwellings (ibid., 173–174). Similarly, chickens raised in caves in the Linfen region averaged one more year of life and produced twenty to thirty more eggs per year than those raised aboveground (ibid., 175).

In Hongtong xian County, chickens raised by cave dwellers in holes dug beneath the heated brick beds within their cave dwellings produced larger eggs all year round. Residents of Shibatai cun Village, in Beipiao xian County, Liaoning (northeastern China), raised chickens in caves they built on the slopes. In the winter when the outdoor temperature was −30 °C the indoor temperature ranged between 13 and 15 °C and egg production increased by 85 percent year-round. It was also found that when an epidemic of chicken pests occurred, the cave-raised hens resisted disease and survived.

In the USSR, "cave therapy" has been practiced since 1968 in the Trans-Carpathian Mountains. Patients are accommodated in caves 300 meters beneath the surface of the earth. Treatments ranging from 200 to 300 hours in length are reported to have had curative effects—especially on patients with neurasthenia, insomnia, and fidgets. Patients were able to sleep fourteen to twenty hours and seemed relaxed and vigorous when they awoke. The fresh air of the belowground environment had a curative effect also on patients suffering from bronchitis and asthma, with the cure rate reaching 84 percent among adults and 96 percent among children (ibid.).

SEISMIC IMPACT

Construction of a brick facade and brick vault in cave dwellings would help to ease the effects of earthquakes. When the seismic waves of an earthquake reach a mountain, they are reflected and refracted. It is not recommended that cave dwellings be built at the foot of loess hills in a region subject to seismic activity. Cliff caves, located on the sides of slopes or gullies, are mainly subject to reflective action and are resistant to earthquakes. In normal cases, there is a thick layer of soil above a cave dwelling. Such loess layers will have a horizontal movement under earthquake conditions. The horizontal shearing stress at the lower part of the arch is greater than the horizontal shearing stress experienced at the bottom of the cave. The soil can withstand the horizontal shearing force at the two sides of the cave. Consequently, the arch in these cave dwellings is very stable. The ability to support a vertical load is related to the curvature of the arch. The greater the curvature, the better the support will be. This explains why the pointed arch is the most stable. The ability to resist earthquake stress is greater in cave dwellings than in aboveground housing built of stone and earth (Ren 1982b, 33–34).

The vault form, which has a limited capacity for resistance, should be reexamined and redesigned. All parts of a cave unit should be built at one time to avoid disintegration of weak joints. Timbers should be used to support the vault. The chimney should be built as an independent unit outside the wall. Large windows, doors, and niches weaken the walls. To resist stress, the design of the cave dwelling should take into consideration the vertical and horizontal shear, as well as tension or compression forces, of a potential earthquake. Forms that resist pressuring symmetrically, such as the spherical shape, should be integrated into cave dwelling design and construction.

The greatest risk under earthquake conditions is the collapse of the front part of the cave dwelling (fig. 6.8). The floor of the courtyard should be designed at a lower level than the entrance of the cave dwelling. This way—should a collapse occur—there is less likelihood that the inhabitants will

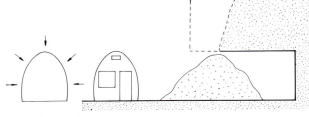

a   Commonly used

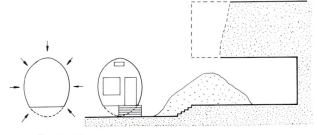

b   Proposed

Fig. 6.8   Curved walls, vaulted ceilings, and elevated entrances to minimize seismic effects

be trapped inside the cave. The following design measures are recommended to increase the structural stability and safety of cave dwellings:

Cave facade. The facade should be of stone or brick, not earth. Also, the cliff above should be faced with brick. If the cliff is very high, it should be terraced every three to five meters above the facade level.

Span. The span of a room unit should not exceed three to 3.5 meters. If a wider span is desired, separate structural procedures should be undertaken to provide for the vault arch such as coverings and central support columns built of cement, brick, or stone. The wall thickness between rooms should be at least three meters.

Niches. These should be avoided, as they weaken the walls.

Maintenance. A program of regular maintenance should be performed in order to eliminate or minimize cracks, cavities, or holes and thus to minimize the danger of wall or ceiling collapse.

DESIGN ALTERNATIVES

The pit-type cave dwelling should be eliminated because it occupies a large area of arable land and introduces design problems that result in a deficit of sunlight penetration and air circulation. The cliff-type dwelling should be encouraged because of a broad range of advantages, including land conservation. It is preferable to develop design types that enable use of the soil above the cave for agriculture, or use of the cliffs above for development. These alternatives can include one form or another of earth integration.

The basic concepts for three promising new alternatives are presented here. It is the author's belief that the proposed designs can meet Chinese expectations and requirements (fig. 6.9).

(1) A subsurface dwelling, where the structure is fully excavated from the terraced cliff and covered by one-half to one meter of earth (fig. 6.9A). The top is level with the terrace above, which is used for pedestrian traffic, light agriculture, or both. Special waterproofing is provided with the enveloping earth, especially at the top. The vault is built with stone or brick and then is covered with earth.

(2) An earth-sheltered habitat is a vaulted structure built completely aboveground, made of stone or brick, and then covered with one-half to one meter of earth (fig. 6.9B). Here too, the top can be used for light agriculture, although less efficiently than over the subsurface dwelling and only if waterproofing is undertaken. This type of habitat is increasingly popular in China today, in flat areas as well as on terraced sites.

(3) A semi-belowground dwelling is a half-belowground and half-aboveground structure, the aboveground portion being covered with earth after construction (fig. 6.9C). The structure is built of stone or brick in vault form. It can be built either on a flat or cliff site and provides good exposure to available sunlight.

The three alternatives suggested occupy a minimal area, use construction techniques commonly available in China, and use the vault form that has typically been employed in existing cave dwellings. They are easy to construct, affordable, use minimum amounts of energy, and provide for

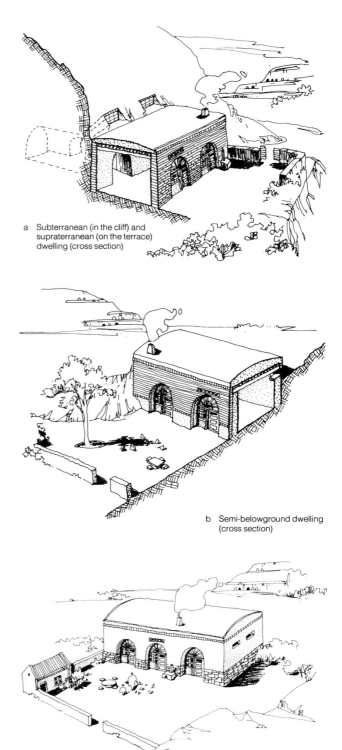

a Subterranean (in the cliff) and supraterranean (on the terrace) dwelling (cross section)

b Semi-belowground dwelling (cross section)

c Aboveground earth-sheltered habitat

Fig. 6.9   Three design concepts with earth integration

dual land use in varying degrees. Cave dwelling construction, maintenance, heating, and cooling require very little expenditure of energy as opposed to aboveground dwellings. Normally, no manufacture or transportation of building materials is necessary unless the dwelling is covered with brick. Within a newly designed modern cave dwelling neighborhood or village, a network of subterranean pedestrian walkways and streets can be planned. Such a network can also include the services and amenities of a conventional neighborhood.

Construction of earth-sheltered dwellings should be adjusted to the topographical configurations of the site, especially when large-scale development is required (fig. 6.10). Such integration

should be in harmony with the environment and rely on a problem-solving approach to design.

The main problems associated with cave dwellings arise in the summer season, when heat and humidity combine to make living conditions uncomfortable. However, these technical problems can be overcome. If, for some reason, the required improvements are not possible then it would be necessary to explore an "annual living cycle" design concept similar to that employed in Iranian or Baghdadian habitats. Such a habitat is planned around supraterranean living in the winter and semi-belowground connected with aboveground living in summer, in a structure that combines one floor below the ground with one above. Such dwellings can be developed in highly urban-

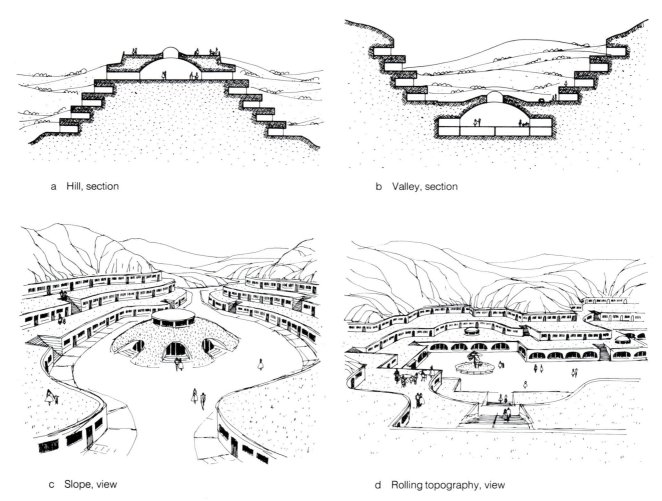

a   Hill, section

b   Valley, section

c   Slope, view

d   Rolling topography, view

Fig. 6.10   Alternatives for integrating earth-sheltered dwellings with the topography

ized regions, and the buildings can be attached to one another.

Although every region has unique climatic and geographical conditions, most existing cave dwellings are similar in their basic design patterns and dimensions. It is recommended that designs should be further adapted to suit the conditions of the region. Each region has its distinctive features and it follows that the designs, regulations, and building codes for cave dwellings should be localized to suit each context.

Cliff dwellings designed with the patio floor at a lower level than the rooms of the cave have cer-

tain psychological advantages for the residents (fig. 6.11). In this regard, cliff cave dwellings are preferable to pit cave dwellings. This standard cliff dwelling design feature permits residents to enter the cave rooms by ascending several steps. To enter a pit cave dwelling, residents must descend rather than ascend a stairway and this can create uncomfortable feelings of claustrophobia. Also, cliff cave dwellings allow more sunlight and air to enter the cave unit, contributing to the psychological well-being of the residents.

In an attempt to solve many of the previously discussed problems, the author designed a subsur-

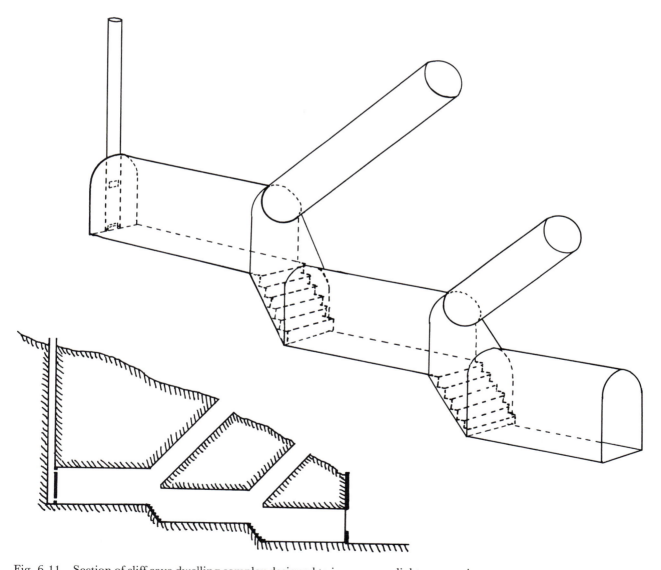

Fig. 6.11 Section of cliff cave dwelling complex designed to improve sunlight penetration

face earth-sheltered dwelling for construction in China that could accommodate a family comfortably. The dwelling was built near the city of Linfen in Shanxi, in collaboration with the Architectural Scientific Academy of Shanxi Province. The goal was to provide a design that was affordable and practical for the average Chinese citizen (especially the rural dweller), for a habitat that

would meet modern needs and could accommodate an extended family of four or five. The type of dwelling that was realized from this design is a sub-cliff earth-sheltered habitat (fig. 6.12). The author does not recommend the development of cave dwellings on flat terrain for reasons explained earlier in this volume. It is his conviction that a cliff cave dwelling in the form of an earth-

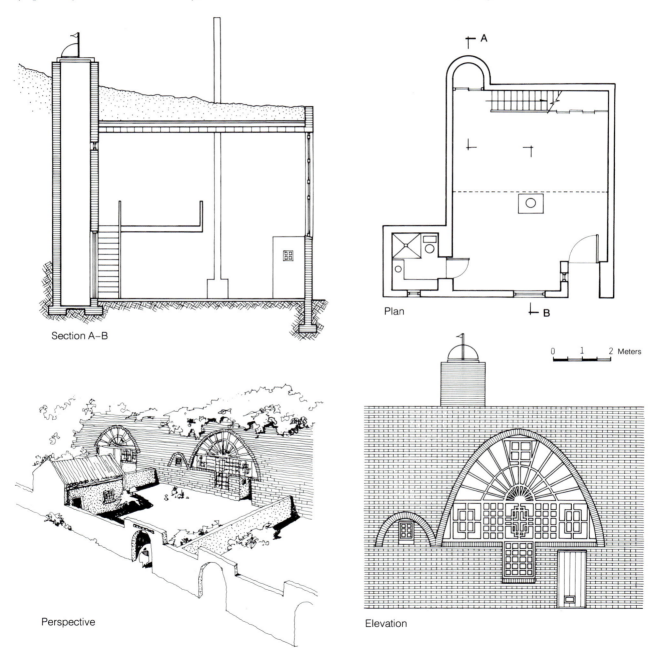

Fig. 6.12   Plan of earth-sheltered cave dwelling designed by the author. The dwelling was constructed near Linfen, Shanxi province, by the Architectural Scientific Academy of Shanxi.

sheltered habitat has optimal advantages and should be explored for development in China. This type of dwelling does suit the Chinese context of prevailing climatic conditions and limited resources.

The construction method recommended by the author's design, if it is to be developed on a larger scale, should make use of available technology, first establishing wide terraces on the cliff site, made from the soil that has been removed from cutting into the cliff. The second stage should be to cut a space within the cliff that is 5.5 meters in width, 7.5 meters in depth, and 7.5 meters high and open to the sky. The third stage involves construction of a vaulted form that is seven meters high, made of bricks, and covered with approximately one-half meter of earth. According to this recommendation, construction should start from the highest terrace and proceed to the lowest out of consideration for the weight of the machines.

The facade of the dwelling at Linfen is covered with bricks. Its two floors provide larger accommodations than usual and a division of room functions, with space for a living room at ground level and bedrooms on the second level. There is also space for a shower and lavatory, not commonly found in existing traditional cave dwellings. In addition, the design of this habitat minimizes the threat of collapse resulting from erosion. The width of the rooms is greater than that found in standard cave dwellings and they can therefore accommodate modern furniture and appliances. The design allows maximum exposure to available sunlight, especially during winter, and the structure is well ventilated.

FUTURE TRENDS

In spite of the multiple advantages, many young Chinese citizens do not want to continue living in cave dwellings. This is a matter of self-image, since historically cave dwellings have been associated with poverty, and in the minds of many people they still are stigmatized. It is said, for example, that a young man living in a cave has difficulty attracting a wife. In any case, although no statistics are available yet, there is a noticeable trend toward abandoning the caves today in China. On the other hand, there has also been a considerable amount of new cave dwelling construction and improvement of existing ones. The Architectural Society of China is concerned about this matter and has appointed a special investigation group to study it. For economic reasons particularly, they recommend that reconstruction and renovation of existing cave dwellings be pursued as well as construction of new units.

Future demands on housing, especially in rural areas where cave dwellings constitute the major housing type, will continue to increase both quantitatively and qualitatively. Standards of living are improving much more rapidly in China's rural society than in its urban communities. The cave dwelling life-style has the vitality to adapt to accelerated housing needs. The crucial question is whether scientists, architects, and urban designers can provide modern, high-quality, and affordable cave dwellings for the average Chinese citizen. Research on improving cave dwelling designs for modern China should be based on an understanding and analysis of the historical vernacular cave dwelling tradition, which can be applied to solutions for modern design.

In conclusion, it has been the author's ultimate goal to record, analyze, and define the problems posed by Chinese cave dwellings, and to introduce relevant solutions to improve upon these unique indigenous habitats. Until now, there has been only limited information about them in the general literature. Interestingly, the Chinese cave dwelling incorporates some design principles that can be applied in modern architecture. There are far-reaching advantages to be realized in land use, health conditions, economics, and energy savings that we should be aware of in applying those design principles to modern habitations. One common problem shared by people all over the world is a psychological bias against the use of belowground space for living. But it is this author's conviction that an innovative designer can certainly introduce a belowground habitat that provides all the advantages of the aboveground house, that is flooded with sunshine and light, accessible, and allows direct eye contact between the indoor and the outdoor environment.

It is also this author's conclusion that there are design elements in traditional belowground space usage that should be introduced into modern urban design. The author views the integration of belowground space into urban design as a challenge. In this context, two questions should be posed: Can belowground space usage respond to our modern urban design problems and be found suitable, yet still provide a pleasing urban environment? If so, what are the other associated design principles that must be integrated along with this concept in order to promote a higher quality in modern urban design?

The following section is an attempt to introduce belowground space usage, in combination with other traditional design practices, into modern urban design.

Contributions of Belowground Space to Modern Urban Design

Our study shows that there has been renewed contemporary interest in, as well as practical design and construction of, belowground space throughout the world. Although originally motivated by the energy crisis of 1973, interest in belowground space use has also gathered support from other arguments not predominantly related to the energy crisis. The new arguments are strongly and integrally associated with issues affecting the basic policy of urban design and construction, issues which have become increasingly important to urban designers over the last century. The introduction of belowground space usage to modern urban design can solve or ameliorate some pressing urban problems if the approach is comprehensive, innovative, unconventional, courageous, and oriented toward the long-term future. This amounts to a demand for the revolutionary revision of public land use policy in urban design. This revision should be related to the use of belowground space and be strongly influenced by the need for environmental ambient comfort and satisfactory human performance. It must be socially motivated and community oriented rather than strongly individualistic, and should consider long-range economic benefits over the immediate "cost benefit" of dollar returns.

THE TRINITY CONCEPT

To achieve optimal advantages of urban belowground space usage, its integration with other

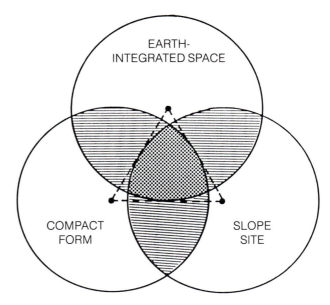

Fig. 6.13   The new urban trinity concept

design concepts should be considered. Belowground urban development should be viewed as triune in nature. The integration of two other design elements with belowground space usage can ease or eliminate problems traditionally associated with this type of space use. A "trinity concept" of urban design and construction is based on the integration of slope site selection, compact city form, and use of earth-integrated space (fig. 6.13). This concept should be viewed, analyzed, and implemented in urban design as a cohesive integral unit, but one that offers a variety of design principle applications within the city itself. Using the trinity concept, designers have the option to apply each of the principles in single or combined form. The designer can use each of the three principles side by side in isolated form (one principle), in semi-integrated form (two principles), or in their fully integrated form (all three principles together). Approached in this way, subterranean space usage can provide comprehensive solutions to some of the more pressing urban problems we face.

SLOPE SITE SELECTION

The selection of a city's site has the greatest long-range impact on future urban development. The impact is diverse and goes beyond what are normally seen as the physical implications. Urban growth and evolution is achieved through a complex of diversified forces. In selecting the site, a planner must consider its influence upon many different factors including social, economic, and environmental considerations. Basically, even in planning a small-scale design and construction project (such as a single building), the architect is not making a physical decision only. Rather, but perhaps unconsciously, he or she is making social, economic, and environmental decisions as well. The impact is much greater when considering the influence the city's site selection will have on urban life after hundreds, perhaps thousands, of years have passed, even while the structures themselves may last only a few decades.

Study of urban site selection throughout history reveals that two types of site selection have been realized, either by intention or through the operation of historically complex forces. Each type of urban site has been the common and dominant choice for its own historical era, but both types are treated here in relation to topographical positioning.

The first type of site selection is the slope site, commonly found in the Middle East, the Mediterranean region, Asia, and Europe. This type of site was generally selected during the period of the rise and development of the village settlement. The other type selection is the flat site, commonly found in North America and developed during the last several centuries throughout the contemporary world.

It is important to recognize that there are advantages and disadvantages associated with each type of site selection. However, their characteristics should be reviewed and analyzed with long-range and comprehensive considerations in mind. Against the "cost-benefit analysis" approach often introduced, we should recognize that there is also a price to be paid for social quality, health, well-being, and comfort. Even environmental and energy-consumption costs are affected by the site selection of a city.

This author emphatically recommends selection of the slope site usually to be found in a mountainous region. This type of site selection would leave flat and rolling topographical forms free for the uses of agriculture, forestry, major transportation, environmental preservation, or other similar types of function. The benefits to be associated with a slope site are varied and complex (table 6.1).

Although selection of a slope site for development would appear to involve a higher initial

Table 6.1 Pros and Cons of Slope Site Selection for Urban Development

PROS	CONS
• Good ventilation • Low risk of air inversion • Unobstructed sunshine penetration • Relatively low land cost • Safe from problems associated with major transportation routes • Saves agricultural lowland • Easy sewage disposal • Attached to natural environment • Direct eye contact with open spaces of lowland • Privacy • Low pollution impact • Varied landscape environment • Low water table • Low risk of flooding • Potential accomplishment of neighborhood entity and identity • Fresh air and little dust • Healthy • Tranquil environment • Optimal integration of belowground space usage concepts	• Possible seismic risk • Lengthy construction time • Possible energy consumption for pumping water • Limited accessibility • Possibly windy • Requires initial investment for access roads, utilities, and some other construction • Low winter temperatures may require energy consumption for active heating

investment than development of a lowland site, this investment would be offset by the lower cost of acquiring the slope site. Apparently, the slope site can improve the overall quality of life and self-image of inhabitants. It provides a pleasing environment for all age groups and can foster improved social interactions on a neighborhood basis, compared to the quality of interaction that is common in the contemporary individualistic and urban society. Introduction of the concept of slope site selection for new urban development should be associated with the use of belowground space. There are comprehensive and long-range benefits to be gained by integrating the two concepts of slope site usage and belowground space.

COMPACT CITY FORM

The compact city form has been commonly used throughout the history of human settlements—often without particular regard to topography, using flat, hilly, or sloping sites. The development of the compact city occurred for a variety of reasons, including need for defense, conservation of arable land, as protection from climatic conditions, as a labor-saving strategy in city wall construction, and to strengthen territoriality. In some regions, especially arid and semiarid zones, the compact city has emerged as the dominant city form having evolved over many millennia. But it was also introduced, and has been present for many centuries, in temperate climatic regions such as Europe and the Mediterranean region. During this century, the compact city has been reintroduced in the search for an optimum city design by urban designers, architects, and social scientists such as Ebenezer Howard, Frank Lloyd Wright, Le Corbusier, and Paolo Soleri.

The compact city differs from the dispersed city in that it maintains a sharp line of demarcation between its own physical form and the immediate natural environment. This contrast, inherent in the compact city form, contributes both practically and psychologically to a strong awareness in the inhabitants of the natural environment.

In both theory and practice, urban expansion can take place in three different directions, either simultaneously or separately. These three types of expansion are:

(1) Horizontal expansion, dispersion in all cardinal directions either continuously or consecutively, with or without patches of open space. Such land development, which has been typical in the United States, is extremely costly in economic and social terms, and makes transportation difficult. Because horizontal expansion requires lengthy utility networks of all types, it diverts much of the taxpayers' money to the construction and maintenance of those utilities and away from essential social services, quality-of-life concerns, and education. In addition, it enforces social isolation and increases energy expenditures.

(2) Vertical upward expansion, the proliferation of high-rise buildings, has been introduced throughout this century primarily in the large and medium-sized urban centers of the West. A good example of this is provided by the twin towers of the World Trade Center in lower Manhattan, New York City, which accommodates more than 100,000 people a day and is used for multiple purposes. Another good example (although a hypothetical one) is Paolo Soleri's proposal for one high-rise building to accommodate four million people as the sole structure of a city. Similar to this, but on a much smaller scale, is Le Corbusier's high-rise building design.

(3) Vertical expansion downward, which exploits subterranean space for multiple uses. Typically, development of belowground space has been limited to uses such as storage and parking. More recently, coinciding with the energy crisis and the increasing cost and scarcity of land in our urban centers, planners/designers have begun to explore the possibilities of expanding their use of subterranean space. Although modern societies are technologically advanced enough to support such construction on a single-unit scale, the theoretical and practical designs for implementation and maintenance of such a large-scale development as a subterranean

city are still lacking (Golany 1989, 54). But regardless of technological feasibility, the greatest complex of problems arises when social, economic, and environmental issues are considered. In regard to these problems, the Japanese seem to have accumulated the beginnings of useful experience.

Throughout this century, horizontal and vertical urban expansion has been introduced extensively and intensively into modern civilization along with the improvement of building technology and transportation.

Commonly, discussion of the compact city is associated with high density of people per unit. However, a distinction should be made between person density per house unit, and house unit density per city. The compact city should not be associated with high density of people per dwelling unit beyond the conventional and expected density of modern standards and norms. The proposed compact city form does not call for a density increase of people per house unit. Rather, a higher density in the number of habitat units for a given city space, which will not detract from the quality of indoor privacy, is suggested.

The compact city should avoid combining the two densities. If the two types of density are combined they will minimize privacy, increase noise, limit the possibility of movement, and may contribute to disruptive behavior among the inhabitants. However, careful design of dwelling units in combination with other land uses can improve the physical and psychological environment of the residence. The Russians have developed a new-town plan for compact cities that range from fifty to 116 people per acre of living unit (house unit without open space), with an average of twelve new towns of 88.7 people per neighborhood acre. The Russian experience indicates that a higher-density city is cheaper to heat in a cold climate and generally requires less energy (Jack Underhill 1978, 409–410).

Some assumptions associated with the compact city are outlined below. Homogeneous groups are usually more tolerant of high-density living than heterogeneous groups because they enjoy better communication. Adaptability to limited space

conditions depends on the existence of communally shared elements of national origin, culture, and life-style. Also, the importance of preserving private space for individuals and families is greater indoors than outdoors in the street, marketplace, or other public open space. Aside from the importance of personal space within the house itself, space priorities differ between one family and another and usually are related to the size of the family and the age and number of children. But it can also be assumed that similar differences exist outdoors in relation to public open space, shopping centers, cultural centers, and educational institutions.

The urban planner/designer should offset the high unit density of the compact city by incorporating the needs of residents for frequent open spaces and green areas, safety of movement for children and adults, proximity to services, and distance from sources of noise and pollution (table 6.2).

In cultures of the Middle East and Mediterranean regions, people are accustomed to high levels of physical closeness. This is mostly a result of strong tribal and kinship ties rooted in the historical society. It can also be attributed to harsh climate and the need for protection. In such a society, personal commitment, mutual responsibility, sharing, and communality provide the assurance of security and survival. On the other hand, Western industrial society places a greater emphasis on privacy and individualism. It is likely that younger generations in the West would be more receptive to a higher degree of physical closeness, and presumably, to the compact form of neighborhood. But this does not necessarily mean that older generations would resist such a change, if it conformed to existing standards of living density.

Within the compact city it is assumed that personal contacts in shopping centers and other public areas of activity will be more extensive than those experienced in the conventional city, because of the mutual proximity of these centers within the neighborhood. However, it is likely that people of different societies might react differently to living in a compact city, and the mutual contact established by proximity may not

Table 6.2   Pros and Cons of the Compact City

PROS	*CONS*
PHYSICAL	
• Proximity of land use for daily needs • Significantly reduced transportation network • Shortened utility length • Increased use of pedestrian network • Proximity to nature	• Congestion may take place and lead to loss of some privacy if detailed design is not considered carefully and with social consciousness in mind
ECONOMIC	
• Conserves land for agriculture and other uses • Energy consumption reduced: less heat exchange than the dispersed city, and less fuel consumed for transportation • Efficient land use • Shortened commuting time • Significant savings in design, construction, maintenance, and operation	• Land price can escalate when building density is increased
SOCIAL	
• Increased social closeness and interaction • Increased interaction among age groups • Improved urban self-image supported by familiarity with total environment • Increased use of public institutions and open space • Encourages pedestrian movement	• Requires adaptability and takes time
HEALTH AND WELL-BEING	
• Reduces pollution • Protects against stressful climates: intense radiation or extreme cold, diurnal changes in temperature, extreme dryness, cold or hot winds, dust storms	• Potential increase of noise generated from public space
ENVIRONMENT	
• Decreased land consumption preserves delicate ecosystem • Creates pleasing urban environment	• Innovative design is necessary and can be costly

be fully acceptable to some groups. It is also assumed that social, economic, and habitation norms are not static, but rather are subject to changes that are related to social expectations. The challenge for the urban planner/designer is to anticipate these future changes by introducing a flexible plan.

The compact city has been presented here within a trinity concept of urban design that is integrated with urban belowground space. If we combine the compact city form with belowground space, both concepts become more meaningful, with a greater likelihood of realization and mutual reinforcement than if they were introduced singly. The historical tradition of compact city form still requires further research and understanding from the social and economic points of view, even

though modern societies have the technological capacity to construct the compact city already.

EARTH-INTEGRATED SPACE

In addition to the Chinese case analyzed here, there have been many historical belowground agricultural villages and a few such urban communities, and some of these are still in existence today. They are: Cappadocia (central Turkey), the Matmata plateau (southern Tunisia–northern Sahara), and Gharyan, Nalut, and Ghadamis (cities in northern and western Libya) (Golany 1983, 1–50).

The use of underground space in cities is motivated by many conditions that prevail in most contemporary cities (ibid., 145–215). These include escalating land prices, shortages of space for expansion, the need for proximity of land uses, transportation congestion, utilities development, urban inefficiency, and high maintenance expenditures.

Earth shelter is a general term for space built within the earth. However, there is variety in the forms that may be assumed by such space: earth-enveloped, subsurface, earth-integrated, semi-subterranean, and subterranean (Golany 1988b, 19–25). The plan for a subterranean city offers positive solutions to some existing urban problems.

The proposed subterranean city design would be integrated with use of a slope site and compact form. As such, it should be subterranean rather than of the earth-enveloped type. Belowground space should envelop habitats on five sides, leaving the sixth side for direct exposure to the outdoor aboveground environment. Such a setting alleviates the problem of claustrophobia, which is commonly introduced as a "con" argument against the windowless environment. In fact, an average of fifty percent of land use in modern cities is *nonresidential* and much of that is often in a windowless environment regardless of having been built aboveground (table 6.3). Consequently, at least nonresidential land use can be introduced into the subterranean environment. The contribution, of course, will be greater if dwellings are introduced into the subterranean space. Single dwelling unit design should utilize a combination of above- and belowground space. Two fundamental design principles are suggested for the subterranean habitat of such a city:

Indoor-outdoor eye contact. Since the proposed city is located on a slope, the indoor living environment will permit direct eye contact with the out-of-doors. Thus, residents will experience the rhythm of the outdoor movement (birds, clouds, wind, trees, people, etc.) and feel themselves part of the natural setting. In addition, the indoor space, if it is properly oriented, will enjoy much of the available natural sunlight.

Access. Belowground city habitats should be accessed by ascending rather than descending. This design principle and approach will ameliorate, or will at least diminish, the claustropho-

Table 6.3   The Urban Windowless Environment

Educational Facilities
- Classrooms: schools, universities, training centers
- Libraries
- Museums (of all types)
- Cultural centers
- Exhibition halls

Entertainment Centers
- Theaters
- Opera halls
- Concert halls
- Bowling alleys
- Skating rinks: roller, ice
- Sports arenas

Agriculture
- Mushroom raising
- Chicken raising

Storage
- General storage
- Equipment
- Garages
- Agricultural
- Refrigeration

Service
- Restaurants
- Shopping centers (of all types)
- Some offices
- Hospitals: surgery and recovery rooms

Industries and Factories
- Processing plants

bic feeling a person could experience when descending into a habitat. The location on a slope will support this type of design.

Most people, regardless of their culture and standard of living, are biased against belowground space usage especially for habitats. Historically, subterranean space usage has been psychologically associated with dampness, darkness, lack of ventilation, an unhealthy environment creating an overall negative feeling—with some justification. However, the proposed belowground space for living and other uses should counteract the historical bias. Exploiting the trinity concept, a designer can offer a subterranean space with plenty of natural sunlight, efficient passive ventilation, and direct indoor-outdoor eye contact that will meet most modern norms and standards of living.

The nature of the subterranean city construction debate is psychological and it involves the potential biases of the potential inhabitants. All practical issues can be overcome with modern and sophisticated technology that is readily available. The key is the urban design pattern to be introduced by the urban planner. It is of great importance to educate the public to appreciate this innovative and beneficial urban environment, and the urban designer can do much to contribute to this education process.

Urban belowground city construction, as an innovative venture, requires that many conventional approaches to urban design be reexamined. These include the urban design concepts of site selection criteria, physiography, orientation to available natural sunlight, macro- and micro-climatological systems, geological limitations, drainage patterns, accessibility, and, last but not least, environmental constraints.

Subterranean cities offer many benefits and some limitations. Unfortunately, people may argue these issues without weighing the relative arguments and without keeping long-range considerations in mind. Also, there is an acute deficit in the theory and modern practice of such an endeavor, in addition to a lack of published work. In the opinion of this author, decisive research in this field is justified both economically and practically, from the point of view of urban development strategy. Underground cities are a revolu-

Table 6.4 Pros and Cons of Subterranean Space Usage

PROS	CONS
PROTECTION FROM STRESSFUL CLIMATE	
• Weatherproofing against extreme diurnal and seasonal climates, protective against strong winds, dust storms, and tornadoes	• Risk of cover by dust storm
• Temperature fluctuation resistance, heat storage benefit, stable diurnal temperature, indoor-outdoor seasonal temperature contrast	
• Temperate ambient environment	
• Survival under extreme weather disaster	
• Suitable for stressful climate	
ENERGY COSTS	
• Heat gain and loss is minimal or none	• Natural lighting can be minimal if not carefully designed and some sections will require electricity
• Energy consumption is zero in the summer and minimal in the winter	
• Refrigeration is optimum	
CONSTRUCTION COSTS	
• Land cost reduced through dual use—sub- and supraterranean	• Blasting increases costs
• Design costs lower relative to dual space use	• Excavation removal costs
• Fewer building materials required (less windows and landscaping)	• Geological and soil mapping costs
• Floor has increased load capacity	• Construction duration costs
• Significantly shortens all urban utilities	
LAND USE	
• Preserves land and natural landscape	• Increased density of structures per overall urban land
• Conserves land for use as open green space or for future expansion	• Cultural bias may cause acclimatization difficulties
• Compact land use significantly reduces energy consumption, transportation time, and pollution	• Privacy potentially lost if innovative, socially conscious design is lacking
• Proximity to nature	
• Proximity of land use encourages social interaction and pedestrian movement	
• Improved agricultural and poultry production (mushrooms, eggs)	

tionary concept, compared with conventional cities, and they address a complex of concerns: protection from the climate, energy costs, construction costs, maintenance costs, land use type, safety concerns, health conditions, and environmental impact. To familiarize the reader with the relevant arguments, the basic pros and cons of the subterranean city endeavor are presented in table 6.4.

RETURN VALUES

As with any other project there are both pros and cons to building the trinity city. The overall return value of combining the concepts of slope usage, compact form, and subterranean space is greater than with the conventional urban design. Such an endeavor should be comprehensively evaluated in long-range terms. The benefits include economic, social, health, transportation, and other considerations.

The economic return value is diverse and in general the compact city project lowers economic costs. First, and above all, land price is reduced by half, resulting from dual use of the land. Second, the design and construction of the compact city, although innovative, will reduce overall expenditures. It is the integration of the three concepts of slope site, compact form, and subterranean space usage that results in such benefits. Third, operation and maintenance expenditures

PROS	CONS
MAINTENANCE COSTS	
• Low maintenance costs for overall structure (external) painting, repairs, remodeling, window and roof replacement) • Durability is extended due to the enveloping earth • Housekeeping is reduced because of decreased dust • Fire insurance rate should be less • Utility costs reduced significantly	• Higher expenditures for utility repair may be required • Water supply pumping may increase costs
SAFETY	
• Protection from man-made and natural disasters: vandals, air attack, shelling, tornadoes, some earthquakes, storms and radioactive fallout • Water utilities will not freeze, burst, or cause flooding • Fire resistance and containment enhanced • Flood risk is minimal due to slope configuration and good drainage	• Fire evacuation difficulties due to slope topography and limited accessibility • Geological faults (commonly associated with the slope) increase earthquake impact risk
HEALTH	
• Comfortable ambient climate provides relaxing environment • Quietness stimulates creativity especially among writers and artists • Distractions and obstructions are minimal which contributes to decreased stress	• Dampness risk increased, especially in humid regions, when design and building construction are not carefully implemented • Claustrophobia can develop among some people and requires special design
ENVIRONMENTAL IMPACT	
• Minimum impact on the natural environment and the ecosystem • Pollution decreased significantly: soundproof from noise and vibration, air pollution reduced • Productive labor conditions: stable, ambient microclimate (temperature and humidity) and windowless environment • Reduces external post-surgical recovery period by 20% • Wind impact reduced significantly and heat gain and loss minimized	• Radon exposure potential increased, requiring frequent observation and effective ventilation • Special design of passive or active ventilation required • Special indoor landscaping needed for some spaces • Transportation vibration of heavy movement such as railroads may affect indoor environment

for the compact city should provide relief to tax-payers and divert the gains to improvement of the social quality of life and the environment. In addition, it is expected that this design pattern will ease the financial, management, and (possibly) political crises that most contemporary urban centers increasingly experience.

The author researched and concluded the simple exercise of designing 19.42 hectares (forty-eight acres) using three separate design models comparatively: "conventional sprawl" (on a flat site), compact form (on a slope site), and combined form (compact form with subterranean space on a slope site) (fig. 6.14). The goal of this research and exercise was to compare the economic gains in terms of land use, infrastructure, and urban fixtures (fig. 6.15). Although it was already known that some economic gain is realized through reduced urban fixtures, it was only after the statistical results of this exercise were compiled that the magnitude of the gain became apparent. Combining the supraterranean and subterranean models resulted in greater savings than found with the conventional model (table 6.5).

Social benefits of the combined design model

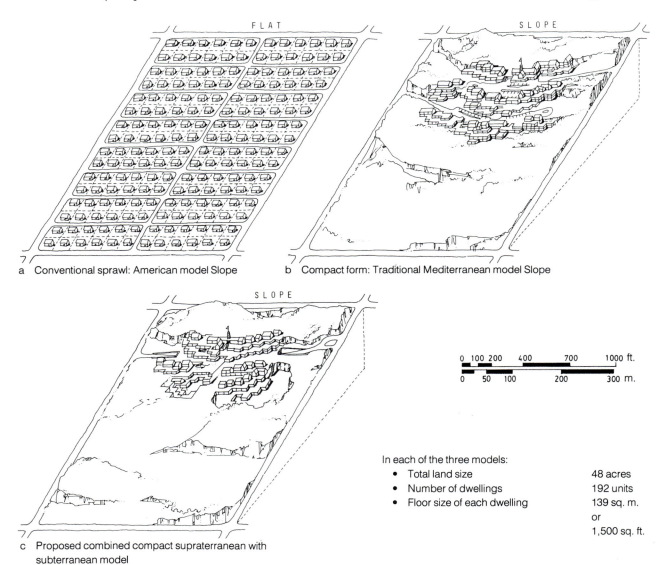

a Conventional sprawl: American model Slope

b Compact form: Traditional Mediterranean model Slope

c Proposed combined compact supraterranean with subterranean model

In each of the three models:
- Total land size — 48 acres
- Number of dwellings — 192 units
- Floor size of each dwelling — 139 sq. m. or 1,500 sq. ft.

Fig. 6.14 Economic profile comparison for three 48-acre urban design sites

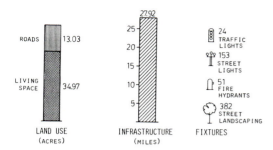

A. CONVENTIONAL SPRAWL: AMERICAN MODEL

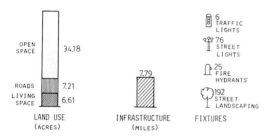

B. COMPACT FORM: TRADITIONAL MEDITERRANEAN MODEL

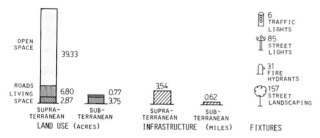

C. PROPOSED COMBINED FORM: COMPACT SUPRATERRANEAN WITH SUBTERRANEAN MODEL

Fig. 6.15 Benefit comparison for the three 48-acre urban sites

Table 6.5   Comparison of Economic Return Values for Three Different Design Models

Item	Conventional Sprawl: American Model	Compact Form: Traditional Mediterranean Model	Proposed Combined Form: Compact Supraterranean with Subterranean Model
Land Use			
Living units	194	194	194
Living space*	34.9 acres	6.6 acres	6.6 acres**
Road space	13 acres	7.2 acres	7.5 acres
Open space	none	34.1 acres	39.3 acres
Infrastructure Length***	27.9 miles	7.7 miles	4.1 miles
Urban Fixtures			
Traffic lights	24	6	6
Street lights	153	76	85
Fire hydrants	51	25	31
Street landscaping	382 trees	192 trees	157 trees

*Living space includes the house unit with the private open space of the lot surrounding it in the case of the conventional American model. In the other two cases living space includes the living structure only, without the surrounding lot. The 194 units of each model are equal in floor size.

**The compact supraterranean living space was 2.87 acres and the subterranean was 3.75 acres.

***Infrastructure length includes the total length of interior roads and peripheral streets, pedestrian paths, sewage network, water network, telephone lines, gas lines, television cables, and central heating network.

also present significant advantages. First, the commuting time between places of work, residences, and access to shopping is significantly reduced, with positive psychological effects. Second, social interaction is increased, an effect that may offset the common complaint of loneliness that prevails among modern city dwellers. Third, children and especially the elderly are nearer to the urban atmosphere and can become more familiar with the city's urban geography, resulting in improvements to the quality of their social life. In addition, economic gains to the public sector

can be used to make significant contributions to the improvement of services and the overall quality of social life. Open active space, both supraterranean and subterranean, should be plentiful and in close proximity to pedestrian access. Such a city will become more pedestrian oriented than the conventional city. Still, with the combined pattern of slope site, compact form, and subterranean space, there will be some degree of trade-off in benefits to individuals as well as to the community, due to cultural differences and differing personal expectations.

PUBLIC POLICY

Although the optimal realization of the trinity city concept can only take place in a new town built from scratch, it is possible, too, that it can be integrated with the expansion of an existing city if the new site is located on a slope. Traditionally, use of each one of the three elements of the trinity (slope location, compact form, and subterranean space) has evolved singly in the history of human settlements. The trinity city concept as presented here combines the three elements purposefully into a cohesive and comprehensive pattern. The general public's response may be negative only as a result of bias, lack of knowledge, inexperience, short-sightedness, lack of a holistic view, and short-range planning. To counteract this profile there is a need for focused public awareness, enlightened public policy, and coordinated design enforcement.

The support of common public opinion would require awareness. Without this awareness it would be difficult, if not impossible, to introduce such an innovative, nonconventional trinity concept. Public awareness can be increased through study, research, dissemination of knowledge through all forms of communications media, and through planned interactions, discussions, and the display of a practical model. Public policy should follow the public's awareness and be estab-lished as part of the legislation where appropriate. Moreover, new zoning ordinances combined with incentives are necessary in order to achieve enforcement and to protect the public interest. Coordination is essential throughout the design and implementation of a trinity city development project. Such a project would require the effort and contribution of almost every sector of the community.

Conclusions

The trinity concept for urban design introduced here is based on the study of historical vernacular urban design with an attempt to learn from it those lessons that are relevant to our modern needs and norms. Although it represents the integration of an ancient concept into modern urban design, its validity for modern times is shown by its practicality and applicability to contemporary urban design problems. The innovativeness of the trinity concept requires the collaboration of aggressive designers, social scientists, economists, and (last but not least) politicians. It is the author's belief that to pursue the urban project along these lines must involve a trade-off of cost benefits between the social and economic spheres, and that for every social experiment there must be an economic price.

APPENDIX 1

Chronology of Chinese Dynasties

Xia	c. 21st century–16th century B.C.
Shang	c. 16th century–11th century B.C.
Zhou	c. 11th century–221 B.C.
Western Zhou	c. 11th century–770 B.C.
Eastern Zhou	770–221 B.C.
Spring and Autumn Period	770–476 B.C.
Warring States Period	475–221 B.C.
Qin	221–207 B.C.
Han	206 B.C.–A.D. 220
Western Han	206 B.C.–A.D. 24
Eastern Han	25–220
Three Kingdoms	220–280
Wei	220–265
Shu	221–263
Wu	222–280
Jin	265–420
Western Jin	265–316
Eastern Jin	317–420
Southern and Northern Dynasties	386–589
Southern Dynasties	420–589
Song	420–479
Qi	479–502
Liang	502–557
Chen	557–589
Northern Dynasties	386–581
Northern Wei	386–534
Eastern Wei	534–550
Western Wei	535–557
Northern Qi	550–577
Northern Zhou	557–581

Continued

Appendix 1: Chronology of Chinese Dynasties *(Continued)*

Sui	581–618
Tang	618–907
Five Dynasties and Ten Kingdoms	907–979
Song	960–1279
Northern Song	960–1127
Southern Song	1127–1279
Liao	916–1125
Jin	1115–1234
Yuan	1271–1368
Ming	1368–1644
Qing	1644–1911

Source: Foreign Languages Press, ed., *China facts and figures: 4,000-year history* (Beijing, 1982)

APPENDIX 2

Linear and Square Measure Equivalences

Linear Measure (Length)
  1 inch = 2.54 centimeters
  1 foot = 12 inches = 0.3048 meter
  1 yard = 36 inches = 0.9144 meter
  1 mile = 1760 yards = 1609.3 meters = 1.6093 kilometers
  1 knot (nautical mile) = 6080.27 feet = 1853 meters = 1.853 kilometers

Square Measure (Area)
  1 square inch = 6.452 square centimeters
  1 square foot = 144 square inches = 929 square centimeters
  1 square yard = 9 square feet = 0.8361 square meters
  1 acre = 4840 square yards
  1 square mile = 640 acres = 2.59 square kilometers
  2.471 acres = 1 hectare

APPENDIX 3

Temperature Equivalences

°C	°F	°C	°F	°C	°F
-20	-4	5	41	30	86
-19	-2.2	6	42.8	31	87.8
-18	-0.4	7	44.6	32	89.6
-17	1.4	8	46.4	33	91.4
-16	3.2	9	48.2	34	93.2
-15	5	10	50	35	95
-14	6.8	11	51.8	36	96.8
-13	8.6	12	53.6	37	98.6
-12	10.4	13	55.4	38	100.4
-11	12.2	14	57.2	39	102.2
-10	14	15	59	40	104
-9	15.8	16	60.8	41	105.8
-8	17.6	17	62.6	42	107.6
-7	19.4	18	64.4	43	109.4
-6	21.2	19	66.2	44	111.2
-5	23	20	68	45	113
-4	24.8	21	69.8	46	114.8
-3	26.6	22	71.6	47	116.6
-2	28.4	23	73.4	48	118.4
-1	30.2	24	75.2	49	120.2
0	32	25	77	50	122
1	33.8	26	78.8	51	123.8
2	35.6	27	80.6	52	125.6
3	37.4	28	82.4	53	127.4
4	39.2	29	84.2	54	129.2
				55	131

Source: *Metric system guide,* vol. 3 (Neenah, Wisc.: J. J. Keller and Associates, 1982)

BIBLIOGRAPHY

Abbreviated Titles

Conference on underground space
Tongji University Press, ed. 1988. *Proceedings of the third international conference on underground space and earth sheltered buildings: New developments of underground space use.* Shanghai.

Earth sheltered buildings conference
Texas A&M University, Department of Architecture, ed. 1986a. *Proceedings of the second international earth sheltered buildings conference: Advances in geotectural design.* College Station, Tex.

Surveys of cave dwellings in China
Gansu Cave Dwelling and Soil Construction Survey and Research Group, ed. 1982. *A collection of theses on surveys of cave dwellings and buildings in earth in China* (Zhongguo yaodong ji shengtu jianzhu diaoyan lunwen xuanji). Lanzhou: Architectural Society of China.

Symposium on earth architecture
Architectural Society of China, ed. 1985. *Proceedings of the international symposium on earth architecture, 1-4 November, 1985, Beijing.*

Beijing Daily
Beijing ribao.

People's Daily
Renmin ribao.

Works Consulted

Adachi, T.
1986 Geotechnical report on the Seikan tunnel. *Tunnelling and Underground Space Technology* 1.3-4: 351-356.

Andreadaki-Chronaki, Eleni
1986 Earth sheltered architecture as an alternative for environmental planning: The experience of Santorini. In *Earth sheltered buildings conference,* 6-11.

Aoki, Shiro, and Toshimasa Konishi
1985 Types and locations of earth construction. In *Symposium on earth architecture,* 17-19.

Architectural Journal, ed.
1981 First symposium on cave dwellings and buildings in earth (Zhongguo jianzhu xuehui yaodong ji shengtu jianzhu: Di yi ci xueshu taolun huiyi jiyao). *Architectural Journal* (Jianzhu xuebao) 10:29-30.

Architectural Society of China, ed.
1985 *Proceedings of the international symposium on earth architecture, 1-4 November 1985, Beijing.*

Architectural Society of China and Tianjin University, Department of Architecture, eds.
1985 *Earth sheltered architecture in China* (Zhongguo shengtu jianzhu). Tianjin: Tianjin Science and Technology Press.

Arledge, Pat H., and Cora F. McKown
1985 Innovativeness and risk-taking characteristics of owners of earth sheltered houses. In *Symposium on earth architecture,* 41-46.

Asanga, Cletus T., and Robert B. Mills
1985 Changes in environment, grain quality, and insect populations in pearl millet stored in underground pits. In *Underground Space* 9.5-6:316-321.

Attewell, P. B., and A. R. Selby
1988 The effects of large ground movements caused by tunnelling in compressible soils. In *Conference on underground space,* 316-326.

Autio, Jorma
1988 Economic and functional operating characteristics of rock caverns used for various purposes in Finland. In *Conference on underground space,* 31-36.

Baggs, Sydney A.
1984 The first international earth shelter building conference. *Underground Space* 8.3:149.
1985 Environmental factors possibly influencing attitude in Australians living in above- and below-ground dwellings in an arid region mining town. In *Symposium on earth architecture,* 47-54.
1988 Survey and analysis of interior/exterior environments of nine case studies of "dugout" dwellings, Coober Pedy, South Australia. In *Conference on underground space,* 441-446.

Baggs, S. A., and C. F. Wong
1986 Survey of radon in Australian geotecture and architecture. In *Earth sheltered buildings conference,* 111-116.

Bai Mingxue
1985 Earthquake hazards to the earth buildings in Ningxia. In *Symposium on earth architecture,* 55–63.

Banks, H. J.
1981 Effects of controlled atmosphere storage on grain quality: A review. *Food Technology in Australia* 33:335–340.

Bansal, N. K., and M. S. Sodha
1986 An earth-air tunnel system for cooling buildings. *Tunnelling and Underground Space Technology* 1.2:177–182.

Bartz, Janet G.
1986 Attitudes and residential satisfaction of earth sheltered housing consumers. In *Earth sheltered buildings conference,* 137–142.

Beijing City Office of Air Defense
1982 The use of air raid shelters in Beijing (Beijing renfang gongcheng de liyong). *Architectural Journal* (Jianzhu xuebao) 11:40–41.

Blick, Edward F., and J. G. Eyerman
1986 R factor for earth bermed buildings. In *Earth sheltered buildings conference,* 175–182.

Bowers, Douglas A.
1986 Geocomposites: A systems approach. In *Earth sheltered buildings conference,* 103–106.

Boyd, Andrew C. H.
1962 *Chinese architecture and town planning, 1500 B.C.– A.D. 1911.* Chicago: University of Chicago Press.

Boyer, Lester L.
1986a Daylighting performance of an earth covered dwelling at high altitude. In *Earth sheltered buildings conference,* 252–256.
1986b Design and construction of a remote, fully passive, two-story earth covered residence at high altitude. In *Earth sheltered buildings conference,* 230–233.

Boyer, Lester L., and Morad R. Atif
1988 Comparison of daylighting distribution in an underground dwelling high in the Rockies using computer algorithms, scale models, and on-site measurements. In *Conference on underground space,* 470–475.

Boyer, Lester L., and W. T. Grondzik
1986 Sunlighting, daylighting, and passive solar heating for earth covered dwellings. In *Earth sheltered buildings conference,* 220–223.

Britz, Richard D.
1986 Modular method of making a building "earthship" structure. In *Earth sheltered buildings conference,* 263–266.

Broch, Einar, and Jan A. Rygn
1988 Recreational facilities in rock in Norway. In *Conference on underground space,* 502–508.

Brown, R. L.
1974 Japan: Under land and under water. *Building* 226:87–88.

Cai Xiaohong and Lu Younian
1987 Calculation of elastic-plastic stress for hydro-technical pressure tunnel (Shuigong yali suidong tansuo xingying li jisuan). *Underground Space* (Dixia kongjian) 1:29–38.

Cai Xiuyue
1988 The utilization and development of the space in subway stations—Some ideas on the plan of Xi Dan Station. In *Conference on underground space,* 110–115.

Cao Guiquan
1988 Application of installation with heating pipes and heat air supply in underground construction (Refeng reguan zhuangzhi zai dixia gongcheng de yingyong). *Underground Space* (Dixia kongjian) 8.3:68–72.

Carmody, John, and Douglas Derr
1982 The use of underground space in the People's Republic of China. In *Underground Space* 7.1:7–15.

Carmody, J. C., L. S. Shen, Y. J. Huang, L. G. Goldberg, and George D. Meixel, Jr.
1988 A comprehensive method for predicting residential energy savings due to basement insulation. In *Conference on underground space,* 404–409.

Carmody, J. C., and R. L. Sterling
1986 Design strategies to alleviate negative psychological and physiological effects in underground space. In *Earth sheltered buildings conference,* 127–136.

Cave Dwelling Survey and Research Group
1982 *Sunken cave dwellings in Gong county* (Gong xian de xiachen shi yaodong jianzhu). Construction Committee of Kaifeng Region, Henan.

Cena, K., L. Sliwowski, and J. R. Spotila
1988 Thermal comfort of humans in normal and special environments. In *Conference on underground space,* 492–495.

Central Meteorological Bureau, ed.
1978 *Climate of China,* [with] *diagrams and illustrations.* Beijing: Cartographic Press.

Chan Bingshan, Jian Wenbin, and Wu Qiong
1988 The resource significance of the karst underground space. In *Conference on underground space,* 280–282.

Chang, Kwang-chih
1977 *The archaeology of ancient China.* 3d ed. New Haven: Yale University Press.

Chatani, Masahiro, and Koji Yagi
1985 Analysis of hillside and pit type dwellings. In *Symposium on earth architecture,* 20–23.

Chatani, Masahiro, Koji Yagi, Kiyoshi Ishikawa, Naomi Ando, Katsuhiko Yashiro, and S. Nonaka
1988a Analysis of recognition of route in underground shopping areas of Tokyo and Yokohama. In *Conference on underground space,* 433–436.

Chatani, Masahiro, Koji Yagi, Kiyoshi Ishikawa, T. Nakazawa, Katsuhiko Yashiro, and T. Taniguchi
  1988b Research on spatial perception in underground shopping areas of Tokyo and Yokohama. In *Conference on underground space,* 437–440.

Chatani, Masahiro, K. Yagi, T. Nakazawa, and K. Yashiro
  1986 Underground dwellings in the loess land of China. In *Earth sheltered buildings conference,* 36–40.

Chen, B. J., Q. Y. Chi, and X. K. Li
  1988 Environment and health in [an] underground hospital. In *Conference on underground space,* 399–403.

Chen Benrong and Zhang Yushu
  1983 Glimpse into the underground city of Beijing (Beijing dixiacheng yi pie). *Beijing Daily,* 21 December 1983.

Chen Lidao, Zhang Dongshan, and Shu Yu
  1988 The evaluation of demand for underground space in urban areas and optimal distribution. In *Conference on underground space,* 165–171.

Chen Qigao
  1986a Research on the thermal performance of a sweet orange cellar. In *Earth sheltered buildings conference,* 190–194.
  1986b Theory of heat transfer in a tunnel with natural ventilation. In *Earth sheltered buildings conference,* 205–209.
  1988 A program on wastes control for a heat power plant by an underground system. In *Conference on underground space,* 416–421.

Chen Yanxun, Nie Minggang, and Xiao Mingyan
  1988 Investigation on acoustic environment of underground space (Dixia kongjian de sheng-huanjing diaocha). *Underground Space* (Dixia kongjian) 8.3:38–50.

Chen Zhanxiang
  1981 Cave dwellings and architecture (Yaodong yu jianzhu). *Architectural Journal* (Jianzhu xuebao) 10:31–33.

Chen Ziqiang
  1986 Construction and management of an underground market in the department store Nanfang Dasha (Nanfang Dasha dixia shangchang de shigong yu guanli). *Underground Space* (Dixia kongjian) 4:49–55.

China Handbook Editorial Committee, comp.
  1983 *Geography, China handbook series.* Beijing: Foreign Languages Press.

Chinese Academy of Sciences, Institute of Geology
  1965 *Chinese loess soil distribution map* (Zhongguo huangtu fenbu tu). Beijing: Cartographic Press.

Chongqing University, Tongji University, Harbin Architectural Engineering Institute, and Tianjin University, eds.
  1928 *Underground architectural structure in rocks* (Yanshi dixia jianzhu jiegou). Beijing: China Building Industry Press.

Cui Zhensheng and Gu Zuming
  1988 The Ep-pur elastic sealer—A sealing material for underground engineering. In *Conference on underground space,* 208–210.

Denda, Atsushi, Toshiaki Mimuro, and Michi Noda
  1988 Slaking characteristics and mechanical behaviours of soft rock in Japan. In *Conference on underground space,* 366–371.

Deng Qisheng
  1985 Traditional measures of moistureproof in raw soil architecture in China. In *Symposium on earth architecture,* 64–68.

Di Cristofalo, S., S. Orioli, G. Silvestrini, and S. Alessandro
  1988 Thermal behaviour of "Scirocco Room" in ancient Sicilian villas. In *Conference on underground space,* 45–47.

Duddeck, Heinz
  1988 Guidelines for the design of tunnels. In *Conference on underground space,* 180–188.

Duddeck, Heinz, Dieter Rabe, and Dieter Winselmann
  1988 Design criteria for immersed tube tunnels: Experiences gained by the Autobahn-Tunnel under the river Ems. In *Conference on underground space,* 172–179.

Dunkel, Florence V.
  1982 Grain storage in south China. *Cereal Foods World* 27:409–414.
  1985 Underground and earth-sheltered food storage: Historical, geographic, and economic considerations. In *Underground Space* 9.5–6:310–315.

Dunkel, Florence V., Zhe Lung Pu, Chuan Liang, and Fan-yi Huang
  1982 Insect and fungal response to sorbic acid-treated wheat during storage in south China. *Journal of Economic Entomology* 75:1083–1088.

Dunkel, F., R. Sterling, and G. Meixel
  1986 Underground bulk storage of shelled corn in Minnesota. In *Earth sheltered buildings conference,* 78–85.

Dunkel, F. V., R. L. Sterling, G. D. Meixel, and L. D. Bullerman
  1988 Underground structures for grain storage: Interrelatedness of biologic, thermal, and economic aspects. In *Conference on underground space,* 1–6.

Eberspacher, Warren
  1986 The earth systems structural forming system. In *Earth sheltered buildings conference,* 257–262.

Editing and Writing Group, ed.
  1983 *Handbook for the design of heating and air conditioning in underground buildings* (Dixia jianzhu nuan tong kongtiao sheji shouce). Beijing: China Building Industry Press.

Eisenhofer, F.
1988 Ferro cement domes set on coastal sand dunes in New Zealand. In *Conference on underground space,* 16–21.

El Bartali, Houssine
1986 Underground storage pits in Morocco. In *Earth sheltered buildings conference,* 68–73.

El Bartali, Houssine, and Said Afif
1988 Temperature variations in underground grain storage structures. In *Conference on underground space,* 488–491.

Esaki, Yoichiro, and Ryuzo Ohno
1985 A morphological analysis of underground rooms. In *Symposium on earth architecture,* 24–26.

Fairhurst, Charles, and Raymond Sterling
1983 Session report: Subsurface storage of food. *Underground Space* (Dixia kongjian) 7.4–5:249–250.

Fan Jiancheng and Kang Ning
1986 Analysis of probability of existence for underground construction (Dixia gongcheng de shengcun gailu qianxi). *Underground Space* (Dixia kongjian) 4:19–40.

Feng Zhongwen
1987 Scientific management of utilization of underground tunnel air (Didaofeng liyong de kexue guanli). *Underground Space* (Dixia kongjian) 1:55–63.
1988 Strategic transition and future development of civil air defense (Renfang zhanlue zhuanbian he weilai fazhan). *Underground Space* (Dixia kongjian) 8.3:14–16.

Foreign Languages Press, ed.
1982 *China facts and figures: 4,000-year history.* Beijing.
1984 *China facts and figures: Population.* Beijing.

Freeman, S. Thomas, et al.
1982 Tunnelling in the People's Republic of China. *Underground Space* 7.1:24–30.

Fujita, K., K. Ueda, and Y. Shimomura
1978 An empirical proposal on stability of rock cavern wall during construction in Japan. *Storage in Excavated Rock Caverns, Rockstore 77.2,* Magnus Bergman, ed., 309–314. Oxford: Pergamon Press.

Fukuchi, G.
1986 Guest editorial. *Tunnelling and Underground Space Technology* 1.3–4:223–224.

Fuller, Myron L., and Fredrick G. Clapp
1924 Loess and rock dwellings at Shensi. *Geographical Review* 14:215–226.

Future Press, ed.
1987 *Scenic spots of Shaanxi Province: Qianling Tomb.* Xi'an: Future Press.

Gansu Cave Dwelling and Soil Construction Survey and Research Group, ed.
1982 *A collection of theses on surveys of cave dwellings and buildings in earth in China* (Zhongguo yaodong ji shengtu jianzhu diaoyan lunwen xuanji). Lanzhou: Architectural Society of China.

Gao Boyang and Geng Yonghang
1988 Research on the psychological condition of people working and living in underground circumstances. In *Conference on underground space,* 428–432.

Gao Hewei and Zhang Changquan
1988 Shanghai People's Square underground parking. In *Conference on underground space,* 133–137.

Gazetteer Research Office, Survey Science Research Institute, National Survey Bureau, ed.
1983 *Gazetteer of China: An index to the atlas of the People's Republic of China* (Zhongguo diminglu: Zhonghua Renmin Gongheguo dituji diming suoyin). Beijing: Cartographic Press.

Gilman, G. A., and R. A. Boxall
1974 The storage of food grain in traditional underground pits. *Tropical Stored Products Information* 28:19–38.

Goding, Lloyd A.
1986 Ferrocement as a building material for earth shelter. In *Earth sheltered buildings conference,* 100–102.

Golany, Gideon S.
1983 *Earth-sheltered habitat: History, architecture and urban design.* New York: Van Nostrand Reinhold.
1985a Below-ground dwellings in China and Tunisia. In *Symposium on earth architecture,* 75–81.
1985b Earth architecture in perspective. In *Symposium on earth architecture,* 10–16.
1986 Below-ground dwellings in China, Tunisia, and Turkey: A comparative study. In *Earth sheltered buildings conference,* 18–27.
1988a Contributions of below-ground space to urban design: A trinity concept. In *Conference on underground space,* 194–201.
1988b *Earth-sheltered dwellings in Tunisia: Ancient lessons for modern design.* Newark: University of Delaware Press.
1989 *Urban underground space design in China: Vernacular and modern practice.* Newark: University of Delaware Press.
1990 *Design and thermal performance: Below-ground dwellings in China.* Newark: University of Delaware Press.

Gonner, D. H. W.
1988 Prevention of industrial accidents and damage to property. In *Conference on underground space,* 509–514.

Granit, Michael
1988 Underground design in urban areas. In *Conference on underground space,* 116–121.

Gu Fubao
1982 *Cave dwellings in west Henan* (Yuxi yaodong minju). Zhengzhou: Civil Engineering Department, Zhengzhou Engineering College.

Guan Lijun
1985   Research on thermal environments inside loess cave dwellings in China. In *Symposium on earth architecture*, 82–92.

Gudehus, G.
1988   Geotechnical innovations for an underground garage in soft soil. In *Conference on underground space*, 86–89.

Guo Yunfu, Yang Nanfang, and He Tienan
1987   Design and economical benefit of cavern oil storage with double approach (Danshuang yin-dao shantong shiyouku sheji yu jingjixiao yi fenxi). *Underground Space* (Dixia kongjian) 1:5–16.

Hait, John N.
1988   Passive annual heat storage. In *Conference on underground space*, 476–481.

Hanamura, Tetsuya
1990   Japan's new frontier strategy: Underground space development. *Tunnelling and Underground Space Technology* 5.1–2:13–22.

Hane, Tadashi
1988   Application of solar daylighting system to underground space. In *Conference on underground space*, 464–469.
1989   Application of solar daylighting systems to underground space. *Tunnelling and Underground Space Technology* 4.4:465–470.

Hanegreefs, P., S. Clarke, and F. Dunkel
1986   Underground bag storage of dry edible beans in Rwanda (east Africa). In *Earth sheltered buildings conference*, 74–77.

Hasegawa, F., H. Yoshino, and S. Matsumoto
1987   Optimum use of solar energy techniques in a semi-underground house: First year measurement and computer analysis. *Tunnelling and Underground Space Technology* 2.4:429–436.

Hashimoto, K., and Y. Tanabe
1986   Construction of the Seikan undersea tunnel—II: Execution of the most difficult sections. *Tunnelling and Underground Space Technology* 1.3–4:373–380.

Hayashi, Yasuyoshi
1985   Effect of village improvement on earth architecture. In *Symposium on earth architecture*, 93–99.
1986   The future of earth-sheltered architecture in China's farming villages. *Tunnelling and Underground Space Technology* 1.2:167–170.

He Lianghai
1987   Deformation and state under forces of enclosing rock during cavern excavation (Dongshi kaiwa weiyan de bianxing yu shouli fenxi). *Underground Space* (Dixia kongjian) 1:17–28.

Higashikata, Yoshio
1986   Under urban units in Japan. In *Earth sheltered buildings conference*, 316–322.
1988   Living in the urban under unit. In *Conference on underground space*, 144–149.

Hiyeda, Tetsuya, Hajime Ogi, and Kazuo Nakamura
1988   Differences in thermal environmental characteristics of basements among districts. In *Conference on underground space*, 482–487.

Hiyeda, T., H. Ogi, M. Yoshioka, K. Nakamura, and K. Iwai
1986   Physical environment properties of the basement and its simulation. In *Earth sheltered buildings conference*, 117–121.

Hou Jiyao
1982   Cave dwellings in Shaanxi Province (Shaanxi yaodong minju). *Architectural Journal* (Jianzhu xuebao) 11:71–74.
1985a   The architectural arts about the cave dwellings in Shanxi Province. In *Symposium on earth architecture*, 107–114.
1985b   The new development of earth dwellings in Fujian and Guangdong provinces. In *Symposium on earth architecture*, 100–106.
1986   Development and utilization of cave dwellings and earth buildings in China. In *Earth sheltered buildings conference*, 55–61.

Hou Jiyao, Feng Xiaohong, and Zhao Xiaobou
1988   Affiliation innovation and exploitation of hidden space: A study on the underground exhibition hall of bronze chariot and horses at Qin Shi Huang's museum. In *Conference on underground space*, 22–26.

Hou Xueyuan and Su Yu
1986a   Stability and indoor environment of loess cave dwellings. In *Earth sheltered buildings conference*, 44–54.
1986b   Urban underground space environment and human performance. In *Earth sheltered buildings conference*, 307–315.
1988   The model of underground space of the city. In *Conference on underground space*, 74–85.

Hou Xueyuan and Sun Yiming
1985   Stability analysis for loess cave dwellings. In *Symposium on earth architecture*, 124–134.

Hu Fan
1988   China's underground commercial constructions. In *Conference on underground space*, 156–161.

Huanghe River Conservancy Commission, Ministry of Water Conservancy, ed.
1982   *The Huanghe river*. Shanghai.

Huo Fuguo and Cao Shaokang
1985   The precautions against earthquakes and the anti-seismic for Ningxia's architecture of immature soil. In *Symposium on earth architecture*, 115–123.

Huo Yan
1985   Cave dwelling and human health. In *Symposium on earth architecture*, 135–144.
1986   The effects of cave dwelling on human health. *Tunnelling and Underground Space Technology* 1.2:171–176.

Hyde, M. B.
1973   Scientific principles of airtight storage: Airtight grain storage (with particular reference to hot climates and developing countries.) *FAO Agricultural Service Bulletin* 17:1–15.

Hyde, M. B., and N. J. Burrell
1969   Control of infestation in stored grain by airtight storage or by cooling. In *Proceedings of the fifth insecticide and fungicide conference, Brighton, England, 17–20 November 1969.* London: British Crop Protection Council.
1982   Controlled atmosphere storage. In *Storage of cereal grains and their products.* St. Paul: American Association of Cereal Chemistry. Pp. 443–478.

Hylton, Joe
1986   An analysis of the effect of plant materials in controlling heat flow through the roofs of earth sheltered buildings. In *Earth sheltered buildings conference,* 183–189.

Inaba, Kazuya, Akihiko Miyano, Akio Mizutani, Akira Koyama, and Takuzo Sakamoto
1985   Investigation and improvement of living environment in cave dwellings in China. In *Symposium on earth architecture,* 145–152.

Inada, Y., T. Manabe, S. Ohashi, and M. Yoshikawa
1988   Stability of underground openings due to storage of heated water. In *Conference on underground space,* 338–343.

Inoue, Takashi, Yoh Matsuo, and Toshiteru Honma
1985   Estimation of the thermal performance of underground architecture. In *Symposium on earth architecture,* 153–159.

Inoue, Tomoyuki, and Nobuhiro Yamahata
1985   Life styles in pit type dwellings. In *Symposium on earth architecture,* 35–37.

Inoue, Toshitaka
1986   Survey of the Seikan tunnel. *Tunnelling and Underground Space Technology* 1.3–4:333–340.

Ishihara, K.
1979   Earth pressure balanced shield tunnelling method: Water pressure type. *Underground Space* 4.2:95–102.

Janitsary, M.
1988   Shield tunnelling and tunnel lining with new type of precast concrete segments. In *Conference on underground space,* 262–266.

Jansson, Birger
1988a   Habitation for homeless in earth-covered cabins. In *Conference on underground space,* 519–522.
1988b   Water and sewage in caverns and tunnels—30 years' experience. In *Conference on underground space,* 94–99.

Jansson, Birger, and Torbjorn Winqvist
1977   *Planning of subsurface use.* Stockholm: Liber Tryck.

Japan Tunnelling Association
1988   Single-shell in-situ concrete tunnel lining: Experience in Japan. *Tunnelling and Underground Space Technology* 3.1:51–54.

Japan, underground movement.
1966   *The Economist* 221: 1323.

Japanese firm markets portable "pod houses" as disaster shelters.
1980   *Underground Space* 4.5:320.

Jia Kunnan
1985   Sintered cave for living-room. In *Symposium on earth architecture,* 160–164.

Jin Oubo
1983   Living space gained from earth (Xiang dixia zhengqu juzhu kongjian). *Architects* (Jianzhushi) 15:63–74.
1985   Non-residential earth architecture in China. In *Symposium on earth architecture,* 165–171.

Jin Shixu
[n.d.]   *The Ming Tombs.* Beijing: People's Fine Arts Publishing House.

Jing Qimin and Anthony Vacchione
1985   Architectural patterns of Chinese cave houses. In *Symposium on earth architecture,* 172–182.

Kang Ning
1986   Futurology in construction of civil air defense (Weilaixue zai renfang jianshe zhong de yunyong). *Underground Space* (Dixia kongjian) 3:29–41.
1988a   The Baoshi hall in Hangzhou (Hangzhou Baoshi huitang). *Underground Space* (Dixia kongjian) 8.3:25–29.
1988b   The Precious Stone auditorium in Hangzhou. In *Conference on underground space,* 150–155.

Karisaka-Swedish technology and Japanese expertise.
1990   *World Tunnelling* 3.3: 173–176.

Kawashima, Horishichiro, Akio Nakatani, and Hiroshi Ito
1985   Natural lighting design in earth architecture. In *Symposium on earth architecture,* 183–190.

Kawashima, H., K. Iwai, H. Furukawa, K. Ito, K. Umemoto, T. Kumazawa, G. Shigaraki, and R. Imamura
1986   Geodata check system of sites for Japanese housing with basements. In *Earth sheltered buildings conference,* 94–99.

Khalili, E. Nader
1985   Timeless materials, timeless principles. In *Symposium on earth architecture,* 191–197.

Kim, H. G., and R. L. Sterling
1983   Integrating earth-sheltered design into the Korean terrain and tradition. *Underground Space* (Dixia kongjian) 7.6:381–386.

Kimber, Wayne J.
1986   Liveability, comfortability, flexibility, affordability, and longevity of "total wood" earth covered structures. In *Earth sheltered buildings conference,* 267–272.

Kitamura, Akira
1986   Technical development for the Seikan tunnel. *Tunnelling and Underground Space Technology* 1.3–4:341–350.

Kojima, Keiji
1990 Underground space use in Japan—Recent and near-future developments. *Tunnelling and Underground Space Technology* 5.1–2:3–6.

Konishi, T., and K. Watanabe
1988 Study on utilization of underground space of Ohya. In *Conference on underground space,* 90–93.

Kusumoto, Yuji, and Koyoshi Ishikawa
1985 Typological analysis of plans and approaches. In *Symposium on earth architecture,* 27–29.

Kuwajima, F. M., and A. Negro, Jr.
1988 Ground movements around underground openings in gravitational stress field. In *Conference on underground space,* 332–337.

Lan Jian
1985 The space and landscape of earth architecture in China. In *Symposium on earth architecture,* 198–201.

Lee, C. F.
1987 Performance of underground coal mines during the 1976 Tangshan earthquake. *Tunnelling and Underground Space Technology* 2.2:199–202.

Lee, Shi Woong, and Jang Yeul Shon
1988 The thermal environment in an earth-sheltered home in Korea. *Tunnelling and Underground Space Technology* 3.4:409–416.

Lemley, J. K.
1986 Keynote address to the Seikan Colloquium. *Tunnelling and Underground Space Technology* 1.3–4:225–228.

Li Chenggao and Cui Tiejun
1986 Experiments on arched trough panel ferrocement (Gangsi wang shuini caoxing gongban shiyan yanjiu). *Underground Space (Dixia kongjian)* 3:21–28.

Li Chunling
1982 *Reinvestigation of the yellow soil (loess) cave dwellings in west Henan* (Yuxi huangtu yaodong minju zai diaocha). Zhengzhou: Henan College of Architectural Design and Research.

Li Dage
1986 The nation's largest underground ring street market built in Jilin (Quan Guo zuida dixia huanxingjie shangchang zai Jilin shi jiancheng). *Underground Space (Dixia kongjian)* 3:45.

Li Guixian, and Wang Zhongqi
1988 Prediction of seismic effect of underground space. In *Conference on underground space,* 356–361.

Li Jinle, Zhang Congrong, and Li Liangsheng
1985 An experiment in cave-dwelling reformation. In *Symposium on earth architecture,* 202–208.

Li Jinle, Zhang Congrong, Liu Yi, and Luo Wenbao
1982 *Summary of improvements in cave dwellings in Shikusi (Stone Cave Temple) Elementary School* (Shikusi Xiaoxue yaodong gaizao xiaojie). Zhengzhou: Henan College of Architectural Design and Research.

Li Ning and Zhang Haidong
1988 The visco-plastic FEM analysis for underground openings in layered expansive rock. In *Conference on underground space,* 352–355.

Li Shihui
1988 The scientific methodology of tunnel surrounding rock stability analysis. In *Conference on underground space,* 216–220.

Li Xiaoqiang
1985 The origin and development of cave dwellings in China. In *Symposium on earth architecture,* 209–215.

Li Youguo and Jiang Dingyang
1988 On feasibility of construction of underground railway through utilization of passage for civil air defense (Shilun kaifa liyong renfang tongdao, jianshe dixia yougui jiaotong kexingxing wenti). *Underground Space (Dixia kongjian)* 8.3:1–5.

Li Yunpeng, Wang Zhiyin, and Liu Huaiheng
1988 Three dimensional back analysis of viscoelastic creep displacements. In *Conference on underground space,* 382–387.

Li Yuxiang
1987 Secondary utilization of the suburban quarry (Chengshi jinjiao caikuang shichang de erci liyong). *Underground Space (Dixia kongjian)* 1:1–4.
1988 A suggested underground tramline in the West Lake area in Hangzhou. In *Conference on underground space,* 138–143.

Liang Jiongyun
1986 An enlightenment from the development of tunnel construction (Cong suidao fazhanshi zhong dedaode qifa). *Underground Space (Dixia kongjian)* 3:1–3.

Lin Bozhong, Gao Boyang, Wang Zhenjia, Li Shun, and Qi Ruifang
1988 Basic approach to analysis of reliability of underground construction for civil air defense (Dixia renfang jiegou kekaoxing fenxi de jiben fangfa). *Underground Space (Dixia kongjian)* 8.3:73–75.

Lin Jing
1985 The vitality of earth architecture—Past and present of earth architecture in Ningxia, China. In *Symposium on earth architecture,* 216–223.

Littlejohn, G. S.
1988a Rock anchorages for underground support. In *Conference on underground space,* 227–233.
1988b Sprayed concrete for underground support. In *Conference on underground space,* 234–240.

Liu Chunhan
1982 A discussion on the problems of the modernization of cave-dwellings in loess-land (Huangtu yaodong minju jianzhu xiandaihua de jige wenti de taolun). In *Surveys of cave dwellings in China,* 74–101.

Liu Wenbin
1982   Recommend a residential area of soil constructions: Xiangyang Xincun in Baiyin District,
Lanzhou (Jieshao yige shengtu jianzhu de
jumindian: Lanzhou shi Baiyin qu Xiangyang
Xincun). In *Surveys of cave dwellings in China*,
142–154.

Liu Yuegeng
1986   Evaluation and optimization of the plan for utilization of underground construction both in
ordinary time and during war (Dixia gongcheng pingzhan jiehe fangan de pingjia he
youxuan). *Underground Space* (Dixia kongjian)
4:9–18.

Lopez de Asiain, Jaime
1988   One earth sheltered village in Andalucia,
Spain. In *Conference on underground space*, 72–73.

Loubes, J. P.
1985   For a contemporary troglodytic architecture:
Underground climate parameters. In *Symposium on earth architecture*, 224–231.

Lu Bingjie
1988   The strange buildings: The building group of
Tu-Lou in Tian-Liao Keng. In *Conference on
underground space*, 63–71.

Lu Shixi
1986   Insulation practice for subsurface cold storage.
In *Earth sheltered buildings conference*, 273–276.
1988   Energy saving design for underground refrigeration (Dixia lengku jianzhu jieneng). *Underground Space* (Dixia kongjian) 8.3:30–37.

Lu Younian
1988   A general formula for calculating the rock
resistant factor K of hydraulic pressure tunnel.
In *Conference on underground space*, 362–365.

Lundstrom, Bertil
1983   Demand and technical requirements for food
storage in developing countries. *Underground
Space* 7.4–5:251–256.

Luo Wenbao
1981   *Earthquake protection problem of Chinese loess soil
cave dwellings* (Woguo huangtu yaodong de
kangzhen wenti). Henan Group, Cave Dwelling and Soil Construction Survey and Research
Section, Architectural Society of China, Earthquake Engineering Society of Henan Province.
1985   The seismic problems of cave dwellings in loess
region in China. In *Symposium on earth architecture*, 232–241.
1987   Seismic problems of cave dwellings on China's
loess plateau. *Tunnelling and Underground Space
Technology* 2.2:203–208.

Luong, M. P.
1988   Tensile and shear characteristics of rock materials. In *Conference on underground space*, 327–331.

Luoyang City Cave Dwelling Investigation Group
1981   Cave dwelling in loess-land, Luoyang (Luoyang huangtu yaodong jianzhu). *Architectural
Journal* (Jianzhu xuebao) 10:41–47.

McHenry, Paul G., Jr.
1985a   Earth architecture in the southwestern United
States: Past–present–future. In *Symposium on
earth architecture*, 248–254.
1985b   Preliminary proposal for research and development of low cost housing in China. In *Symposium on earth architecture*, 255–258.

McKown, Cora
1985   Lighting earth sheltered spaces. In *Symposium
on earth architecture*, 259–266.

Madryas, C.
1988   Some problems of the underground grids re-
building. In *Conference on underground space*, 275–
279.

Maidl, B., and K. Gebhardt
1988   The planning of the 4th shaft of the Elbtunnel
in Hamburg. In *Conference on underground space*,
189–193.

Manandhar, Ramesh
1985   Lessons from earth roofing projects in Australia
and Nepal: A blow to technology transfer. In
Symposium on earth architecture, 242–247.
1986   People's earth sheltered architecture in Nepal.
In *Earth sheltered buildings conference*, 28–32.

Maru, Y., and T. Maeda
1986   Construction of the Seikan undersea tunnel—I:
General scheme of execution. *Tunnelling and
Underground Space Technology* 1.3–4:357–372.

Matsuo, Shogo
1986   An overview of the Seikan tunnel project. *Tunnelling and Underground Space Technology* 1.3–4:
323–332.

Maurenbrecher, P. M., and P. N. W. Verhoef
1988   Review of research into structural stability of
underground space in abandoned building
stone mines in the Cretaceous limestones of
southeast Holland. In *Conference on underground
space*, 372–376.

Miyaguchi, Korehide
1986   Maintenance of the Kanmon Railway tunnels.
Tunnelling and Underground Space Technology 1.3–
4:307–314.

Miyano, Akihiko
1985   On the present state of underground towns and
the environmental disasters in Japan. In *Symposium on earth architecture*, 267–274.

Morishita, Kiyoko, and Hitoshi Nakamura
1985   An overall view of pit type settlement. In *Symposium on earth architecture*, 30–31.

Moro, T.
1990   Methodology of geological and rock mechanics
studies for underground nuclear plants. *Tunnelling and Underground Space Technology* 5.1–2:103–
109.

Mulligan, Helen
1985   Performance prediction of excavated dwellings.
In *Symposium on earth architecture*, 275–282.

1986 The rock-cut dwelling in a temperate climate: Occupational patterns and heating demand. In *Earth sheltered buildings conference,* 12–17.

1988 Estimating the energy consumption of cave dwellings: The profile factor method. In *Conference on underground space,* 458–463.

Murakami, Yoshimaru
1988 Types of utilization of underground space—History, present and tomorrow. In *Conference on underground space,* 286–291.

Murakami, Yoshimaru, and Tokio Arai
1988 Present status of the shield-tunnelling method developing in Japan. In *Conference on underground space,* 292–297.

Nakashima, M., A. Hirata, and Y. Hori
1988 Design and construction of a subway line under large permanent structures by underpinning. In *Conference on underground space,* 251–256.

Nakazawa, Toshiaki, and Katsuhiko Yashiro
1985 The spatial organization of pit type settlement. In *Symposium on earth architecture,* 32–34.

Nan Yingjing
1982a A preliminary attempt to explore the structure, composition, and construction of cave dwellings in the Qingyang region (Gansu sheng Qingyang diqu yaodong jiegou, gouzao ji shigong chutan). In *Surveys of cave dwellings in China* 56–74.

1982b A preliminary discussion on the future of the "poor cave dwelling" (Dui "hanyao" qiantu de qianyi). In *Surveys of cave dwellings in China* 109–116.

1984 *Discussion on the reduction of moisture in cave dwelling yards (Yaodongyuan luo chushi wenti tantao).* Gansu Academy of Sciences, Institute of Natural Energy Resources.

Navarro, Hugo
1985 Earth construction technologies applied to the humid tropics. In *Symposium on earth architecture,* 283–290.

Neumann, Joachim, and Dietmar Paul
1988 The first parking cavern with shelter in the Federal Republic of Germany. In *Conference on underground space,* 515–518.

Newman, J. O., and L. C. Godbey
1986 Soil temperatures adjacent to a South Carolina earth sheltered residence. In *Earth sheltered buildings conference,* 158–168.

Nie Bihua
1988 On the design of entrances to underground space. In *Conference on underground space,* 298–301.

Ning Zhuzhi, Liu Qiaobao, Wang Denggao, Shi Kai, Qi Shangwen, and Xiang Huaiqiang
1988 Complex signs of reaction on environment of underground space under air-conditioning (Kongtiao tiaojian xia de "dixia kongjian fanying zonghe zheng"). *Underground Space (Dixia kongjian)* 8.3:55–59.

Nishi, Junji, Fujio Kamo, and Kunihiko Ozawa
1988 Rational use of urban underground space for surface and subsurface activities. In *Conference on underground space,* 257–261.

1990 Rational use of urban underground space for surface and subsurface activities in Japan. *Tunnelling and Underground Space Technology* 5.1–2:23–32.

Noguchi, Masao, and Yasushi Kakiuchi
1985 An introduction to hillside type settlement. In *Symposium on earth architecture,* 38–40.

Nordgren, Ingemar
1988 Cold storage in rock. In *Conference on underground space,* 122–126.

Odul, Pascal
1985 Earth construction technologies appropriate to developing countries. In *Symposium on earth architecture,* 291–299.

Ogi, Hajime, Tetsuya Hiyeda, and Kazuo Nakamura
1988 Simulation system for environmental property of man: Basement system. In *Conference on underground space,* 447–452.

Okuda, M., and K. Iwai
1986 An analysis of needs for basements in Japanese housing. In *Earth sheltered buildings conference,* 146–151.

1987 An analysis of needs for basements in Japanese housing. *Tunnelling and Underground Space Technology* 2.4:437–440.

Oliver, David L.
1986 User acceptability and marketing strategies for rammed earth in developed countries. In *Earth sheltered buildings conference,* 143–145.

Osborne, Graham
1986 Low cost self-help earth shelter. In *Earth sheltered buildings conference,* 152–157.

Pan Dingyuan
1986a A study on development and utilization of underground space by means of system engineering (Yong xitong gongcheng fangfa yanjiu dixia kongjian de kaifa yu liyong). *Underground Space (Dixia kongjian)* 3:4–14.

1986b Multipurpose decision on construction of the tunnel through a river (Yuejiang suidao de duomubiao jueze wenti). *Underground Space (Dixia kongjian)* 4:1–8.

Paulson, Boyd C., Jr.
1981 Japan's Nakayama tunnel. *Underground Space* 5.6:337–343.

1984 Urban tunnelling in Japan. *Underground Space* 8.3:185–190.

Petersen, D., C. Nelson, R. Emanuelson, N. Podas, and M. Marshak
1986 Outfitting an underground science laboratory. In *Earth sheltered buildings conference,* 245–251.

Pinzón-Isaza, Hernando
1988 Eurotunnel—A tunnel beneath the English Channel. In *Conference on underground space,* 530–536.

Qian Daren
1988   Construction of the Yan'an Road underwater tunnel in Shanghai. In *Conference on underground space*, 162-164.

Qian Fuyuan
1988   An experimental study of the CO_2 concentration criterion for air in underground shelters. In *Conference on underground space*, 422-427.

Qian Fuyuan and Su Yu
1985   Research on the indoor environment of loess cave dwellings. In *Symposium on earth architecture*, 300-308.

Qiao Zhen and Hou Jiyao
1986   Development and utilization of loess cave districts in urban China. In *Earth sheltered buildings conference*, 288-294.

Qu Zhenliang
1985   Solar sunk yard cave dwelling. In *Symposium on earth architecture*, 314-317.

Qu Zhenliang, Nan Yinjing, and Liu Guangliang
1985   Solar earth house in Dunhuang, China. In *Symposium on earth architecture*, 309-312.

Quarmby, Arthur
1986   Principles and practicalities of design. In *Earth sheltered buildings conference*, 215-219.
1988   The design of earth-sheltered and underground developments. In *Conference on underground space*, 37-42.

Raetzman, Ronald, and Suzanne Wadsworth
1982   Atrium and courtyard houses: Forms expressive of Chinese social organization. *Underground Space* 7:14.

Rahamimoff, A., A. Silberstein, D. Faiman, A. Zemel, and D. Goaver
1986   Earth integrated educational center in the Israeli desert. In *Earth sheltered buildings conference*, 241-244.

Rejeski, David
1986   Energy sensitive land-use planning in urban environments. In *Earth sheltered buildings conference*, 282-287.

Ren Zhenying
1982   Give a new lease on life to the "poor cave dwelling" on the loess plateau (Wei huangtu gaoyuan de "hanyao" zhaohuan chuntian). In *Surveys of cave dwellings in China*, 1-5.
1985a Call for spring for "bleak cave dwelling" on loess plateau of China. In *Symposium on earth architecture*, 318-324.
1985b Earth construction and man. In *Symposium on earth architecture*, 1-9.

Ren Zhiyuan
1982a A preliminary discussion of sunken loess land cave dwellers' courtyards (Xiachenshi huangtu yaodong minju yuan luo chuyi). In *Surveys of cave dwellings in China*, 102-109.
1982b A survey on the cave dwellings in loess area in the Qingyang region of Gansu province (Gansu sheng Qingyang diqu huangtu yaodong diao-

cha baogao). In *Surveys of cave dwellings in China*, 7-55.
1983   A preliminary discussion of sunken loess land cave dwellers' courtyards (Xiachenshi huangtu yaodong minju yuan luo chuyi). *Architects (Jianzhushi)* 15:75-82.
1985a Distribution and classification of cave dwellings in the loess regions of China. In *Symposium on earth architecture*, 331-342.
1985b Tibetan dwellings in Gansu, China. In *Symposium on earth architecture*, 325-330.

Rizzo, Gianfrance, and Antonino Giaccone
1988   Modeling tools for approaching energy and environment analysis of earth sheltered buildings. In *Conference on underground space*, 453-457.

Rottier, Guy
1985   About a new earth architecture. In *Symposium on earth architecture*, 343-350.

Rylander, Rod
1986   Adaptation of the vertical crawl space technique to conditions in Nepal. In *Earth sheltered buildings conference*, 33-35.

Saari, Kari
1988   Public subsurface buildings in Finland. In *Conference on underground space*, 11-15.

Shaanxi Province Revolutionary Committee, ed.
1979   *Architectural code of the damp sunken loess region (Shixianxing huangtu diqu jianzhu guifan)*. Beijing: China Building Industry Press.

Shang Kuo
1978   Analysis of design approach to landscape architecture of Reed Flute Cave at Guilin (Guilin Ludiyan fengjing jianzhu de chuangzuo fenxi). *Architectural Journal (Jianzhu xuebao)* 3:211-215.

Sharma, B. D., and R. K. Bhandari
1988   Subterranean ancient structures of India. In *Conference on underground space*, 48-53.
1989   Subterranean ancient structures of India. *Tunnelling and Underground Space Technology* 4.4:475-480.

Shen, Lester Sheng-wei, Yu Joe Huang, and Jana Poliako
1988   The effect of soil thermal and moisture properties on building foundation heat loss. In *Conference on underground space*, 410-415.

Shi, Y.
1988   Developing earth sheltered buildings to improve Lanzhou city's development. In *Conference on underground space*, 43-44.

Sigaut, F.
1980   Significance of underground storage in traditional systems of grain production. In *Controlled atmosphere storage of grains, an international symposium held from 12-15 May 1980 at Castelgandolfo (Rome), Italy.* J. Shevbal, ed. Pp. 3-13. Amsterdam: Elsevier.

Smoot, Ralph C.
1986 Design and construction process of an earth sheltered home in Austin, Texas. In *Earth sheltered buildings conference*, 234–240.

Soil Construction Survey and Research Group
1982 *Recognition of soil construction in Gong County* (Gong xian shengtu jianzhu qianshi). Kaifeng: Henan Province, Construction Committee of Kaifeng Region.

Soil Mechanics Office, Northwest Water Conservation Research Institute, ed.
1961 On the relation of the settlement of loess with its density, water contents and pressure (Huangtu de shixianxing he midu, shidu, yali de guanxi). *Architectural Journal* (Jianzhu xue-bao) 1:23–26.

Song Hailiang
1982 Facts recorded about the investigation of cave dwellings in the eastern Gansu area (Longdong yaodong diaocha jishi). In *Surveys of cave dwellings in China*, 155–189.

Song Wentian
1988 On development and utilization of urban underground space (Qian tan chengshi dixia kongjian de kaifa liyong). *Underground Space* (Dixia kongjian) 8.3:6–10.

Speltz, Jerome J.
1986 Analysis of thermal comfort conditions in earth sheltered buildings. In *Earth sheltered buildings conference*, 122–126.

St. John, C. M., and T. F. Zahrah
1987 Aseismic design of underground structures. *Tunnelling and Underground Space Technology* 2.2: 165–198.

Stauffer, T.
1980 Grain, seed, food storage, and farm machinery manufacturing tie Kansas City's use of underground space to the U.S. agricultural Midwest. In *Subsurface space, proceedings of Rockstore 80, Stockholm*. Oxford: Pergamon Press. Vol. 1, 407–414.

Sterling, Raymond L.
1980 *Delegation journal: Underground space use delegation to the People's Republic of China 7*. Minneapolis: University of Minnesota, Underground Space Center.
1985 Earth-sheltered building research in the United States: A selective state of the art review. In *Symposium on earth architecture*, 351–359.

Sterling, Raymond, B. Anderson, A. Cisewski, and J. Bidwell
1986 Waterproofing design and installation for the underground telecommunications facility at the University of Minnesota. In *Earth sheltered buildings conference*, 277–281.

Sterling, Raymond, John Carmody, and Walter H. Rockenstein II
1988 Development of life safety standards for large mined underground space facilities in Minneapolis, Minnesota, USA. In *Conference on underground space*, 496–501.

Sterling, Raymond, Charles Fairhurst, Magnus Bergman, and John Carmody
1982 China tour initiates information exchange on underground applications. *Underground Space* 6.6:319–322.

Sterling, R. L., et al.
1983 Underground storage of food. *Underground Space* 7.4–5:257–262.

Stevens, Andre
1985 Ancient cities and earth architecture through the history of the world. In *Symposium on earth architecture*, 360–369.

Su Yu and Hou Xueyuan
1988 The interaction between underground environment and mankind. In *Conference on underground space*, 393–398.

Suh, Jungkyu, Hyungsik Chung, and Cheehwan Kim
1988 Study on the gas containment criterion in unlined rock caverns. In *Conference on underground space*, 127–132.

Sun Jun
1988 The characteristics of rock nature and the surrounding rock stability analysis of tunnel opening in overstressed ground regions. In *Conference on underground space*, 307–309.

Suzuki, Tokio
1985 The origin of *tianjing* and *tianjing*-type *yaodong*s in China. In *Symposium on earth architecture*, 370–373.

Tan Qixiang, ed.
1982 *The historical atlas of China* (Zhongguo lishi dituji). Vols. 1–7. Shanghai: Cartographic Press.

Tani, Takuro, and Shin-ichiro Matsudome
1985 Use of bamboo lath-and-mud construction in Japan. In *Symposium on earth architecture*, 374–389.

Tao Zhenyu
1986 Design and performance of shotcrete-bolting support for a tunnel in a special weak rock. *Tunnelling and Underground Space Technology* 1.1: 49–52.

Tao Zhenyu and Mo Haihong
1988 Under cyclic loading the experimental study and the numeric simulation of constitutive relation of rock. In *Conference on underground space*, 310–315.

Tatsukami, T.
1986 Case study of an underground shopping mall in Japan: The east side of Yokohama Station. *Tunnelling and Underground Space Technology* 1.1:19–28.

Terman, Maurice J.
1974 *Tectonic map of China and Mongolia*. Boulder.

Texas A&M University, Department of Architecture, ed.
1986a *Proceedings of the second international earth sheltered buildings conference: Advances in geotectural design.* College Station, Tex.
1986b Concrete as a structural material in underground structures subject to dynamic loads. In *Earth sheltered buildings conference,* 107–110.

Theunissen, P. M. A.
1985 Discussion on some institutional aspects of the use of earth as a building material. In *Symposium on earth architecture,* 390–398.

Thomas, T., R. Lentz, D. Look, D. Elifrits, and L. Sieck
1986 The earth as insulation. In *Earth sheltered buildings conference,* 86–93.

Thomas, William
1982 Land-use planning in the People's Republic of China. In *Underground Space* 7.1:21–23.

Tian Yujia
1988 Study of downstream sidewall anchorage effect in Baishan underground powerhouse. In *Conference on underground space,* 211–215.

Tian Zhiqian, Feng Yueduan, and Yuan Daiguang
1988 Improvement of environment with radon and atmospheric ions in underground engineering is in urgent need (Dixia gongcheng zhong dong ji kongqi lizi huanjing jidai gaishan). *Underground Space* (Dixia kongjian) 8.3:60–67.

Tianjin University, Department of Architectural Engineering, Education and Research Office of Underground Architectural Engineering, ed.
1979 *Statics calculation on underground structures* (Dixia jiegou jingli jisuan). Beijing: China Building Industry Press.

Tong Linxu
1981 *Architectural planning and design of underground buildings.* Beijing: Qinghua University.
1988a On the main experiences in construction of underground shopping center in Japan (Lun Riben dixiajie jianshe de jiben jingyan). *Underground Space* (Dixia kongjian) 8.3:76–83.
1988b Urban underground shopping malls: The essential experience of Japan. In *Conference on underground space,* 100–104.

Tong, L. X., and H. Jing
1986 Developing underground shopping space in the Qianmen business district of Beijing. In *Earth sheltered buildings conference,* 295–300.

Tongji University, Tianjin University, Harbin Architectural Engineering College, Xi'an Metallurgy and Architecture College, and Shanghai Tunnel Construction Company, eds.
1982 *Underground Architectural Structures* (Tuceng dixia jianzhu jiegou). Beijing: China Building Industry Press.

Tongji University Press, ed.
1988 *Proceedings of the third international conference on underground space and earth sheltered buildings: New developments of underground space use.* Shanghai.

Underhill, Jack
1978 Soviet policy for new towns and its implementation, achievements, and problems. In *International urban growth policies: New-town contributions.* New York: John Wiley & Sons. Pp. 397–437.

Vallabhan, C. V. G., and E. W. Kiesling
1986 Boundary element methods for heat transfer analysis in earth sheltered buildings. In *Earth sheltered buildings conference,* 201–204.

Veach, K. C., and L. F. Goldberg
1986 A simplified experimental evaluation of an earth-coupled heating tube in Minnesota. In *Earth sheltered buildings conference,* 210–214.

Wada, Kanji
1986 Maintenance and control of the Kanmon Highway tunnel. *Tunnelling and Underground Space Technology* 1.3–4:315–322.

Wada, Yuji, and Hinako Sakugawa
1990 Psychological effects of working underground. *Tunnelling and Underground Space Technology* 5.1–2:33–38.

Wakayama, Shigeru, and Yoshihiro Yamada
1985 Distribution of materials, building system and natural environment in the case of mud architecture. In *Symposium on earth architecture,* 399–403.

Wan Guo'an
1988 Specific features of the layout of mausoleums in China and the thinking behind them. In *Conference on underground space,* 59–62.

Wang Dongyun
1986 Calculation of heat energy storage in water-bearing formation (Hanshuiceng reneng chucun de jisuan wenti). *Underground Space* (Dixia kongjian) 3:15–20.

Wang Fu
1982 A preliminary exploration of safety in soil cave dwellings (Chutan tuyaodong de anquan). In *Surveys of cave dwellings in China,* 117–125.
1985 Approach to safety of loess caves. In *Symposium on earth architecture,* 404–414.

Wang, H. S.
1988 Boundary element analysis for viscoelastic contact problems in underground geotechnical engineering structures. In *Conference on underground space,* 388–392.

Wang Haiwen
1988 On calculation of air conditioning capacity and energy saving in underground market (Dixia shangchang kongtiao fuhe jisuan yu jieneng de qianjian). *Underground Space* (Dixia kongjian) 8.3:51–54.

Wang Tingmin
1987   A new material for waterproofing walls of a dam: A concrete with cationic bituminous emulsion (Bati fangshenqiang xin cailiao: Yanglizi ruhua liqing hunningtu). *Underground Space* (Dixia kongjian) 1:47–54.

Wang Weiping
1985   Earth houses and rural construction in China. In *Symposium on earth architecture,* 415–419.

Wang Weizhong and Liu Wenbin
1982   Earth structures (Shengtu jianzhu). In *Surveys of cave dwellings in China,* 126–141.

Wang Yongnian
1988   Analysis of in-situ test results of rock stress and deformation in the Thirteen-Tomb underground power station, Beijing. In *Conference on underground space,* 344–351.

Wang Yongyan and Zhang Zonghu, eds.
1980   *Loess in China.* Xi'an: Shaanxi People's Art Publishing House.

Wang Zuoyuan and Tong Linxu
1985   Waterproofing and dampproofing for cave dwellings in loess regions. In *Symposium on earth architecture,* 420–426.
1986a   Water damage and its control for cave dwellings in loess. In *Earth sheltered buildings conference,* 62–67.
1986b   Waterproofing and dampproofing of cave dwellings in China. *Tunnelling and Underground Space Technology* 1.2:163–166.
1988   Control of water damage in cave dwellings built in loess. *Tunnelling and Underground Space Technology* 3.1:71–74.

Wang, Z. X.
1988   The first metro line in Shanghai. In *Conference on underground space,* 105–109.
1989   The first metro line in Shanghai. *Tunnelling and Underground Space Technology* 4.4:461–464.

Watanabe, Toshiyuki, Yoshimi Urano, Tetsuo Hayashi, and Yuji Ryu
1985   Case study of thermal institution systems for the earth-contact floor. In *Symposium on earth architecture,* 427–434.

Watanabe, Yoshiro
1990   Deep underground space—The new frontier. *Tunnelling and Underground Space Technology* 5.1–2:9–12.

Wright, David
1986   Earth—How much? In *Earth sheltered buildings conference,* 1–6.

Wu, Nelson I.
1963   *Chinese and Indian architecture.* New York: George Braziller.

Wukasch, Eugene
1982   Underground population defense structures in China. *Underground Space* 7.1:16–20.

Xia Yun, S. Guang, Y. Cheng, and Y. Shi
1986   Experiences in using earth sheltered buildings and underground spaces in Shaanxi, China. In *Earth sheltered buildings conference,* 41–44.

Xia Yun and Hou Jiyao
1982   *Preliminary discussion on comprehensive management of loess (yellow soil) cave dwellings* (Huangtu yaodong zonghe zhili de tantao). [Xi'an]: Architectural Society of China, Shaanxi Cave Dwellings and Soil Construction Survey and Research Section.
1985   Comprehensive treatments on loess caves in China. In *Symposium on earth architecture,* 435–442.

Xia Yun, and Y. R. Zhang
1988   Go underground to get building space. In *Conference on underground space,* 7–10.

Xianyu Fanggeng
1986   An example of handling serious collapse of a tunnel (Kengdao da tafang chuli shili). *Underground Space* (Dixia kongjian) 4:41–44.
1987   Exploration on technique of drainage and waterproofing in basements (Loufang dixia shifang paishui jishu de tantao). *Underground Space* (Dixia kongjian) 1:39–46.
1988   Today and tomorrow in development and utilization of construction for civil air defense in Wuhan (Wo shi renfang gongcheng kaifa liyong de xianzhuang yu qianjing). *Underground Space* (Dixia kongjian) 8.3:11–13.

Xiao Tihuan
1982   New spring for the "winter caves"—New hope for cave dwellers (Wei "han yao" zhaohuan chuntian). *People's Daily,* 27 December.
1983   Investigation of Yan'an cave dwellings—Editorial note (Yan'an yaodong kaocha ji). *People's Daily,* 4 June.

Xu Guangliang
1988   Design of inspection passage to power tunnel for Yuzixi Hydropower Station. In *Conference on underground space,* 283–285.

Xu Ronglie and Wu Jialiu
1984   Technical policies concerning China's building construction. In *Building in China: Selected papers.* Beijing: China Building Technology Development Centre. Pp. 1–6.

Xu Sishu
1981   *Design and structure of architecture under the rock ground* (Yanshi dixia jianzhu sheji yu gouzao). Beijing: China Building Industry Press.
1982   Utilization of underground urban space (Chulun chengshi dixia kongjian de liyong). *Architectural Journal* (Jianzhu xuebao) 11:37–39.
1986   Development and utilization of underground space for public entertainment and cultural activities in China. In *Earth sheltered buildings conference,* 301–306.
1987   Development and use of underground space for entertainment and cultural activities in the People's Republic of China. *Tunnelling and Underground Space Technology* 2.3:269–274.

1988   Development and utilization of underground space in Chinese cities. In *Conference on underground space*, 241–245.

n.d.   *Cave dwelling habitat* (Yaodong shi xueju). Chongqing: Chongqing Institute of Architecture.

Yagi, Koji
1985   Analysis of settlement and houses of the central Sahara. In *Symposium on earth architecture*, 443–446.

Yamada, Koichi
1985   The features of Japanese earth walls. In *Symposium on earth architecture*, 447–452.

Yan Ke'an
1986   Application of monolitic placing for waterproofing concrete (Fangshui hunningtu zhengtijiao zhufa de yunyong). *Underground Space* (Dixia kongjian) 4:61–63.

Yan, S. H., and C. Y. Wang
1988   Seismic stresses and displacements of underground circular tunnel. In *Conference on underground space*, 377–382.

Yang Hongxun
1981   Discussion on energy-saving underground residential areas in the loess land belt in China (Shilun zhongguo huangtudi dai jieyue nengyuan de dixia junmin dian). *Architectural Journal* (Jianzhu xuebao) 5:68–73.

Yang Linde, Tao Sunbo, and Wang Yu
1988   Design and construction of TES Project. In *Conference on underground space*, 267–271.

Yang Nanfang and He Tienan
1986   Three examples of prevention from waterpermeability in underground cavern oil storage (Shantongshi dixia youku guanshi de shenlou shuifang zhi sanli). *Underground Space* (Dixia kongjian) 4:56–60.

Yang Yuecheng and Yang Liu
1985   Earthquake damage and aseismic measures for earth buildings in contemporary China. In *Symposium on earth architecture*, 453–463.
1987   Earthquake damage to and aseismic measures for earth-sheltered buildings in China. *Tunnelling and Underground Space Technology* 2.2:209–216.

Yoshino, H., S. Matsumoto, and F. Hasegawa
1986   Optimum utilization technique for solar energy in semi-underground houses. In *Earth sheltered buildings conference*, 224–229.

Yoshioka, M., H. Ogi, K. Nakamura, T. Hiyeda, and K. Iwai
1986   Measurement of thermal behavior of a basement and its surroundings. In *Earth sheltered buildings conference*, 195–200.

Yu Andong
1988   An improved shape of underground triangle shell. In *Conference on underground space*, 272–274.

Yu Fuwei and He Guanbao, eds.
1982   *Hanjia storehouse in the east capital of the Sui and Tang dynasties* (Sui Tang dongdu Hanjia cang). Beijing: Cultural Relics Press.

Yuan Chimin, ed.
1979   *Underground grain storage* (Dixia liang cang). Beijing: China Building Industry Press.

Yuan Zhibing
1986   On the design and construction of box-type foundations for high buildings used as waterproofing basements for civil defense (Shilun gaoceng jianzhu xiangxing jichu jianzuo renfang dixiashi kangshen fangshui de sheji yu shigong). *Underground Space* (Dixia kongjian) 4:45–48.

Zartman, R. E., and K. S. Hutmacher
1986   Temperature variation within the soil envelope above an earth sheltered church. In *Earth sheltered buildings conference*, 169–174.

Zhai Lisheng
1983   *Essentials of structural engineering: Geological properties of China damp-sinking loess* (Zhongguo shi-xianxing huangtu quyu jianzhu gongcheng dizhi gaiyao). Beijing: China Academy of Building Research.

Zhang Mi and Jing Shiting
1988   Recent developments in railway tunnelling in China. In *Conference on underground space*, 202–207.
1989   Recent developments in railway tunnelling in China. *Tunnelling and Underground Space Technology* 4.4:455–460.

Zhang Yuhuan
1981   Chinese aeolian soil architecture: Cave dwellings in eastern Gansu (Zhongguo fengtu jianzhu: Longdong yaodong). *Architectural Journal* (Jianzhu xuebao) 10:48–51.
1985   An overview of the historical development of earth construction in China. In *Symposium on earth architecture*, 464–476.

Zhang, Yuhuan, ed.
1986   *History and development of ancient Chinese architecture*. Beijing: Science Press.

Zhao Sude
1985   Researches on the improvement and development of immature soil engineering in China. In *Symposium on earth architecture*, 477–484.

Zhao Yanming, Zuo Guohua, and Liu Dongsheng
1988   Analysis of the stability of the supporting system in the fill section of the "August 1" tunnel in Chongqing (Chongqing "Ba-yi" suidao duiji tuduan zhi hutixi de wendingxing fenxi). *Underground Space* (Dixia kongjian) 8.3:17–24.

Zhao Zhangxian
1986   A brief description of dehumidification–noise elimination and noise elimination–dewetting in underground construction (Dixia gongcheng chushi xiaoyin, xiaoyin chulu gaishu). *Underground Space* (Dixia kongjian) 3:42–44.

Zheng Chen
1985   Analysis of damages to earth buildings in Hei-
        longjiang, China. In *Symposium on earth architec-
        ture,* 485–492.

Zheng Chen and Zhao Yunduo
1985   A study on construction of earth architecture in
        Heilongjiang, China. In *Symposium on earth
        architecture,* 493–499.

Zheng, G. R., and S. C. Yang
1989   The effect of thermal insulation and moisture
        control in underground cold storage. *Tunnelling
        and Underground Space Technology* 4.4:503–508.

Zheng, Y. R., and Y. F. Lin
1988   Application of the semi-analytical finite ele-
        ment method to analysing stability of the three-
        dimensional elasto-plastic problem in under-
        ground openings. In *Conference on underground
        space,* 302–305.

Zhong Baiyi, Shi Zhugao, and Jiang Naifeng
1988   The application of diaphragm walls in China.
        In *Conference on underground space,* 221–226.

Zhou Peinan et al.
1981   New spaces gained from the loess land (Xiang
        huangtu diceng zhengqu heli de xin kongjian).
        Architectural Journal (Jianzhu xuebao) 10:34–40.

Zhu Jie and An Jin
1985   A report on investigation of earth dwellings in
        Inner Mongolia. In *Symposium on earth architec-
        ture,* 500–506.

Zhu Keshan
1982   The upsurge in China's use of underground
        space. *Underground Space* 7.1:3.

Zhu Keshan, Hu Zhenying, Zhu Zuorong, Zhong
Yougui, and Wang Qingming
1988   Multipurpose uses of a street traffic tunnel in a
        mountainous city. In *Conference on underground
        space,* 246–250.

Zhu Keshan and Xu Sishu
1981a   A promising solution to surface congestion:
        Using the underground. *Underground Space* 6.2:
        96–99.

1981b   *The utilization of underground space in Chongqing*
        (Dixia kongjian zai Chongqing de yingyong).
        Chongqing: Chongqing Architectural Engi-
        neering Institute.

Zhu Qianxiang
1985   Technique and experience in building houses
        with beaten clay walls. In *Symposium on earth
        architecture,* 507–511.

Zuo Guobao
1985a   Loess cave dwelling in Shanxi, China. In *Sym-
        posium on earth architecture,* 521–530.
1985b   Research into the measures taken to prevent
        humidity in the loess caves. In *Symposium on
        earth architecture,* 512–518.
1988a   Loessial dwelling cave—Its covering pressure
        and excavation span. In *Conference on underground
        space,* 54–58.
1988b   Stability of the caves excavated in loess and
        their reinforcement measures. In *Conference on
        underground space,* 27–30.

CREDITS

Figures

CHAPTER 1

1.1 Based on Zhang Yuhuan 1986, 7–28. A redrawn from Yang Hongxun 1981, 68. B redrawn from Li Xiaoqiang 1985, 213. C redrawn from Kwang-chih Chang 1977, 102.
1.2 Redrawn from Tan Qixiang 1982, vol 1, 5–6.
1.3 Redrawn from Chang 1977, 101 (photo of the model at Banpo Museum, Xi'an).
1.4 Ibid., 98.
1.5 Redrawn from Tan 1982, 7–8.

CHAPTER 2

2.4 Redrawn from Chinese Academy of Sciences, Institute of Geology, *Chinese loess soil distribution map* (Beijing, 1965).
2.6 Wang Yongyan and Zhang Zonghu 1980 [unpaginated].
2.8 Ibid.
2.9 Data from Zhai Lisheng 1983, 12.
2.11 Photograph from Huanghe River Conservancy Commission, Ministry of Water Conservancy, 1982 [unpaginated].
2.12 Photograph from Wang and Zhang 1980.
2.13 Ibid.
2.15 Data from Central Meteorological Bureau 1978 [unpaginated].
2.16 Ibid.
2.17 Ibid.
2.18 Ibid.
2.19 Ibid.
2.20 Ibid.
2.21 Ibid.
2.22 Ibid.
2.23 Ibid.
2.24 Ibid.

CHAPTER 3

3.3 Redrawn from Ren Zhiyuan 1982b, 8a.
3.4 Redrawn from Nan Yingjing 1982a, 56.
3.6 Ibid., 61.
3.15 Courtesy Professor Hou Jiyao.
3.17 Data gathered with the assistance of architect Zuo Guobao.
3.21 Courtesy Liu Zenzhong.

CHAPTER 4

4.2 A, B, C, E, F, and G redrawn from Ren Zhiyuan 1982b, 47, 50–53. D and H redrawn from Zuo Guobao 1985a, 523–524. I redrawn from Deng Qisheng 1985, 64.
4.3 Courtesy Su Yu of Tongji University, Shanghai.
4.4 A redrawn from Xu Sishu n.d., 128. B, C, and D redrawn from Masahiro Chatani and Kogi Yagi 1985, 22. G redrawn from Yang Hongxun 1981, 73. H redrawn from Zuo Guobao 1985a, 524. I, L, and N redrawn from Tomoyuki Inoue and Nobuhiro Yamahata 1985, 35, 37. J and K redrawn from Ren Zhiyuan 1985a, 341. M redrawn from Luoyang City Cave Dwelling Investigation Group 1981, 43. E, F, and O redrawn from Ren 1982b, 45–46, 53.
4.11 Nan Yingjing 1982a, 71.
4.13 Based on Gideon S. Golany 1990, 40–41.
4.19 Redrawn from Hou Jiyao 1982, 73. Also Hou Xueyuan and Sun Yiming 1985, 130.
4.28 Courtesy Professor Hou Jiyao.
4.41 Partially based on Ren 1982b, 38.
4.43 J redrawn from Hou Jiyao 1985a, 108.

CHAPTER 5

5.1 Redrawn from Maurice J. Terman 1974, 1–2.
5.2 Redrawn from Hou Xueyuan and Sun Yiming 1985, 125. Also Luo Wenbao 1985, 236.
5.4 Based on Gideon S. Golany 1990, 39.
5.5 Ibid., 39–41.
5.6 Ibid., 112–113.
5.7 Data from Zuo Guobao, et al. 1985b, 512.
5.9 Based on Gideon S. Golany 1990, 110–112.

CHAPTER 6

6.1 Redrawn from Wang Zuoyuan and Tong Linxu 1985, 421–422.
6.2 Ibid., 423.
6.6 Based partially on Cora McKown 1985, 262–263.
6.8 Redrawn from Luo Wenbao 1985, 241.
6.10 Based on Gideon S. Golany 1983, 180–181.
6.12 Gideon S. Golany 1990, 136–139.
6.14 Based on Gideon S. Golany 1983, 163.
6.15 Ibid.

Tables

CHAPTER 2

2.1 Zhai Lisheng 1983, 15.

CHAPTER 3

3.1 Ren Zhiyuan 1982b, 12.

CHAPTER 6

6.5 Based on Gideon S. Golany 1983, 164.

INDEX

About the Author

GIDEON S. GOLANY is an internationally recognized specialist on earth-sheltered habitats, urban design in arid zones, and new town design/planning. He received a Ph.D. from Hebrew University, Jerusalem, an M.Sc. from Technion-Israel Institute of Technology, and a Dip.C.P. from the Institute of Social Studies, the Hague. Currently Distinguished Professor of Urban Design/Planning in the Department of Architecture at the Pennsylvania State University, Professor Golany has taught at a number of universities throughout the world. He is a recipient of honorary professorships from four Chinese academic institutions, including the China Academy of Sciences. He is also a recipient of the Faculty Scholar Medal for Outstanding Achievement in the Social and Behavioral Sciences and the Research/Creative Development Award at the Pennsylvania State University and has been awarded Fulbright grants to India, Turkey, and Japan. In addition to twenty-seven monographs and numerous articles, Golany has written or edited eighteen books, including *Urban Underground Space Design in China, Earth-Sheltered Dwellings in Tunisia,* and *Earth-Sheltered Habitat: History, Architecture and Urban Design.*

Production Notes

This book was designed by Paula Newcomb.
Composition and paging for this book were
done on the Quadex Composing System and
typesetting on the Compugraphic 8400 by
the design and production staff of
University of Hawaii Press.

The text typeface is Baskerville and the
display typeface is Paladium.

Offset presswork and binding were done by
The Maple-Vail Book Manufacturing Group.
Text paper is Glatco coated matte, basis 70.